CLASSIC

Coastal Walks

OF BRITAIN

by Martin Collins

Acknowledgements

Sincere thanks to Rennie McOwan, Fred Gordon, Katie Mowat and Màiri MacDonald for their contributions on coastal walks in Scotland, and to Aileen Evans for her walk on the Isle of Man.

Thanks are also due to Richard Kreutzmann of Colwyn Bay, Clwyd, for his technical photographic advice and for superlative processing of my colour film.

For Paul—that the glories of our coastline remain unsullied for him and future generations to enjoy.

First published by Oxford Illustrated Press Limited, Haynes Publishing Group.

This edition published 1995
by The Promotional Reprint Company Limited,
Deacon House, 65 Old Church Street,
London SW3 5BS

ISBN 1 85648 209 X

Printed in Malaysia

Contents

All photography by the author unless otherwise stated

Introduction

Ever since, aeons ago, life forms crawled from the ocean's nutrient-rich depths and learned to survive on land, the sea's restless rhythms have echoed through the shadowy world of our collective unconscious. In evolutionary terms the sea is, indeed, 'in our blood'; even those living far from its edge experience the passage of weather systems generated by the presence of salt water covering seventy per cent of our planet's surface.

As an island nation, Britain's destiny has been shaped by the sea. From early invasion by the Romans, Vikings and Normans to the development of maritime trade, naval power and the exploitation of marine resources, the waters surrounding us have played a crucial role. Unhappily, man's ages-old reliance upon fishing and the sea's ability to purge the coast of his waste at each tidal ebb and flow could not last forever. Contamination by industrial and agricultural processes threaten the long term health of Britain's shoreline, even that of our offshore waters. New fishing technology is achieving catches beyond the dreams of traditional fishermen and in so doing has upset forever the delicate balance between harvesting and regeneration.

In many parts of Britain, the coastal landscape is under enormous pressure. Saltmarsh is 'reclaimed' for agriculture and building development, huge industrial installations despoil scenically valuable shoreline with dust and fumes, military ranges monopolise miles of glorious clifftop, estuaries are poisoned by agricultural run-off or 'modified' to accommodate the burgeoning growth in pleasure craft marinas, and our beaches are polluted by raw sewage. Everywhere, dunes and fragile foreshore are at risk from over-use as greater personal mobility and leisure time increase public demand for more car parks, more accommodation, more amenities. Even remote locations are not immune from degradation by plastic flotsam and the consequences of oil spillage.

Fortunately this bleak scenario, an ecological Armageddon, has its obverse. The effects of neglect and misuse do not go unnoticed and many agencies—the National Trust, Friends of the Earth, the Nature Conservancy Council, the Marine Conservation Society and the RSPB among them—are working hard for wildlife conservation and the reinstatement of damaged environments. Their collective mission—one that we should all heartily subscribe to—is helped by the existence of Nature Reserves, Areas of Outstanding Natural Beauty, stretches of Heritage Coast and, of course, National Parks. Here at least the public's attention is drawn to the need for positive action to protect vulnerable habitats.

However, to paraphrase Paul Theroux in his acid account of Britain's seaside, *Kingdom by the Sea*, we British do what we like beside the uncomplaining sea; it belongs to everyone and seems to inspire anarchy. Most of us, thank goodness, behave responsibly, but my travels researching this book uncovered the deeds of some who do not: junk dumped from the seaward edge of farmland, campfires lit on grassy clifftops, tents pitched thoughtlessly near public footpaths, and the ubiquitous rash of litter—from beer cans to tissues, chocolate wrappers to soft drinks bottles—that constitutes something like a national disease.

Despite this, our coastline is an asset of inestimable value, scenically more varied and arguably more beautiful than anywhere else in the whole of Europe. Undeniably, many coastal communities have suffered from the decline in fishing and shipbuilding, their once-vigorous populations now swamped by second-home owners and the elderly retired—or else simply left to face the vagaries of an uncertain future. Yet often there is cause for optimism as stronger links than ever before existed are forged between the coast and recreational activities. Sailing, water-sports, sea- cliff climbing and walking enjoy immense popularity alongside more leisurely, traditional seaside pursuits.

Perhaps because it allows us to encompass both land and sea simultaneously, the coastal margin—that primordial battleground between irresistible forces and immovable objects—is particularly compelling. Here, close to our watery origins, the shaping of islands and continents assumes fresh significance as we witness the crumbling of cliffs here, the deposition of shingle there. On no other stage do geology, meteorology, oceanography, marine biology and botany play such interconnected roles—roles which, together, contribute to our understanding of the planet's great evolutionary processes.

The attractions of coastal walking are hard to overstate. As well as offering all the variety of inland routes—even, in many places, the gradients and rugged terrain of hill country—it is enhanced by proximity to an element whose moods and appearance are infinitely changeable. Half the experience of coastal walking takes in features untouched by human feet: rock reefs and islets, waterfalls and estuaries, precipitous cliff faces and inaccessible caves. They, and the vast, animated plane of water always at one side, add an absorbing extra dimension to the landscapes through which we move.

Casual strollers who turn back half a mile from their cars will not, generally speaking, gain access to the finest sections of Britain's coastline; such delights are the reward for a little enterprise! Only those who set out equipped against the weather and prepared for a modicum of exertion will discover the essence of this primeval frontier where land meets ocean. Whether your coastal walk is a modest jaunt or an ambitious, long-distance trek matters not. Waiting for you is the acquisition of new perspectives, an invigoration of the senses and the chance to develop a keener appreciation of the complex interplay between nature and the activities of industrious *homo sapiens*.

The Evolution of Coastal Paths

Mesolithic man, foraging on beaches for shellfish and flints at the dawn of civilisation, would have worn the first, tentative trods around our shoreline. With the diversification of man's activities grew networks of coastal pathways, enabling communities to launch and beach their fishing craft, reach coves and headlands and travel to neighbouring villages. For centuries, life on or near the coast remained abrasively hard; to the rigours of fishing and basic agriculture could always be added the unpredictability of coastal weather and a frequently hostile sea.

As time progressed, more tracks and paths appeared, established by workers in coastal mining and quarrying industries. Trade of all kinds increased and, prior to the advent of railway transport, harbours became major sources of employment: there were ships to build and repair, cargoes to load, men to be housed and fed. Ports played a vital role in the nation's economy, involving regional populations in the comings and goings of trade and providing an infrastructure for crews and port workers.

It is safe to assume that a good deal of Britain's shoreline was already familiar to our predecessors as they fished, laid nets, walked to work, gathered plants and herbs, followed ships in distress and searched for survivors or valuable wreckage after gales. Even so, long stretches of cliff and strand would seldom see a human visitor. It should be remembered that until the nineteenth century, when an expanding railway network heralded the era of mass tourism for an increasingly industrial society, the common man had little time, energy or inclination to travel for its own sake. The concept of 'holidaymaking' had yet to emerge and only individuals with money, time and education would be found travelling on foot by choice.

Early in the eighteenth century, an event took place which would revolutionise the lives of many coastal communities and which led directly to the evolution of coastal footpaths. That event was the government's imposition of heavy customs duties on imported luxury goods—especially wines and spirits—in order to generate much needed revenue.

Quick to seize any opportunity that would raise their standard of living above subsistence level, fishing communities turned to smuggling. Intimate knowledge of sea and shore gave fishermen an immediate advantage which they were not slow to exploit. Even by 1724, Daniel Defoe observed '. . . that smuggling and roguing . . . is the reigning commerce of all this part of the English coast, from the mouth of the Thames to Land's End'.

Faced with such lawlessness, Parliament introduced an Act in 1736 that set out severe penalties—including flogging and hard labour—for anyone found within 5 miles (8km) of the sea who, in the opinion of the authorities, had no good reason to be there. The act was to remain in force for almost a century, a powerful deterrent against coastal walking of any kind other than for the purposes of legitimate work.

Despite this, fat profits from smuggling still eclipsed the risks of being caught and illegal trade grew ever more widespread and organised, particularly along the south coast where continental Europe is closest. No responsible government could tolerate such a state of affairs indefinitely and it was not long before stern counter measures were taken. Around 1815, Royal Navy sailors set up a nightly shore patrol of the Kent and Sussex coast; seven years later this was followed by the inauguration of the Coastguard Service. From then on, the entire coastline of the British Isles was systematically patrolled and coastal footpaths were trodden down by the Revenue Men.

Opposite the French coast, Coastguards were stationed, almost unbelievably, at 100 yard intervals, with 'beats' of a few miles being the norm for officers further west and north. Coastguards were bitterly resented by local people whose access to little luxuries in otherwise comfortless times were quickly eroded. Villagers refused to lodge officers in their houses, so specially designed stations were built, affording accommodation and some protection against an aggressive populace.

Conditions of service were arduous, long duty hours being worked mostly at night, over hazardous terrain and in all weathers. Coastguards were armed and violent confrontations with ruthless, determined smuggling gangs resulted in injury and death on both sides. Eventually, however, the rule of law prevailed and smuggling dwindled to small-scale operations. In any case, by the 1850s adoption of free trade principles had dramatically reduced tariffs and associated duties so that contraband was no longer as profitable as it had once been. Coastguard manning levels were lowered and over the ensuing decades the service shifted its attention to safeguarding the passage of shipping and to initiating rescue operations. Although today's trend is away from clifftop observation and towards the establishment of centralised monitoring stations, local knowledge is still essential, with fishermen sometimes employed as auxiliaries in this regard.

Sadly, many Coastguard lookouts have been abandoned to the elements. Footpaths, thankfully, are far more durable and it is largely due to the foot-slogging of those early Coastguard patrols that so much of our coastline is accessible to walkers today.

About the Walks

I embarked upon the compilation of this book well aware that space would not allow the inclusion of all worthwhile walks within the 7000 mile-odd (11,265km) span of Britain's coastline. Doing justice to everyone's favourite corner of seaside would fill a volume this size many times over and, in the end, might serve only to dissipate the 'specialness' of those stretches widely acknowledged as outstanding for one reason or another.

In walking terms, 'classic' is used to denote routes of exceptional and enduring interest. It does not necessarily imply heroic length or the traversing of unsullied wilderness, but rather that the walks are distinctive and characterise the regions they represent. Thus while some are, indeed, wild and remote, others take as their themes unique natural features, matchless scenery or sites of historical significance. What they all have in common is superlative walking quality, whether you seek modest itineraries suitable for young families, or tough, multi-day treks.

On the whole, coastal walking tends to be at its best in the south and west of Britain, though by no means exclusively so. In those regions you will find consistently magnificent scenery, easy access all year round, well established paths and amenities, freedom from serious industrial pollution and an equable climate. Walks in the east and north may be thinner on the ground, but they have been chosen for their incomparable quality.

Just as substantial tracts of the south and west coast (East Anglia too) are included in National Parks or Areas of Outstanding Natural Beauty, much of Scotland's seaboard is designated as of 'Great Value'. Contributions by fellow authors will leave you in no doubt as to the potential for coastal walking in the Highlands and Islands, though difficulties getting there and the often inhospitable terrain are inclined to militate against exploration of the lonelier parts.

The majority of walks in this book are linear—that is, they start at one location and end at another several miles distant; a few are made circular by cutting across the neck of a headland, returning parallel to the coast, or engirdling an island. As far as possible, starting and finishing points have been chosen with an eye to the availability of accommodation (including youth hostels) and relatively straightforward access. More often than not, however, public transport alone will fail to deliver you to the precise location of a walk, in which case private arrangements will need to be made using, perhaps, two cars or relying on a driver to pick you up at the end of a day.

Routes vary dramatically in length, from short outings like Llandudno's Great Orme, or Cumbria's St Bees Head, to multi-day hikes in Cornwall, Norfolk and Pembrokeshire. It is where a coastline is of consistently high quality that selecting walks has posed the greatest problem. Suggesting a longer distance itinerary split into day-stages seems a sensible solution and prepares the ground for either one continuous trek or exploration by instalments, perhaps from a central base.

Terrain, too, reflects the great diversity of our country's geology and climate. Routes such as Hartland Quay to Bude on the Devon/Cornwall border, or Dorset's Lulworth Ranges walk will test the fittest, especially in blustery weather: gradients are long, steep and repetitive, amenities virtually non-existent. The East Anglian coast is certainly the flattest, though shingle foreshore can be tiring to walk on and there is little shelter from wind. Most walks fall into an intermediate category, presenting you with ups and downs, a variety of underfoot conditions and a range of interesting natural features.

Notes on Equipment and Safety

Readers will appreciate, I trust, that walks spread nationwide and potentially enjoyed at all times of the year have little in common regarding clothing and equipment requirements. Detailed advice covering all eventualities lies outside the scope of this book, but the following notes might be of value in pinpointing factors specific to coastal walking.

Even during the summer months when the weather generally encourages walking, precautions need to be taken against the elements. Coastal locations, like hilly ones, are often windy. Combined with rain, wind saps the body's heat and although there is none of the appreciable cooling due to altitude found in mountain country, nevertheless you can become rapidly chilled. Shelter on open coastline is scarce, so before setting out on any of the longer, exposed routes, check you are carrying spare clothing and a waterproof, windproof 'shell'. In spring and autumn, warmer clothing will be necessary except in especially fine conditions.

As with all serious walking, anticipated weather is always easier to deal with than that which takes you by surprise. Obtaining a weather forecast is recommended for all the walks, particularly for those traversing remote and rugged terrain. Shorts and T- shirt may seem adequate on the beach or in shopping streets, but it is astonishing how vulnerable you become unless adequately equipped, once civilisation is left behind.

Burning ultra-violet radiation from summer sunshine is intensified on the coast by reflection off sea and sand. On gloriously sunny days it may be tempting to wear as little as possible, but walkers are just as liable to sunburn as beachgoers. In particular, forehead, nose and shoulders can become painfully scorched while the preoccupations of walking and route finding hold your attention. Good advice is to avoid sleeveless garments, to wear a brimmed sunhat, polarising sunglasses and dress in light, loose clothing. Applying a high-factor suncream to exposed skin is a wise precaution during the summer; even on bright, cloudy days, fair-skinned people and those unaccustomed to the outdoors are likely to burn.

Heatwaves may be the stuff of holidaymakers' dreams, but walking can be purgatory! When you are hot, thirsty and tired, unrelieved sunshine is no less an adversary to be reckoned with than the winter equivalent of bitter cold. Open coast cannot be relied upon for sources of cool drinking water in the way that hill country sometimes can. Streams running to the sea are often polluted by farm effluent, so in hot weather check the availability of drinks along the way and if necessary carry liquid with you. The chance to cool off in the sea is a distinct possibility on some walks when a bathing costume and towel will be prudent additions to the rucksack.

I have always considered a pair of binoculars or a monocular to be worth their weight, not just for viewing along the coast, but for providing close-ups of sea birds, seals, shipping and features such as islands or lighthouses. If you are a keen photographer, a UV filter is essential for colour work and will protect your lens from salt spray which, along with sand, is one of a camera's arch enemies!

Footwear is a vexed subject and not one I am happy to pontificate about! I know long-distance backpackers who swear by trainers, and have used them successfully myself on occasions. They offer little support, however, and not much reassurance on steep, rough ground. Wet feet are a recurrent problem on some coast paths—from rain certainly, but more commonly from moisture- laden grasses and undergrowth which curl over the path during the summer, ensuring you receive a perpetual footbath! Leather boots are no match for this, even well waxed and worn with gaiters; wellington boots, or sandals with shorts, work well enough, though not of course on other kinds of terrain.

It goes without saying that rucksacks should contain other sundry items according to the nature and severity of the walk. Essentials at all times include spare and shell clothing, a first-aid kit, emergency whistle, telephone coins, map and a torch if hiking off-season. Road or habitations are seldom more than a mile or two away—a few routes excepted—and this alone adds a dimension of extra security should an emergency occur either to your own party or to others.

Finally, a word about safety. Not long ago I was fortunate to escape with my life when the cliff edge near Crackington Haven on Cornwall's north coast collapsed in front of my feet taking several metres of path with it. Two walkers ahead, approaching from the opposite direction, had seen the slippage and kept well back but my companion and I had no way of knowing the path was about to fall away: a few seconds earlier and we would have been swept down to our certain deaths.

I do not mention this to scaremonger but rather to underline the need for vigilance, particularly after periods of wet or windy weather. Our old Coastguard paths have survived more than a century's use, but it is a measure of the sea's inexorable power that man is often in constant retreat. Footpaths inland are never subject to so many diversions and such chronic subsidence as those on our coast.

Flotsam – the unsightly litter of the sea.

Rock climbing accidents, getting into swimming difficulties or being cut off by a rising tide are obvious hazards, though the kind of risks facing walkers are more general and can only be effectively safeguarded against by developing an attitude of mind—by becoming, if you like, 'coastwise'. In the unfortunate event of an emergency, contact the police or HM Coastguard and try to give a map grid reference or an equally accurate indication of where the incident has occurred.

Coastal Weather

A book dealing with walks spread across the length and breadth of Britain cannot also analyse the nation's weather in great detail. However, by describing conditions on the coast in broad terms for the months April to September, readers will gain some insight into the kinds of weather to be expected during spring and summer—the main walking seasons for coastal routes. I hope the following notes will prove helpful, but bear in mind that these statistics are based on a 10-year average and that our fickle climate is subject to uncharacteristic episodes at any time of year.

While national weather forecasts on radio and television will provide general, countrywide predictions, local stretches of coastline often create their own unique conditions. For more specific forecasts, British Telecom's regional Weathercall service is useful. If you are familiar with meteorological terminology, the BBC's Shipping Forecasts issued at 1.55 pm and 5.50 pm will furnish you with an up-to-the-minute synopsis and invaluable data on barometric pressure, wind speed and direction, and visibility. Relevant Sea Areas are included in the following regional summaries of coastal weather.

Wales (Sea Areas Lundy and Irish Sea): By comparison with its hilly interior, the Welsh coast is relatively dry and sunny, the north coast for example receiving less than a third of the rainfall in adjacent Snowdonia and proportionately more sunshine. Frost and snow are rare but gales occur on exposed, west-facing coasts and headlands such as Anglesey and St Ann's Head on an average of 30 days per year. May and June are the sunniest months, July and August the warmest (18°C, 64°F), August and September the wettest (total 5.9in.), April and May the driest.

South-West England (Sea Areas Lundy and Plymouth): Torbay, the far south-west and the Isles of Scilly enjoy exceptionally sunny and warm weather compared to most of Britain, June being the best month. Sea fog can present problems early and late in the season, but winters are often pleasantly mild with very little risk of frost or snow on the coast. Gales, however, are common in exposed areas like Land's End and The Lizard, predominantly south-westerly in direction and occurring on some 30 days a year. July and August are the warmest months (19°C, 66°F), August and September the wettest (total 7.3in.), April and June the driest.

Southern England (Sea Areas Portland and Wight): Protected from northerly and easterly winds by hills inland, the south coast experiences a very pleasant climate, with little frost or snow. Like the south-west, sunshine hours are long, reaching their average daily maximum of 7.8 hours in June, but rainfall is less and occurs most frequently during September and later. April and June are the driest months, July and August the warmest (21°C, 70°F).

South-East England (Sea Areas Dover and Thames): Temperature differences between summer and winter are greater here than anywhere else on Britain's coast. Rainfall, however, is relatively light, June being the driest month. Sunshine is generous, reaching a peak average of over 8 hours per day in June, particularly along the Sussex coast. Sea fog is more common than usual, occurring on 30 to 40 days a year, with Beachy Head a notably foggy spot!

Eastern England (Sea Area Humber): Though often warm and dry in summer when the rest of Britain is affected by rain-laden south westerlies, snow is more frequent in winter. Rainfall is quite light, but bitter east winds can spoil spring days. Sea fog—the notorious 'roak'—affects 20 to 25 days a year. July and August are the warmest months (21°C, 70°F), April and June the driest, May and June the sunniest.

North-East England (Sea Area Tyne): Frequently overcast and chilly, with snow common in winter, this is one of Britain's least favoured coasts. Strong northerly winds and sea fogs keep temperatures depressed and spring arrives late due to the influence of a cold North Sea. Wettest months are July and August (total 5.1in.), driest April, warmest July and August (18°C, 64°F), sunniest May and June. Bracing when the weather is fine, autumn is usually the most reliable season.

Eastern Scotland (Sea Areas Forth and Cromarty): Relatively low rainfall is caused by high ground to the west, but summers are generally cool, especially under a chilly sea fog or 'haar'. Winter conditions can be snowy and frequent gales occur to the north. May and June are sunniest (especially south of the Moray Firth), July and August warmest (16°C, 61°F), August and September wettest (total 6.5in.).

North-West Scotland (Sea Areas Fair Isle and Hebrides): Despite local exceptions, this is Britain's wettest coastline, with up to 50in. of rain per year. Sunshine hours are good, however, in southern parts of the Inner Hebrides and winters are generally mild, with few severe frosts or heavy snowfalls. Coasts exposed to the Atlantic suffer severe gales, but sea fogs are relatively infrequent. July, August and September are the wettest months (total 11.2in.), July and August the warmest (16°C, 61°F). North-west airstreams of polar origin often produce magnificently clear visibility.

South-West Scotland (Sea Area Malin): Sheltered from Atlantic storms and rain-bearing winds by the hills of Northern Ireland, Kintyre and Arran, this coastline is altogether more favoured than other western parts of Scotland. Warm ocean currents, mild temperatures and good sunshine make it popular with holidaymakers and even in winter, snow, frost and fog are rarely persistent. May and June are the sunniest months, July and August the warmest (19°C, 66°F), August and September the wettest (total 8in.).

North-West England (Sea Area Irish Sea): Spring here is sunny and moderately dry, especially in the south and on the Isle of Man. The climate is usually bracing, with mild winters producing few frosts or snowfalls of consequence compared to high ground inland. Autumns are wet, but where there is shelter from prevailing winds, conditions can be very pleasant. Sunniest months are May and June, the warmest June, July and August (18°C, 64°F).

Because wind speeds and direction are of particular concern to coastal walkers, the table shown here is useful in assessing the strength and effects of a blow. It is known as the Beaufort Scale and forms an international standard for mariners. On exposed coast paths, walking is hampered by winds of around Force 6 and great care is needed near cliff edges. Progress is only achieved with difficulty at Force 7 or 8 and beyond that, walking is virtually impossible, though the sea will present an awe-inspiring sight.

'Rough seas north of Whitby'.

BEAUFORT No.	DESIGNATION/ AVERAGE SPEED IN KNOTS	EFFECTS OF WIND ON THE SEA
0	CALM – under 1	Smooth, glassy sea.
1	LIGHT – 2	Small, scale-like ripples without crests.
2	LIGHT– 5	Small waves, still short and smooth but more pronounced.
3	LIGHT – 8	White caps forming but still mostly smooth. Occasional white foam appearing.
4	MODERATE – 13	Waves still small but longer. White caps fairly general.
5	FRESH – 18	Moderate sized waves now long and more pronounced. White caps everywhere. Occasional spray forming.
6	STRONG – 24	Formation of larger waves. Crests break and leave areas of white foam. Some spray.
7	STRONG – 30	Sea heaps up. Long streaks of foam begin to form along the wind. More spray. Some difficulty walking against the wind.
8	GALE – 37	Large waves with very long crests. Spray blown off crests. Long, thick streaks of foam. Walking considerably impeded.
9	SEVERE GALE – 44	Mountainous seas. Dense streaks of foam along the wind. Wave crests begin to topple and roll over. Spray may affect visibility.
10	STORM – 52	Towering, tumbling waves with long, overhanging crests. Sea white with foam. Visibility restricted by spray. Considerable structural damage on land.
11	VIOLENT STORM – 60	Extremely mountainous seas, white and foaming. Drastically reduced visibility. Widespread damage on land.
12	HURRICANE – 68+	Air filled with driving foam and spray as wave crests are torn off by the wind. Sea completely white and frothy. Visibility very difficult. Devastation on land but rarely experienced.

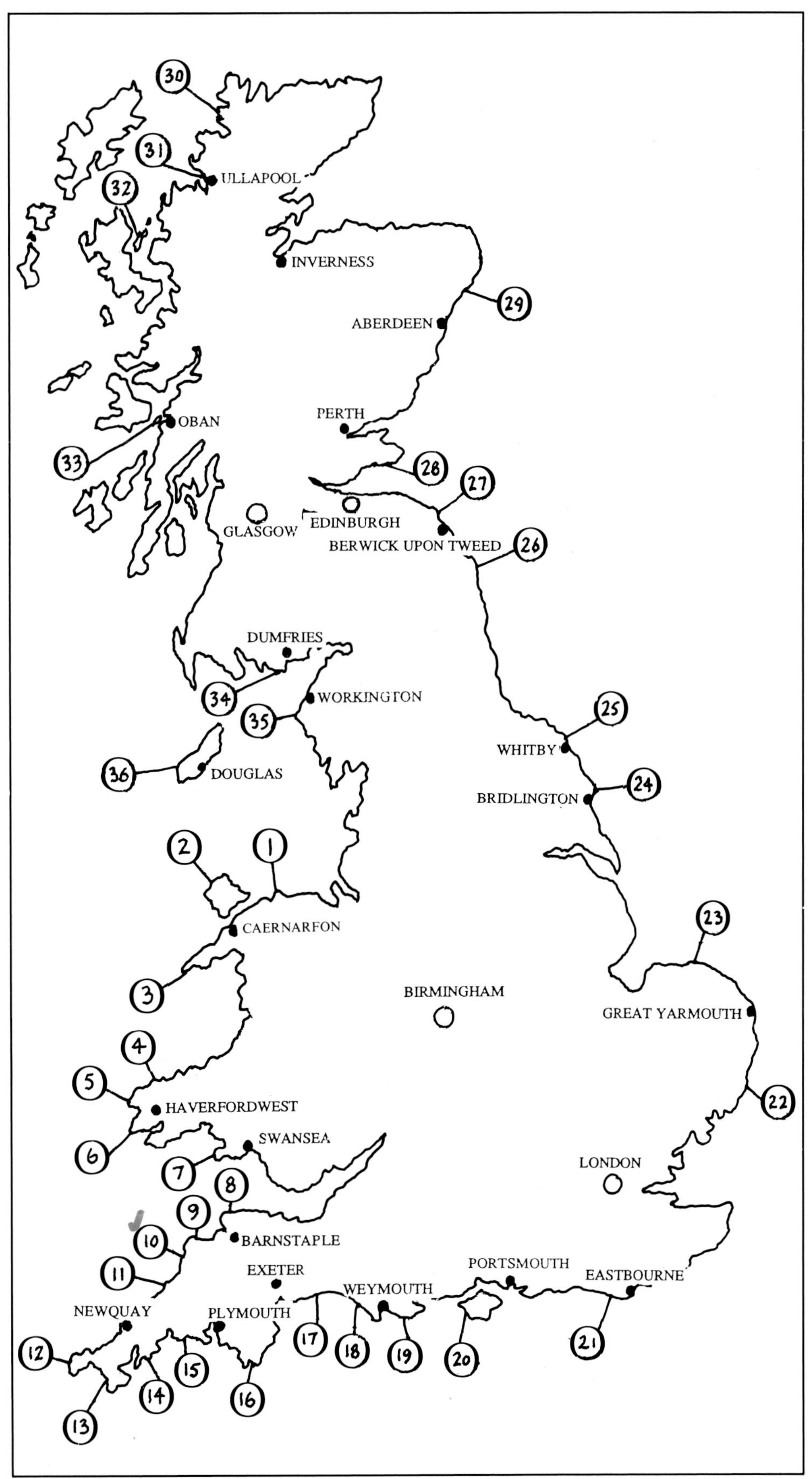
30
31
ULLAPOOL
32
INVERNESS
29
ABERDEEN
OBAN
PERTH
33
28
27
GLASGOW
EDINBURGH
BERWICK UPON TWEED
26
DUMFRIES
34
WORKINGTON
35
25
WHITBY
36
DOUGLAS
BRIDLINGTON
24
2
1
CAERNARFON
23
3
BIRMINGHAM
GREAT YARMOUTH
4
5
HAVERFORDWEST
22
6
SWANSEA
7
LONDON
8
9
10
BARNSTAPLE
11
EXETER
PORTSMOUTH
EASTBOURNE
WEYMOUTH
NEWQUAY
PLYMOUTH
12
17
18
19
20
21
15
14
16
13

Gathering storm over northern Snowdonia and the Conwy estuary, from the Great Orme.

WALK 1: *Gwynedd — The Great Orme, Llandudno*

Map: OS Landranger Sheet 115—Caernarfon and Bangor. **Start & Finish:** West Shore, Llandudno. **Distance:** 4½miles (7.5km)—allow 2 to 3 hours. **Access:** Llandudno is just off the A55 North Wales coast road between Colwyn Bay and Conwy. Nearest railway station—Llandudno. **Type of Walking:** Mixed terrain—rocky paths, farm tracks, surfaced pathways and minor roads; a sizeable climb to begin with, then easy gradients. **Features of Interest:** Superlative views of the Conwy estuary, Snowdonia and Llandudno Bay; limestone pavements; St Tudno's church; ornamental gardens. **Accommodation:** Widely available in Llandudno and the surrounding area.

The Circuit of a Magnificent Limestone Headland

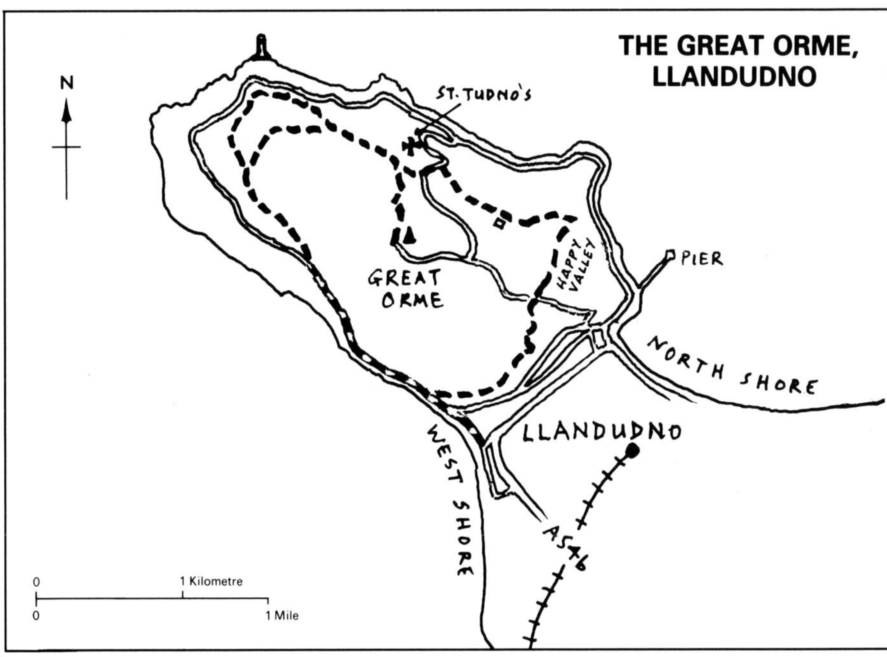

There is a local maxim that whatever the weather over Snowdonia, the Great Orme basks in sunshine. This I can vouch for, having gazed on many occasions from the bleak, overcast summits of the northern Carneddau mountains down to this distant headland, caught in what has seemed like its own improbably theatrical lighting. Such a meteorological advantage is, no doubt, bestowed on the Great Orme by virtue of its bold intrusion 3 miles (5km) into the Irish Sea, its long whaleback dominating the coastline in both directions.

Being limestone, formed from the compressed skeletons of tropical sea creatures during the Carboniferous Period between 300 and 350 million years ago, the Great Orme provides distinctive walking country. Its short grasses, lime-loving flowers and limestone pavements are all reminiscent of the Yorkshire Dales, but there is no mistaking the ozone as you walk out above the 'scars' of dipping rock strata to the call of seabirds. This is a landscape of outstanding importance, designated as Heritage Coast and managed as a Country Park and Nature Reserve.

The Victorian resort of Llandudno, laid out in the mid-1800s by Edward Mostyn and Owen Williams on former marshland, is focused on the wide sweep of promenade and hotels along North Shore. Less than a mile away across the isthmus and facing the lumpy silhouette of Snowdonia lies the less developed West Shore, protected from breaking waves by a terraced sea wall and groynes. Here at low tide, sandbanks in the Conwy estuary merge uncertainly with tidal shallows, setting a trap for the unwary, but most visitors congregate on the sand-and-shingle beach or around the boating lake.

This walk begins along Marine Drive, a toll road circling the Great Orme midway between sea level and the summit plateau. Completed in 1878 for horses and pony traps, it is now surfaced and provided with a pavement throughout its length. Vehicles drive one way (anticlockwise), but a recent rock fall resulting in the freak death of a pedestrian officially closed the Drive, though you can still use it at your own risk. At the time of writing, moves are afoot by the local council to reinstate the toll road after yet another rock fall. Many people walk round Marine Drive, but it lacks so much of the variety and interest of the high route as to be of little value to serious walkers.

Eroded limestone cliffs hang menacingly over the road at first, but you are soon passing private houses and beginning to climb. On the left, Llys Helig Drive leads to select properties along a fringe of almost level ground. During World War II, the Coast Artillery School transferred here from the more vulnerable Shoeburyness and was operational from September 24th 1940, its officers and men housed in local hotels. You can still walk along old concrete roadways to a few huts.

A short distance further up Marine Drive, a footpath leaves to the right. After a rocky start, this ledge of green turf angles excitingly up over less precipitous slopes caused by the dipping of rock strata through a geological fault. The going is without difficulty but grows steeper towards the top, eventually bringing you out near a substantial wall enclosing farmland.

Few coastal locations in Britain offer views as wide-ranging, as varied, or as breathtakingly beautiful as this western rim of the Great Orme. The south-west horizon swells to the northern summits of Snowdonia—notably Conwy Mountain, Tal y Fan, Drum and Foel Fras—while low-lying Anglesey reclines in the west, the Menai Straits which separate it from the mainland barely discernible. Below you, corrugated by breezes, a glittering plane of water spans the mouth of Conwy River, drawing the eye upstream past Deganwy to the grey towers of Conwy Castle.

By following the wall seawards but keeping as near the shattered, rocky edge as is safe, the Great Orme's geological structure becomes clear. During the same great convulsions of the earth's crust which formed the Alps, layers of limestone here moved vertically and horizontally to produce a fault (though the mountains of Snowdonia shielded the Great Orme from more dramatic movement). Such folding allowed molten rock and gasses to intrude and later solidify; veins of lead and copper, in particular, were laid down in the Orme and were mined intensively during the eighteenth and nineteenth centuries from deposits east of the summit.

At a low cairn, the wall swings right and with it the path. Ahead lie several swathes of limestone pavement, the rock laid bare by retreating ice 12,000 years ago and weathered into 'grykes' (deep fissures often occupied by grasses, flowers or dwarf hawthorn) and 'clints' (the remaining raised blocks).

By staying alongside the wall, though pleasant enough, you miss a full appreciation of the headland's northern limits. Numerous pathways and sheep tracks wind hither and thither through beds of gorse, bell heather and ling, including a path from a picnic area over to the left near the highest point on Marine Drive. Probably the most entertaining line is to follow the path to the left of the first limestone pavement and aim for rising ground straight ahead. This leads you over to craggy slopes above Marine Drive and the old lighthouse, now a private residence offering bed and breakfast.

On any suitable trod, or simply by picking a way through obstructions, you can explore the boulders and outcrops which litter this exposed extremity of the Great Orme. A mile to the east are well known rock climbing cliffs, and beyond them the coast of Clwyd melts into the hazy distance. Walking continues, roughly south-east, through an odd landscape of dark vegetation liberally scattered with bleached and eroded rocks, a chaotic surface full of fascinating close-range detail.

Deeper deposits of soil left here by retreating glaciers and known as glacial drift or Boulder Clay, support mature heathland and bracken, and you might expect to find Heath Milkwort, Heath Bedstraw, Tormentil and Heath Speedwell. Elsewhere on the Great Orme, particularly on its south western flanks, more typical limestone grassland is found, containing such springtime species as Salad Burnett, Wild Thyme, Quaking Grass and Common Rockrose, along with many types of butterflies and birds.

Wherever you wander, before long you will meet the field wall again near a cottage-loaf shaped boulder. The way rises as a broad green track which becomes stony and contours above St Tudno's church. Llandudno ('Lands of the Church of Tudno') owes its name to the sixth-century Christian missionary who chose this site for his work. The original timber building was ultimately reconstructed in stone and parts of the existing church date back to the twelfth century.

Panoramic views are obtained from the OS pillar on high ground to the right (679ft/207m), but a steep pull up is involved to reach it; either veer right above a wall on a thin, rocky path or attack the grassy slopes direct. This must rank as an almost obligatory detour for those with time and energy to spare, for at the top is a cabin-lift station, a large café, a Visitor Centre, a children's adventure playground, a car park and the funicular Llandudno Tramway which will return you to the town in sedate fashion for a modest fee!

Resuming the circuit walk, you drop to the road by St Tudno's (just below are tea gardens and toilets) and take to an old bridleway on the right, keeping ahead at a fork. Passing Penmynydd Isa, known locally as Pink Farm, you soon approach open hillside again and by swinging left at the next path intersection you will find yourself climbing gently towards the walk's dramatic *dénouement* above Llandudno Bay. To reach this elevated viewpoint, you skirt above the Happy Valley dry ski slope and climb to a rocky bulge of land, the eastern ramparts of the Great Orme. There is a bird's-eye view of Llandudno pier and the curving flourish of North Shore, culminating in the Little Orme. (This headland, though of smaller stature, is also worthy of exploration on foot.) If a westerly should be blowing—and one often is—refuge can be sought among outcrops below the crest and there is no finer picnic spot!

The Great Orme's sheltered town side is inevitably more built upon and one can expect a descent of different character. Happy Valley contains a popular ski slope and toboggan run, to the right of which a muddy path takes you down past cafés to a road. For a while the route is unprepossessing, but having crossed the tramway rails and walked a hundred metres up the road opposite, escape from the urban is at hand. The footpath in question turns down left and undulates through pleasant deciduous woodland, before plunging down a series of steps into Haulfre Gardens. Interconnected walkways at different heights give access to an aviary and various perspectives over a flat townscape, but the main tarmac path passes a tea room and heads seaward back to Marine Drive.

Below: ***A curious landscape of boulders and limestone outcrops on the Great Orme's eastern flanks.***

WALK 2: *Isle of Anglesey — North Coast*

Map: OS Landranger Sheet 114—Anglesey. **Start:** Cemaes harbour. **Finish:** Point Lynas. **Distance:** 10 miles (16km)—allow about 5 hours. **Access:** Cemaes is on the A5025 north of Holyhead. Nearest railway station—Holyhead. **Type of Walking:** Undulating clifftop with some steep gradients at first; path rocky, boggy and near the edge at times; a little road walking. **Features of Interest:** Llanbadrig church; ruined china-clay works at Porth Llanlleiana; Dinas Gynfor hill fort on the most northerly headland in Wales; Hell's Mouth inlet; ruined Cemaes brickworks at Porth Wen; old Amlwch port; spectacular cliff scenery and rocky foreshore. **Accommodation:** Available at Cemaes, Bull Bay and Amlwch.

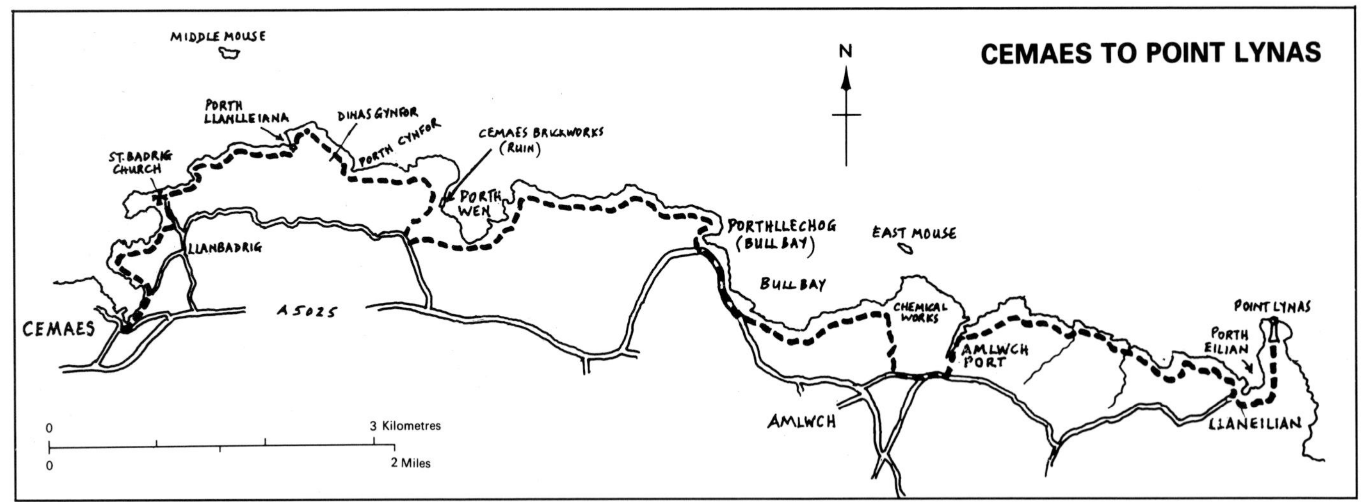

Previous page: ***Cemaes harbour.***

Contrasts Between Nature and the Hand of Man

Anglesey—Ynys Môn to the Welsh— sprawls off the north-west coast of Wales. Cheek by jowl with Snowdonia which lies unfolded like a viewcard across the Menai Straits, southern Anglesey is well populated and eminently accessible thanks to the nineteenth-century bridge building of Thomas Telford and Robert Stephenson. To the north, however beyond the rail and A5 links to Holyhead and the Irish ferry, indeterminate farmland and rough grazing spread between narrow lanes towards the sea. As if subdued by the prevailing 'ocean' winds, this landscape of low pasture and gale-honed copses, of ruined windmills, pinched grey villages and brackish lakes seldom rises above 150 metres.

Were Anglesey's coast as pastorally monotonous as its interior, fewer than do would visit the island, yet the unexpected beauty and seclusion of its bays, beaches, cliffs and headlands draw thousands of holidaymakers during the summer months. Seekers after fine coastal scenery and the outdoor life will find more satisfaction here than those expecting amusement arcades and night-life. But the picture, unsullied though it is for the most part, contains some ugly contradictions. The siting of Wylfa nuclear power station and Amlwch's chemical works on coastline of outstanding natural beauty, or the disturbance caused by low flying aircraft around RAF Valley, for example, are seriously disconcerting. With little need to consider the environmental consequences of their enterprises, our industrious forefathers left their marks here, as elsewhere on Britain's coast. Today, however, the installations are largely ruinous and are explored enthusiastically by students of industrial archaeology.

Although a walking route exists around Anglesey, it is not a continuous coast path as such, often resorting to lanes and tracks where access to the cliffs is unavailable. Several stretches of good length can be found, however. None points up more keenly the essential paradox of Anglesey's shore—great beauty threatened by man's insensitivity past and present—than that between Cemaes and Point Lynas in the north of the island, the walk described below.

Cemaes was the centre of North Anglesey's coastal trade until Amlwch's harbour was developed in the late eighteenth century. Since then, fishing has suffered changes in fortune, augmented these days by trips for the tourists. The bay holds no fewer than five safe bathing beaches: add to that a picturesque little village and harbour and you have a magnet attracting holidaymakers who enjoy getting off the beaten track.

Unfortunately, it is impossible to ignore the blank, rectilinear silhouette of Wylfa nuclear power station on the bay's western headland. While not applauding its position on such a delectable coast, one accepts it—along with the army firing ranges, the military airfields, the sewage outlets, the oil refineries, the mines, quarries and other industrial eyesores that blight Britain's shoreline—with philosophical resignation. At least the bits in between can still be savoured and there is every chance that our increasingly environment-conscious society will refuse to sanction similar developments in the future.

East from Cemaes harbour, a walkway along a low sea wall brings you to a large corrugated-iron café by car parking at the end of a lane. The cliff path is signposted just beyond the café and climbs steeply onto low cliffs owned by the National Trust. Threading round the edges of fields, you pass several idyllic spots, one where the sea has penetrated the outer rocks to pour in through a small cave, filling a pool in a grassy valley behind. The easternmost sandy beach in Cemaes Bay (Porth Padrig) to which you can easily descend, is too far from amenities to become crowded and here the path heads up to a kissing gate at the country road from Llanbadrig; 250m along to the left stands the clifftop church of St Badrig, said to have been founded by St Patrick in gratitude for surviving a shipwreck on Middle Mouse rocks on his way over from Ireland.

The church and its little walled cemetery are perched on the edge of rough pasture where the cliffs turn east. Sadly, the interior was badly damaged by fire and, at the time of writing, is not open to the public. From here the walk's character grows more rugged and spectacular and walkers wishing to start at this point could use the small National Trust car park; there is no verge parking on the single track lanes. Passing through a handgate by the church, you follow the cemetery wall round, cross a stile and contour narrowly above the sea to an overhanging cliff below a rocky knoll. At the top, a wire fence is crossed at a pile of stones and a left turn made alongside old, rusting fence posts towards a wall. The path is poorly defined over close-knit turf but stays outside the tumbledown wall, dropping steeply at first then undulating along, with Middle Mouse rock island not far offshore.

These high, convex hillsides are grazed by sheep whose hooves have worn sundry parallel trods at different levels. By staying lower down on the steeper slopes, there is a more exciting sense of exposure and in fact a plainer path does establish itself as you come round to face the most northerly headland in Wales, atop whose sheer cliffs stands a small monument. Before reaching the inlet, unstable and very steep ground forces you behind the last hump, where the path provides a bird's-eye view of Porth Llanlleiana. Derelict buildings, a chimney and walled bays here at the mouth of a reedy valley are the remains of a diminutive works and harbour which once shipped out locally dug china-clay; the small, pebbly beach is hemmed in by impressive cliff faces.

Seaward of the main ruin, a stiff climb will take you back to clifftop level and on to the monument—a rather un-pretty concrete and brick affair in a state of semi-dereliction but a conspicuous landmark nevertheless. Beyond a series of jutting headlands, the distant lighthouse on Point Lynas marks the walk's eastern terminus.

Winding through heather and bracken, you quickly reach the National Trust's Dinas Gynfor. Limestone outcrops on this high and windy promontory were adapted by Iron Age man to enclose a fortress some 700 x 300m in extent. There are views past quartz-seamed boulders to serrated cliffs ahead, towards which the path descends in a shallow gully. Porth Cynfor (Hell's Mouth) lives up to its name only in rare north-easterly blows and the tiny cove's enclosing rocks would hardly invite landing by boat in all but the quietest seas.

Over a fence stile, there is a stepped climb up rough slopes and the path is soon crossing bracken below rocky bluffs. The highest point—Graig Wen—gleams white with quartz and supports an OS pillar at 298ft (91m). Old winding gear on the right belongs to the long defunct Cemaes Brickworks, above which you soon pass, while over to the left on Torllwyn headland stands a beacon mast used by shipping to determine an exact nautical mile (the other stands 500m north-west of Porthllechog). You crest a rise and drop south past a waymark post on a pleasant grassy track above Porth Wen bay to where the brickworks chimney tops peep above rough ground on the left.

Although not a public right of way, a much used path leads down the old winding ramp to the derelict works (beware crumbling masonry). On a remote and unspoilt sweep of coast below steep hillsides, it is an astonishing location for such an enterprise. However, that it once thrived is evident in the still freshly coloured brickwork of hoppers and kilns, two intact chimneys and a substantial quay. Like all such relics of our industrial past, these remaining buildings will eventually succumb to the elements; sadly, the site is too inaccessible for conservation work to be viable.

The way now climbs inland to reveal a sparsely populated hinterland of low hills; conspicuous to the south-east is Parys Mountain with its windmill tower stump. Reaching a farm road at a gate, you turn left and in 20m left again into a field. A ruined wall leads to the next handgate where you walk ahead half-right and will soon spot the following gate at the field bottom. Continuing thus through fields above Porth Wen, there are good retrospective views of the brickworks; as you pass Castell farm, keep left to resume clifftop walking around Trwynbychan.

The old copper port of Amlwch.

A mile or so of gentle eastward progress ensues above spectacularly inclined rock strata towards Bull Bay (Porthllechog). From a coast path sign, a broad track short-cuts right, but the final little headland offers superior views and delivers you at the road near the Bull Bay Hotel (drinks and snacks here and at the nearby post office/stores). Popular with sub-aqua divers, fishermen and holidaymakers alike, Bull Bay was a busy shipbuilding port at one time; later it became a base for 4-oared pilot boats plying the approaches to Liverpool.

Passing the Yacht Club slipway, you turn left alongside the A5025 for about 800m. There is pavement all the way and underfoot monotony is compensated for by continuing sea views until, opposite the Bull Bay Golf Club entrance, the coast path turns off left over pasture above low cliffs. Soon you are weaving in and out past chaotically bedded foreshore rocks of Pre-Cambrian origins—a feature of this entire walk—with East Mouse islet now offshore. Parallel trods converge by a wall and, beyond a boggy hollow, the path continues over heather and knobbly outcrops.

While nineteenth-century brickworks and china-clay works evoke fascinating images of an industrial era long past, Amlwch's chemical plant, already spied from afar, will provoke groans of disapproval. Mislocated though it undoubtedly seems, this enclave of the petrochemical industry quickly gives way to more coastline of incomparable quality, leaving perhaps an aftertaste of regret tinged with the realisation that we all depend on oil products and should not bury our heads in the sand. Approaching the plant over rough grass, you pass through a wall gap and turn right to an old wall stile by gorse bushes. From here it is inland past houses to the road, turning left along to Amlwch's port inlet.

Originally a modest fishing hamlet, Amlwch became a boom town reminiscent of the Klondike in the late eighteenth century following the discovery of an exceptionally rich copper vein in nearby Parys Mountain. Within 30 years, the settlement's population had swelled to 6000, with an ale-house to every six souls: it was a wonder any work got done at all! Copper was extracted in open-cast workings by men, women and children, the pumps driven by windmill, and Amlwch port was developed to admit ore-carrying vessels. Competition from America and Africa ended the copper boom here (in Cornwall too), but not before the Parys Mountain Copper Company had minted its own distinctive tokens when copper coins of the realm were in short supply during the late 1700s.

Shell's Marine Terminal here receives oil from tankers moored offshore and pumps it via a storage depot at Rhosgoch to Stanilow refinery near Liverpool. Although large ships can be seen off the outer harbour, fishing and pleasure craft dominate the picturesque old port inlet. A path leads down to the quayside which is followed to its seaward end where

Facing page: **Bardsey Island – a view from Pen-y-Cil headland.**

Left: **The Pilot Station and lighthouse on Point Lynas, from the cliffs near Porth Eilian.**

steps behind a building take you to a tarmac road past the oil installation entrance. Beyond a wide turning area, the way veers to the right of the house ahead, passes through a gate and bears right over rough, lumpy terrain to another handgate visible on the cliff edge.

The next 2½ miles (4km) are a fitting climax to this walk; a mellow, friendly stretch (except in a northerly gale!) full of detail and dramatic rock scenery. At first on stony level ground, the path drops through a delightful valley of gorse and bracken to cross a stream on concrete slabs. Knobbly, uneven going precedes the next watercourse which spouts noisily in a waterfall upstream of gravelly shallows where a crossing is easiest. In spate, the stream will almost certainly give you wet feet! Keep to the cliff edge here, for little rocky corners above the sea are more entertaining than the alternative path tens of metres inland. Descending round the back of Porthyrychan can be marshy, but ladder stile and handgate lead onto firm pasture. Three hundred metres up a path to the right stands Llaneilian village whose unusual church possesses many features of note, inside and out.

Never are you more aware of elemental rock than between Amlwch and Point Lynas. Variegated and seductively textural, it thrusts through a skin of vegetation and slants in black reefs beneath the sucking waves. High water on Point Lynas is stained ruler-straight like a fracture line along the promontory. Climbing to a final elevated viewpoint, you are left with a gradual descent through gorse into Porth Eilian, arriving at the road-end turning circle by a slipway above the tiny cove.

To complete this walk, you take a surfaced track veering left. Now just a half mile distant, Point Lynas Pilot Station and lighthouse were established in 1835 by the trustees of Liverpool Docks. Six-oared pilot boats once moored here and ships bound for Liverpool Bay continue to take on pilots to this day. Modern communication masts on Mynydd Eilian—high ground to the south of Llaneilian village—have superseded the original telegraph signal station. The lighthouse complex can be visited and there are rewarding views back to Bull Bay.

WALK 3: *Gwynedd — The Western Lleyn Peninsula*

Map: OS Landranger Sheet 123—Lleyn Peninsula. **Start & Finish:** Aberdaron village. **Distance:** 8 miles (13km)—allow 4 to 5 hours. **Access:** Aberdaron lies at the end of B4413 west of Llanbedrog, itself just west of Pwllheli. Nearest railway station—Pwllheli. **Type of Walking:** Undulating clifftop paths exposed to the weather, at times indistinct or even non-existent. A couple of stiff ascents to around 600ft (180m). Some country lane walking to complete the circular route. **Features of Interest:** Porth Meudwy; Bardsey Island; site of St Mary's chapel and well; Mynedd Mawr and Mynedd Analog summit panoramas; spectacular views of cliffs, islands and the Lleyn Peninsula landscape. **Accommodation:** A few hotels and seasonal guest houses at Aberdaron; several camping and caravan sites in the area. Much more accommodation at Abersoch, Llanbedrog and Pwllheli. No youth hostels on the peninsula.

Round the Tip of Remotest Wales

It is hard to look at a map of the Lleyn peninsula and not be reminded of Cornwall. The Celtic heritage of these double-pronged arms thrusting out into the western seas is a shared one, but while Cornwall's has become all but submerged—to the casual observer at least—by the sheer weight of tourism and second-home ownership, that of the Lleyn remains largely intact. Its farthest extremity, dubbed the 'Land's End of North Wales' (a clumsy analogy the Welsh justifiably resent) and explored by this walk, has changed down the centuries less than most parts of the Principality. Off season, one senses a foreign-ness here—echoes of Brittany or south-west Ireland in the walled pastureland and isolated farms—and a separateness from the mainstream of British countryside that is both quintessentially Welsh and irresistible to lovers of wild places.

Despite a scattering of holiday homes, a thorn in the side of Welsh nationalism, and the busy south coast resorts of Abersoch, Llanbedrog and Pwllheli, the landscape is predominantly agricultural. There has been none of Cornwall's quest for mineral ores and china-clay, none of the pressures inflicted by fast major roads and a frantic holiday industry. Tortuous lanes, an obstructive spine of

Left: **Looking back to Aberdaron from the cliffs above Porth Simmde.**

Right: **Porth Meudwy.**

high, pointed hills and generally low-key development help insulate the Lleyn from trippers in search of instant experience: even in peak season when, admittedly, traffic makes getting around less easy, there is ample scope for escape into solitude.

Aberdaron sits in a fold of its south-facing bay on the threshold of the Lleyn peninsula's western tip—a hilly bastion of land facing Bardsey Island. The final mainland resting place for fourteenth-century pilgrims on their long journey to the Abbey of St Mary on Bardsey was Y-Gegin Fawr (The Big Kitchen), now converted into a café near the old hump-backed bridge. One somehow associates such history with impregnability, yet recent sea defences betray the village's subjugation to centuries of marine erosion. Indeed, the large twelfth-to-fifteenth century church of St Hywyn, whose hillside cemetery rises incongruously above the beach, has been spared from encroaching waves only by the construction of its own sea wall. Visitors to the village are accommodated in a small, seasonal car park; among the few modest shops is a post office designed by Clough William-Ellis of Portmeirion fame.

Our first objective is to reach the cliff path above Porth Simmde at the western end of the bay. At low tide one can simply walk along the beach and climb the stepped path but, if high water prevents this, it is impossible to cross the stream mouth or gain the adjacent cliffs. In that event, a left turn up a lane just past the bridge leads in 500m to a footpath on the left dropping between two bungalows and crossing the Afon Saint, which plunges into an overgrown ravine.

Well waymarked at first the path passes steps from the beach and soon a ruined building, as it undulates along heavily vegetated slopes (mostly unwelcome brambles) with increasingly good views back to Aberdaron. At a kissing gate by gorse bushes, it dives into the shadowy recesses of Porth Meudwy—a slipway and small beach of rocks and pebbles. One or two boats, drawn up by tractor, lie next to lobster pots near a low, stone shed and out between the enclosing cliffs is Trwyn y Penrhyn, the eastern flanks of Aberdaron Bay.

The stream is crossed on stones, steps leading back to clifftop level. If after heavy rain or highest tides the stream is too deep, follow the track inland and where it trends right, look for a path left over a little footbridge. This climbs to Tir Glyn farm. Turn left along the country lane, left again at the next junction and continue to the lane end. Here, the coast path, having passed the tiny inlets of Porth Cloch and Porth y Pistyll, comes up inland by some bungalows.

Angling uphill past farm buildings, the way

takes to a rough track across grass towards a ladder stile on the skyline ahead, the boundary of the National Trust's Pen y Cil headland. Whether or not a detour is made out to the cliff edges, gloriously expansive views can be enjoyed, especially to the east across Aberdaron Bay with its twin rock islands of Gwylan-fawr and Gwylan-bach. Following a wall round to the right through a farm gate, slightly rising ground above unseen Parwyd cove provides the fist sighting of Bardsey Island (unless Pen y Cil was visited). Lying 2 miles (3km) off the mainland and known somewhat prosaically to the Welsh as Ynys Enlli (Isle of Tides, or Eddies), this remote rock mass is seen to better advantage from further along the coast. However, its presence across the treacherous tidal-race of Bardsey Sound is keenly sensed throughout the next mile or two of walking.

There is every reason to pause at the next stile before the path loses height west of Trwyn Bychestyn, for views are unusually wide ranging. White Coastguard buildings on Mynedd Mawr and Mynedd Anelog's bulk to the right monopolise the forward horizon; hillsides around Uwchmynydd are dotted with cottages. Tremendous vistas open out in clear weather, spanning the peninsula's length to the distant mountains of Snowdonia.

Continuing over rough grass alongside an old derelict wall to a gate, a left turn is taken down a grassy track between banks past two traditional Welsh cottages, now holiday homes. Seawards, the track narrows to a path and a metal gate gives access to clifftop land outside an ancient matrix of walled field enclosures

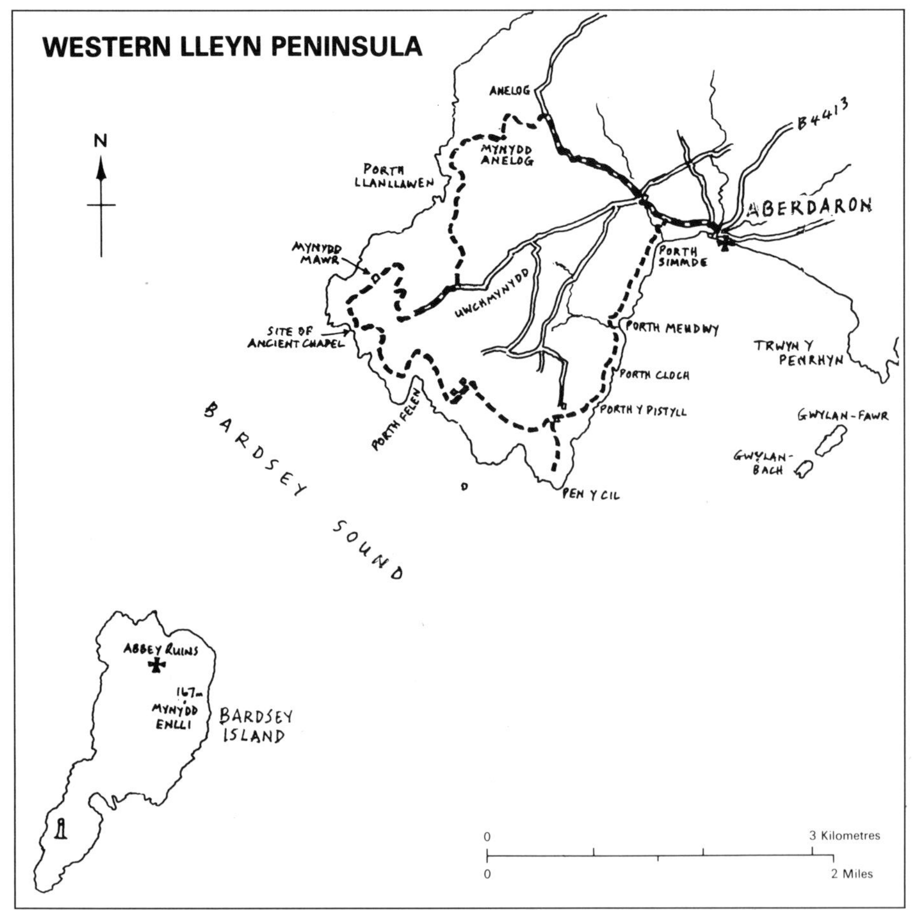

Facing page: ***On the descent from Pen-yr-Afr after rounding Cemaes Head.***

reminiscent of County Kerry in south-western Ireland, though, as with much on the Lleyn peninsula, more intimate in scale.

A barbed wire fence, with no evident stile at my last visit, must be negotiated before a shallow gully is reached at a ladder stile above Porth Felen. (Ordnance Survey rights of way bear little resemblance to existing trods on this rugged section.) Right provides a short cut to the public road-end and car park under Mynedd Mawr, but the walk now swings left into National Trust territory round Trwyn y Gwydell and Trwyn Maen Melyn. A little further on it is possible—with great care and not at high water—to scramble down to sea level and locate the site of St Mary's chapel and well, where Bardsey pilgrims would have prayed and refreshed themselves before crossing to the island.

Without doubt, these slopes of rock and heather offer definitive views of Bardsey Island, bettered only by joining one of the fine-weather boat trips from Aberdaron or Pwllheli during the summer season. Founded in the sixth century, the Abbey of St Mair was a place of pilgrimage for hundreds of years; many pilgrims and holy men stayed and were buried there, giving rise to the title 'Island of 20,000 Saints'. During the early 1900s, Bardsey was still inhabited by a fishing and farming community, but today, apart from a few remaining tenant farmers, it is left largely to the sea birds for which it has become a sanctuary, and to the occasional boatload of ornithologists bound for the observatory. The abbey ruins lie beneath Mynedd Enlli, 548ft (167m), roughly in line with the lighthouse situated $1\frac{1}{2}$ foreshortened miles (2.5km) beyond at the island's south-west tip.

A rough path climbs above Braich y Pwll headland to the foundations of an old wartime radar station, from where a stepped concrete path makes a beeline for the Coastguard buildings and a small car park on Mynedd Mawr's summit, 524ft (160m) above the sea. A motorable track winds downhill, but in clear visibility views from the top should be savoured: they will take in Cardigan Bay to St David's Head, Snowdonia's peaks and even the Wicklow Mountains of Ireland.

During the descent, Mynedd Analog—the walk's culmination—is seen rising beyond an intervening valley, to reach which it is necessary to turn left along the public road for some 600m and turn left past a small lake. After forking right through a gate and swinging left (north-west) into a farm track, pasture and stiles are crossed until, just past the last building, the way veers right above a rocky creek.

Our path, such as it is, stays indistinctly along National Trust-owned, bracken-clad cliff-sides above Porth-Llanllawen. From the north side of this little bay, a direct ascent of Mynedd Analog can be made; concerted legwork is rewarded by a magnificent panorama from the 627ft (191m) top, including the Lleyn's as yet unrevealed north coast. Dropping north to a track and forking left past houses to the road at Analog hamlet, all that remains is a pleasant stroll on country lanes back to Aberdaron, just over a mile (2km) distant.

WALK 4: *Pembrokeshire — Poppit Sands to Newport*

Map: OS Landranger Sheet 145—Cardigan. **Start:** Poppit Sands. **Finish:** Newport harbour. **Distance:** 14 miles (23km)—allow 7 hours. **Access:** Poppit Sands is on the B4546 north-west from Cardigan (bus route). Newport is on the A487 (bus route). Nearest railway station—Fishguard. **Type of Walking:** High and unfrequented clifftops with some strenuous ups and downs: heavy undergrowth a problem in summer; rough underfoot conditions in places; no refreshments or amenities between either end of the walk. **Features of Interest:** The Teifi and Nyfer estuaries; highest cliffs on the Pembrokeshire coast; Witches' Cauldron collapsed sea cave; the historic town and sailing centre of Newport; prolific wildlife and spectacular rock scenery throughout. **Accommodation:** Available at Cardigan, St Dogmaels and Newport.

Majestic, Unspoiled Cliffs linking Two River Estuaries

Compact at around 180 miles (290km) in length and relatively undeveloped as a tourist destination compared with south-west England, Pembrokeshire's coast path possesses some of the finest coastal scenery in Britain, some would say in Europe. The Pembrokeshire National Park was inaugurated in 1952, although 18 years were to elapse before the coast path was completely open to walkers. Despite the county's amalgamation with Cardiganshire and Carmarthenshire in 1974 to form Dyfed, the Pembrokeshire label has stuck!

One can never be sure whether pronouncements about walks are free from subjective bias and it may be misleading to lay great emphasis on what lies in store when everyone's experience of the routes will undoubtedly differ. Nevertheless, after several excursions on the Pembrokeshire coast path, I can recommend it as a mellow, almost voluptuous shoreline, refreshingly free from exploitation and the tawdriness of over-use so often encountered along our hard pressed coast.

That said, the route does have its *bête noire*—a tramp through the oil refineries at Milford Haven—but, being relatively small, it can easily be overlooked. Harder by far is to decide which of the remaining coast to exclude from 'Classic Walk' status! In no sense are the three selected walks 'easy options'. Foul weather and

POPPIT SANDS TO NEWPORT

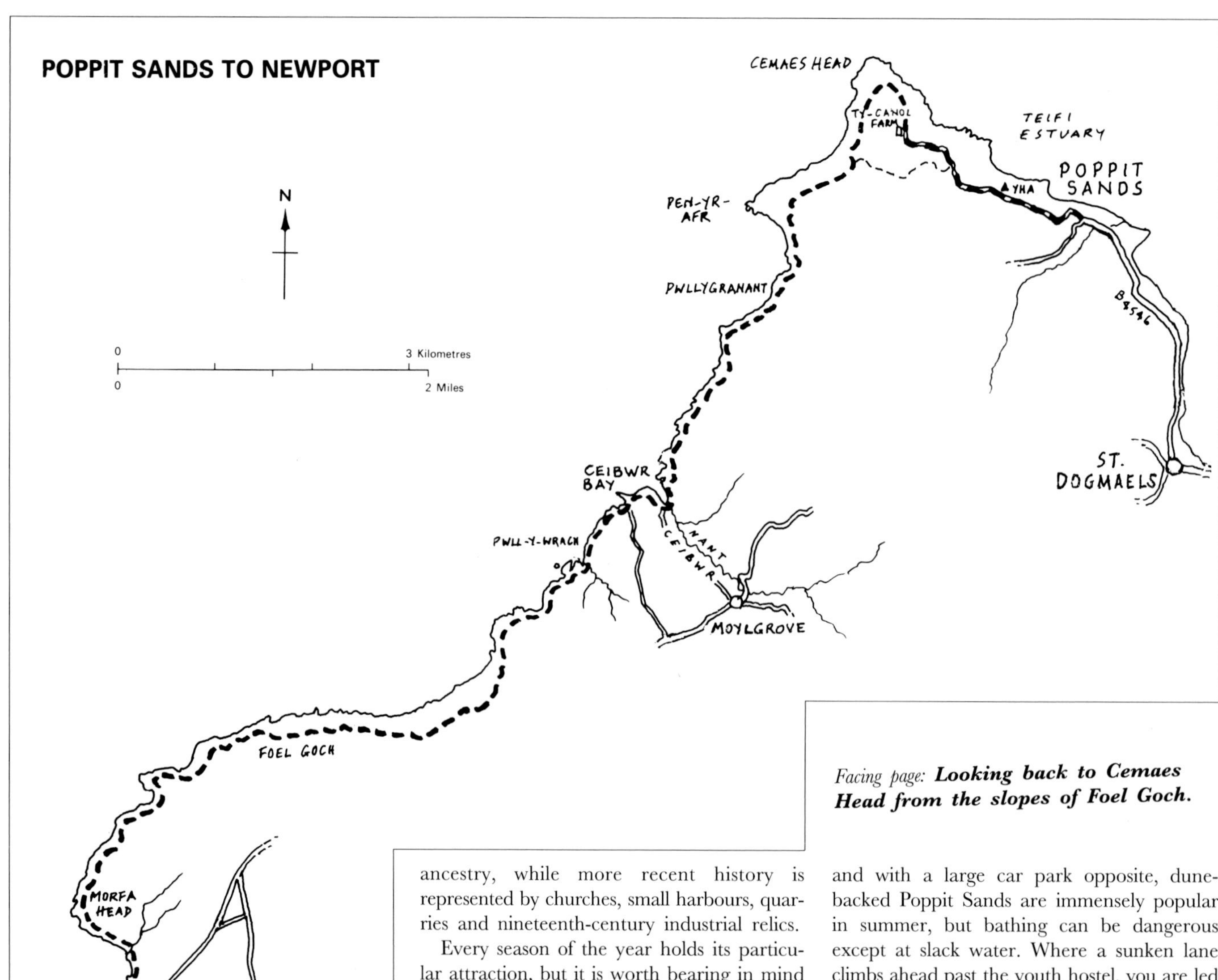

Facing page: ***Looking back to Cemaes Head from the slopes of Foel Goch.***

isolation from the reassuring presence of fellow humans can spice an outing on this exposed coast with enough challenging adversity to satisfy the hardiest among us! Yet the going never gets frustratingly difficult: although the terrain will make demands on legs and lungs, gradients show a certain restraint, with gentle stretches balancing the arduous ones.

Equally as absorbing and beautiful as the wild flowers and seabird colonies passed along the way is the shoreline's geology—a progression of many rock types and features. Iron Age promontory forts, hut circles, *cromlechau* and ancient trackways recall Pembrokeshire's long ancestry, while more recent history is represented by churches, small harbours, quarries and nineteenth-century industrial relics.

Every season of the year holds its particular attraction, but it is worth bearing in mind that accommodation and refreshments are harder to come by in winter. Weather patterns tend to settle down in springtime and the clifftops are embroidered then with a riot of colour. Although some flowers thrive even in mid-winter, May and June see a veritable eruption of blooms from species such as wild foxglove, spring squill, sea campion, horseshoe vetch, common spotted orchid, sea pinks and bluebells.

During high summer, bracken, brambles and gorse can slow progress dramatically and give you a drenching if wet, where the path is not regularly cleared. Autumn sees the southward migration of thousands of birds down the coast, while deep winter expeditions may be reserved for the lovers of solitude and storms.

Although the coast path officially starts at the colourful fishing village of St Dogmaels, built around an ancient abbey not far from Cardigan, there is little virtue in a 2-mile road-bash along the B4546 to reach the point where a proper coastal route for walkers begins. With good access on the coast road to Moylgrove and with a large car park opposite, dune-backed Poppit Sands are immensely popular in summer, but bathing can be dangerous except at slack water. Where a sunken lane climbs ahead past the youth hostel, you are led seawards with ever widening views over the estuary and Cardigan Island. The River Teifi sustains a modest salmon and sea trout fishing industry based on St Dogmaels, but its outflow into the sea is often smothered by extensive surf thrown up by the sandbanks of Cardigan Bay. Steadily gaining height, you pass Ty-canol farm, with its small car park, and join a true cliff path at last.

Cemaes Head, Pembrokeshire's northernmost headland, stands almost 400ft (122m) above the sea and is home to numerous seabirds. In clear visibility, the vast arc of Cardigan Bay is revealed, as far north as Bardsey Island off the Lleyn Peninsula in Gwynedd. Plynlimon swells massively behind Aberystwyth, with the Cader Idris massif further to the north-east.

As the path swings south, in sight will be the low wedge of Dinas Island and the rugged Pen Caer peninsula beyond Fishguard, culminating in Strumble Head lighthouse. Walkers setting out in blustery weather may find southward progress against the prevailing winds has suddenly become less than comfortable! Other than a few hedges at first, there is precious little shelter on these wild and exposed clifftops. Escape routes inland are none too frequent either, although you soon reach one to the left should the day prove unsuitable for a trek to Newport.

Unseen below as you pass a disused Coastguard lookout are rock strata folded on a truly remarkable scale. There is more of the same beneath the Pen-yr-Afr promontory—at 550ft (168m) the loftiest cliffs in the National Park—and these great synclines and anticlines can be seen clearly as the path dips towards Pwllygranant. A stiff climb out from this wild little cove provides a foretaste of many such gradients as the path crosses deep stream valleys, each time rising back to the 200ft (60m) plateau levelled by the Pliocene sea 17 million years ago.

A mile and two streams later, marshy ground precedes your arrival at Ceibwr Bay, distinguished less by its rather unattractive beach of shale and pebbles than by its connection with the coast road at Moylgrove: for the most part, road access to this stretch of coast is conspicuous by its absence. The Nant Ceibwr valley feeding into the bay is choked with glacial overflow deposits from the last Ice Age, while a mile upstream lies the small village of Moylgrove. Once over the footbridge, a little road walking brings you back to the shoreline and a resumption of the cliff path above Carregywylan rocks.

Eight lonely miles (13km) separate Ceibwr Bay from Newport. Less frequented than most other sections of the path, they are for connoisseurs of peaceful places who are undeterred by rough going, steep gradients and a total lack of amenities en route. A clamorous seabird population will soften the edge of isolation with noisy calls and aerobatics, while flowers and less welcome undergrowth flourishes on all sides. The extent to which you enjoy this half of the walk will depend upon conditions and your own preparedness.

Within 800m you are upon the Witches' Cauldron (Pwll y Wrach), an extraordinary sea cave whose roof has collapsed to reveal a tiny bay and several blowholes, all spanned by the path. On the opposite bank of the stream ravine are the indistinct contours of Castell-reryffyd, an Iron Age fort.

Legwork and foot placement are likely to preoccupy you before long as some of the hardest terrain is encountered. Timber steps have superseded muddy scrambles on the steeper slopes—a measure not universally welcomed by purists, although I've yet to hear a word of dissent from laden walkers in rain and wind!

The 500ft (152m) contour is shadowed round the blunt headland of Foel Goch. Invisible far below are caves and rock arches breeding ground for fulmars, choughs, the ubiquitous gulls and seal colonies too. More troublesome by far than the ups and downs are thick beds of brambles, gorse and bracken which both obscure the path line and grow so ferociously in summer that children and casual walkers are effectively denied access. It is the local authority's responsibility to maintain a safe and clear coastal pathway here and one can only assume that an 'out of sight, out of mind' attitude is being adopted.

Foel Goch, in fact, signals a downhill trend, though not uniformly so. Beyond the dark recesses of Godir-rhug and Godir-Tudor, Morfa Head is crossed. Before ambling down to Newport Sands, it is worth casting your eyes south to the knobby moorland crest of the Presely Hills. Well known as the source of bluestone columns quarried and taken to Stonehenge in far-off Wiltshire around 2000 BC, controversy persists over the type of transportation used. Remains from the New Stone, Iron and Bronze Ages are liberally scattered

around the Presely Hills region, nearest to hand being a hill fort and hut circles on Carningli Common behind Newport.

Even from this distance, Newport appears unassuming and pretty, a town of grey and white houses set on the banks of the sheltered Nyfer estuary. To reach it—and the first trappings of civilisation for many a mile—you first descend broken ground to the beach, then cross The Bennett, a triangle of vulnerable sand dunes backed by golf links. Follow waymarks past the Surf Lifesaving Clubhouse and car park and you face a choice of two river crossings. Quickest is a short paddle at low tide and a walk over firm sands to the old granary at Parrog. At other states of the tide, it will be necessary to stay along the riverside and use Newport Bridge, returning seaward on a shady track.

Parrog quay has a long history of coastal trading and was once a sea port of some significance, exporting herrings, slate and wool. Fishing and shipbuilding figured prominently during the nineteenth century and as recently as the 1930s coal and culm (anthracite dust) were being imported.

Newport's Norman castle stands due south of the town centre but is now converted into a private residence. A short distance below—in Long Street—is a National Park Information Centre and signs that, in summer at least, some prosperity is enjoyed by the town, thanks to its reputation as a family resort and dinghy sailing location.

Below: ***Newport.***

Distant St. David's** (top right) **from the summit of Carn Llidi.

WALK 5: *Pembrokeshire — Goodwick to Solva*

Map: OS Landranger Sheet 157—St David's and Haverfordwest. **Start**: Goodwick seafront. **Finish**: Solva. **Distance**: 41 miles (66km)—3 days suggested. **Access**: Goodwick and Fishguard are on the A40 north of Haverfordwest and on the A487 Pembrokeshire coast road west of Cardigan. Solva is on the A487 between St David's and Newgale. Nearest railway stations—Goodwick (Fishguard Harbour) and Haverfordwest. **Type of Walking**: Rugged terrain on high cliffs exposed to bad weather; many ups and downs but few major gradients and some quite easy stretches; only two refreshment points until St David's is reached. **Features of Interest**: Strumble Head; unfrequented little bays; Porthgain's fascinating industrial relics from the last century; Abereiddy slate quarry; Carn Llidi Hill and ancient hut circles on St David's Head; Ramsey Island; St David's Cathedral; Solva's natural harbour inlet. **Accommodation**: At Fishguard and Goodwick, also widely available in the St David's/Solva area. Youth hostels at Pwllderi (south of Strumble Head), Trevine (roughly half way) and near Whitesand Bay (north of St David's).

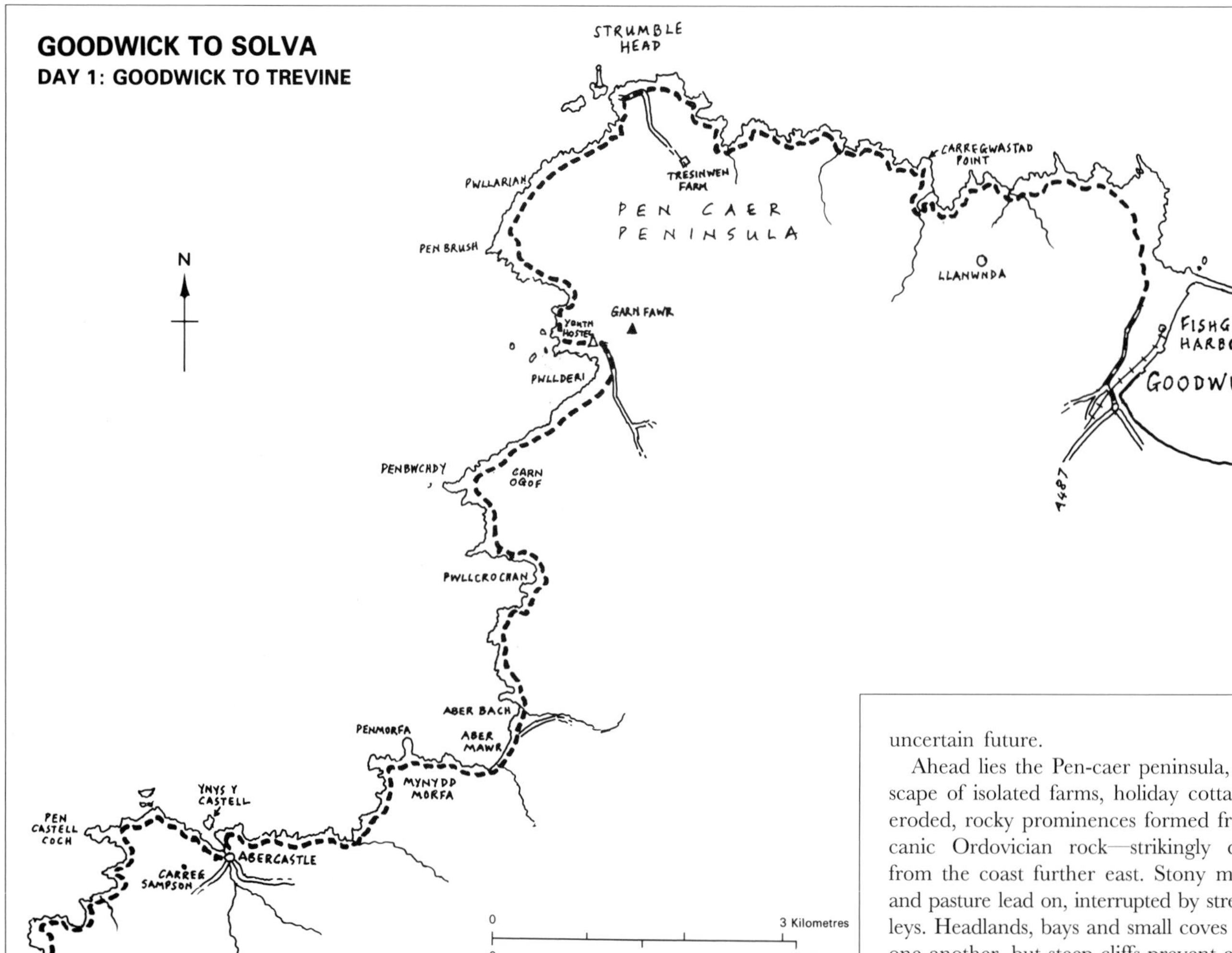

Rugged Grandeur and Relics of the Past
Day 1: Goodwick to Trevine (17 miles/27km)

Although not on this itinerary, Fishguard is only a stone's throw east of Goodwick and is worth visiting, particularly its Lower Town (Cwm Abergwaun) whose picturesque harbour featured in the film of Dylan Thomas's *Under Milk Wood.*

Goodwick (pronounced 'Goodick') is a rather unprepossessing town clustered on a hill-side above the railway and harbour, to which it largely owes its existence. Indeed, both Fishguard and Goodwick were quiet fishing ports until the turn of the century when the Great Western Railway Company adopted them as their terminus for the ferry crossing to Rosslare in Ireland, from here only 54 miles (87 km) distant.

The official coast path crosses the railway from the seafront and forks right, climbing steeply up New Hill to a housing estate above the bay. Alternatively, walk alongside Goodwick Sands, cross the railway footbridge to Quay Road and take either of two footpaths up to New Hill. Continue to the road end where the coast path resumes.

Extensive blasting allowed a new harbour to be accommodated under these precipitous cliffs and stone from the excavations was used to form the great 2000ft (600m) North Breakwater seen below. In 1908, a steamer service was begun.

Aiming to rival Liverpool as a passenger port for the prestigious liners of the day—the so-called 'Greyhounds of the Atlantic'—Fishguard Harbour thrived for a decade and a half. However, World War I heralded the decline in transatlantic trade and, without an industrial hinterland to attract business interests, Fishguard began to look a less attractive proposition. By 1918, long-distance routes had shifted to Southampton and only the Irish services remained; since the removal of the Cork trade to Pembroke Dock, the port faces an uncertain future.

Ahead lies the Pen-caer peninsula, a landscape of isolated farms, holiday cottages and eroded, rocky prominences formed from volcanic Ordovician rock—strikingly different from the coast further east. Stony moorland and pasture lead on, interrupted by stream valleys. Headlands, bays and small coves succeed one another, but steep cliffs prevent access to the shore.

Aberfelin, a modest anchorage sheltered by Carregwasted Point, was the scene of an extraordinary attempt by a French general, Lazare Hoche, to invade Britain with an expeditionary force in 1797. His forays to Ireland and Newcastle ended ignominiously, but 600 troops and 800 convicts were landed here in Wales under the command of an elderly Irish-American renegade named William Tate, with the avowed intention of spreading terror, inciting civil war and sacking Liverpool. Drunk on stolen wine (local farms were well stocked after a recent shipwreck), the unruly French were rounded up with little resistance on Goodwick Sands two days later by the Castlemartin Yeomanry under Lord Cawdor. A stone pillar on Carreg Goffa commemorates the landing, the last by a foreign army on mainland British soil.

A path leads up to Llanwnda hamlet, with no amenities for the walker but containing a fine example of a medieval Celtic church, restored in the nineteenth century. Around and about, the countryside has changed little in the intervening years.

With frequent sinuous twists and undulations

the coast path weaves its way over occasional stiles towards Strumble Head. One still, wet morning I stood hereabouts, transfixed by the haunting call of grey seals echoing through caverns at the foot of the cliffs: such are the privileges afforded to those who can venture off the beaten track.

Public footpaths connect the coastline with Trenewydd and Tresinwen farms and soon the squat, gleaming white profile of Strumble Head lighthouse appears beyond a manned Coastguard station. Built on a rock islet just offshore during the development of Fishguard Harbour for transatlantic liners in the early 1900s, the lighthouse now serves the Irish ferries. Once it was open to public visits, but has been automated and is controlled by radio from the lighthouse on St Ann's Head. The foghorn sounds every 15 seconds and can be deafening while you pass. Strumble Head is a prime site for birdwatchers, especially during the spring and autumn; a narrow lane from Tresinwen farm ends near two small car parks.

A superb stretch of rough walking ensues over the more exposed, west-facing side of this rugged peninsula. Often clothed with bracken, heather and coarse grasses, the skin of farmland is punctuated by the bare bones of volcanic rock which thrusts into sudden outcrops. In places, particularly around Pwllarian and Pen Brush, cairns help define the way which is easily lost in poor visibility.

Once you have swung south-east towards the conspicuous, whitewashed youth hostel above Pwllderi, welcome shelter from wind or rain can be found in a derelict MOD building up to the left. Cliffs and islets below are nesting sites for seabirds and a breeding ground for seals, but eyes will be drawn to the prominent rocky hill just inland. Garn Fawr, at 699ft (213m), is the highest point on the peninsula and its summit incorporates a remarkable Early Iron Age hill fort. Although a path curves up from Tal-y-gaer farm, there is an easier approach from a lane to the east.

Climbing up by the youth hostel makes one appreciate its sensational position, reminiscent of other clifftop hostels such as Tintagel and St Agnes in Cornwall. A roadside memorial stone, just before the path strikes off right, is to the poet Dewi Emrys who died in 1952 and whose poem 'Pwllderi' in local Pembrokeshire dialect celebrates this exquisite part of Wales.

The gentle climb over Carn Ogof to Penbwchdy cliffs is a visual treat, as the path winds over gorse and rocky outcroppings bearing a rich variety of flowers, butterflies and lichens. Views are tremendous, but in poor weather it is an exposed stretch. Aircraft vapour trails converge high to the west, for you are beneath the main air corridor from London Heathrow; just over the Garn hills is 'Green One' homing beacon.

Pwllcrochan, sandy at low tide, is usually deserted, the descent being awkwardly steep. For another mile or so the rugged path continues, bringing you to Aber-bach, a small bay backed by a shingle storm bank. A few hundred metres beyond, you join the one-time coast road at Aber-mawr, but it ends dramatically where storms have undermined the loose cliff over the past 3 decades. The same waves have pushed up a shingle bank here, too, in front of exotic looking marsh plants at the mouth of a wooded glacial overflow channel, a feature of this part of the coast. At its eastern end, the beach is subject to large variations in level—as much as 6ft (1.8m) during the last ten years—but this will not concern the sprinkling of holidaymakers who venture to this neck of the woods and for whom the delightful little bay offers seclusion and fairly safe bathing, except at low water. There are no amenities.

Much easier walking follows round Mynydd Morfa above inaccessible beaches and past an Iron Age fort on Penmorfa. Another glacial overflow channel is crossed and the indented cliff line traced to Abercastle. A flourishing harbour in the sixteenth century and still trading in the 1920s, Abercastle is now reduced to little more than a beach, some cottages and a converted warehouse. However, scuba divers frequent the inlet, as do numbers of summer visitors, but apart from toilets there is little to interest the coastal walker; disappointingly, not one of the three original inns has survived.

At Longhouse Farm, half a mile south-west by road or up from the coast path, may be found perhaps the best known of Pembrokeshire's *cromlechau*—Carreg Sampson. Legend has it that Sampson lifted the mighty capstone of the Megalithic burial chamber onto its six uprights using just his little finger. This was then severed and buried within sight on the harbour island of Ynys-y-Castell.

Hugging the perimeter of farmland, often precariously outside field walls, the coast path to Trevine is notable for magnificent cliff scenery. Coves are virtually inaccessible without risking life and limb and even the clifftop walking is fraught with potential danger as you round Pen Castell Coch. Not only are the cliffs high and vertical, but cracks are continually developing along the narrow ledge of land to which you are confined. The worst is soon over, however, and a lane reached leading to the thoroughly Welsh village of Trevine. The largest settlement between Goodwick and St David's, it offers walkers an opportunity to restock provisions, get a meal or stay overnight. Until it closed in 1918, Trevine corn mill was a focus for the local community and the old millstones, made redundant by changes in farming practice, lie abandoned above the stream which once powered them.

Day 2: Trevine to Whitesand Bay (12 miles/19km)

Leaving the lane which continues inland to Llanrhian, the cliff path leads straightforwardly westwards past small bays and headlands and in less than 2 miles (3km) you are descending towards Porthgain harbour. This must be the most evocative industrial ruin in the whole of Pembrokeshire and provides the coastal walker, as well as visitors who drive down the narrow road from Llanrhian, with an absorbing insight into an industrial era gone forever.

Between 1878 and 1914, Porthgain Village Industries operated a busy quarrying and brickmaking enterprise here. In the early years of this century, the harbour was extended to accommodate the sailing ships and coasters that took on Porthgain stone, as well as slate from nearby Abereiddy. They were heady years during which many millions of tons of crushed roadstone were exported—some to surface London streets—and the brickworks was in full production.

After World War I, business declined and was badly hit by the Depression; the final shipment left the harbour in 1932. Today, the great red-brick crushing plant, with its derelict storage hoppers from which graded cliff granite was shovelled down chutes into waiting coasters, stands gaunt and silent.

Sensitive measures are called for to consolidate what remains at Porthgain for future generations to appreciate. Excessively cosmetic action which removes anything considered 'untidy' is as undesirable as wanton neglect, but now that the site is a scheduled Ancient Monument it is to be hoped that appropriate care will be taken.

The Sloop Inn and harbour café add their own considerable charm and the harbour is popular with boating enthusiasts. You walk back towards the clifftops and for a while follow an old quarry tramway, short-cutting several minor promontories. The way becomes uncomfortably rutted but this is not the imprint of old railway sleepers as you might imagine, but grooves worn by walking cows!

Looking back, you will see navigation cairns on Porthgain's flanking headlands. They were once painted white to mark the harbour entrance which is not only indistinct from offshore, but in heavy swell conditions is very difficult to negotiate. Over to the right are more ruins associated with the roadstone quarries.

If you've time to wander, Treath Llyfn sands can be reached safely down steps cut by Italian prisoners of war during the 1940s: the bay is hemmed in by high rock walls. A considerable surprise awaits round the next headland, for you suddenly encounter the old Abereiddy slate quarry. Worked mainly through the last

Looking back to Strumble Head from Carn Ogof.

half of the nineteenth century when slate was in heavy demand for roofing and flooring, the quarry was ultimately unable to compete with the massive workings above Caernarfon and closed in 1904 after inundation by the sea. A channel was blasted to form a little anchorage for local fishermen and this has become known as the 'Blue Lagoon', after its deep, slate-reflected hues. Still evident are traces of old worker's cottages and quarry buildings on the quay.

Abereiddy Bay, excavated by marine erosion from black Ordovician shales, strikes a Stygian note, its few dwellings braced against the west wind. It also heralds a change from the recent easy-going terrain, as the way ahead is interrupted by a number of sizeable gullies. The path itself, however, is without difficulty, although not easy to reach from the coast road. A gate and stile off the lane at the south end of the bay take you back to the clifftops.

I have always experienced a tingle of anticipation on the approach to St David's. There is a moorland wildness on these seaward slopes as you draw closer to the swelling cones of Penberry and Carn Llidi; their distant outlines seem to slip insistently into the edge of so many views across the flat Pembrokeshire landscape. Volcanic intrusions have shadowed the coast south from Pen Caer and now rear up in these 600ft (200m) 'monednocks' which would have been islands when sea level was 200ft (60m) higher. Despite their modest elevation, the hills resemble small mountains, due partly to the lack of any adjacent high ground.

I once pitched a tent overnight at Aber-Pwll, having searched in vain for any other sheltered spot on these open clifftops. You can reach the shore here but only from the coast path and even then, bathing is not advisable. A long slope angles up across the flanks of Penberry, though its quarried summit (573ft/175m) is best reached from Penberry Farm on the inland side.

Descending through a broad and lumpy stream valley, brambles are soon left behind for unfettered walking towards Carn Llidi (595ft/181m). When the bracken is not too high, tiny fields of an Iron Age settlement can be made out on its lower slopes. It is perfectly possible to scale Carn Llidi from this direction, but paths are often obscured by undergrowth in summer. The orthodox ascent is from a lane behind Whitesand Bay and thence by tracks dating from World War I: a submarine-hunting hydrophone station was installed half way up, its microphones connected to the sea at Porthmelgan.

Climbing Carn Llidi is strongly recommended, for there is no finer viewpoint in this part of Wales. Laid out map-like below you are St David's peninsula, Ramsey Island and the coastline just trodden, while farther afield is the South Bishop lighthouse and—very occasionally visible—the Wicklow Hills of Ireland.

Choughs breed in the vicinity and you might spot the occasional peregrine falcon. Pathside banks are starred with wild flowers in springtime—a delight for the coastal walker—but the cliffs and vicious offshore rocks of St David's Head are much less benign and have claimed numerous shipwrecks over the years. One such was the steamship *Nimrod* which drove ashore on February 28th 1860 on passage from Liverpool to Cork. Heavy seas broke her in two and all 40 passengers and crew were lost.

The OS map shows St David's Head as the point of an anvil-shaped wedge of land and the path makes a beeline for it beyond the shingle inlet of Gesail-fawr. The rough gabbro of these sea cliffs has earned them a high reputation among climbers and the same resistant rock pierces the sea's surface in a treacherous archipelago running north to south 4 miles (2.5km) off the peninsula and known as the 'Bishops and Clerks'.

A short detour out onto St David's Head is worth the time—the path actually short-cuts the point. On the other side of Warrior's Dyke earthwork, once a formidable drystone rampart some 15ft (4.5m) high, are 8 Iron Age stone hut circles reached on ancient trackways. Finds from this exemplary promontory fort include loom weights and blue beads: these and other relics can be seen in Tenby Museum. It is pertinent to recall that St David's Head, named after the saint who spread the Gospel throughout Wales in the sixth century, was the end of the known world for the medieval English and a centre for Christianity long before Canterbury.

Porthmelgan is the first of three sandy beaches which you come to in quick succession, and because it involves a walk from the nearest car park the little cove is usually uncrowded. Porth Lleuog is the next beach and the twentieth century lurks around the next corner! Whitesand Bay (Porth-mawr) faces Atlantic swells four-square and its acres of firm sand draw in holidaymakers galore during the summer. Just how you react to the rows of glittering cars, the ice creams and buckets and spades, the surfers and the general hubbub depends on your state of mind. On one occasion I can remember feeling detached and painfully out of place in walking gear, having tramped miles of gloriously unfrequented cliffs; at another time I was glad of a drink and a snack and the sound of human voices.

Behind dunes before you reach the car park is the site of St Patrick's chapel, once used by sailors and Irish pilgrims and marked by a stone tablet. Up the lane are camp sites and a youth hostel, while St David's itself is less than 2 miles (1.5km) distant by road.

Day 3: Whitesand Bay to Solva (12 miles/19km)

At low tide you can walk right along the sands (Traeth Mawr) to Porthselau, the next little bay; otherwise, a duney footpath leads you above the beach outside a golf course until you swing north-west round Pencarnan headland. Here, flanked by purple bog heather on the easiest of grassy paths, you are taken past Point St John and there, less than a mile offshore, lies Ramsey Island—or Ynys Dewi (David's Island).

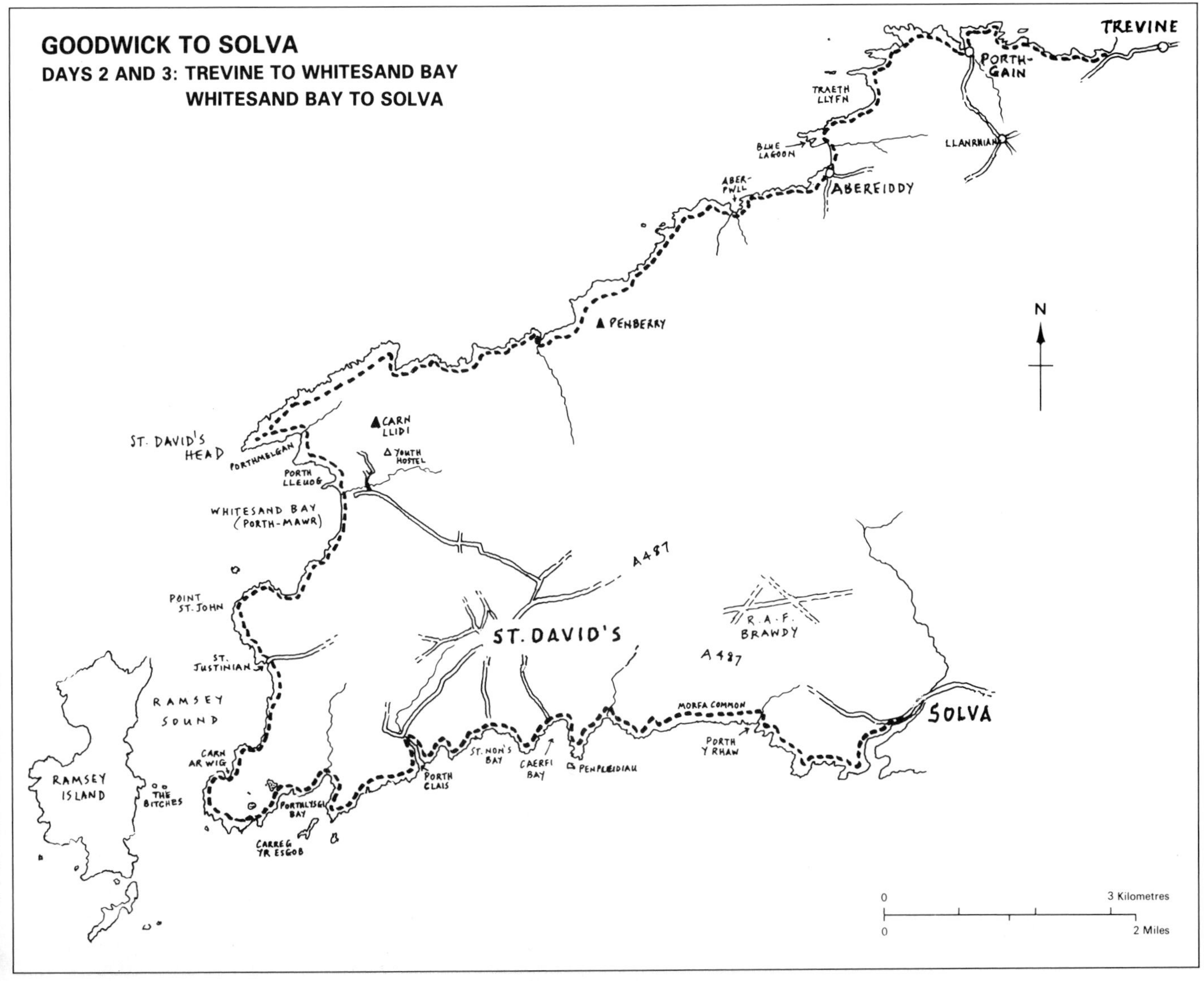

For the next hour or so's walking, Ramsey Island will be a compelling sight, separated from the mainland as it is by an often fearsome tidal race. The island's 600 acres, particularly the more fertile northern half, were farmed until the 1960s, but are now an RSPB nature reserve whose seabirds and grey seals are spied on by boatloads of summer visitors.

The overgrown ruin of St Justinian's chapel above Porthstinian harbour is less likely to draw your attention than the lifeboat station hugging precipitous cliffs just below the path. Established in 1912, the station has a long and distinguished record of call-outs to ships in distress on this malevolent coast. Passenger boats bound for Ramsey Island are based here in summer and the small harbour is used by pleasure craft too, so on fine days there is much coming and going.

Soon you are out on a wilder stretch of path above inclined rock slabs rich with red, green and purple hues, and Porthstinian becomes a background detail. Beyond the tiny cove of Carn ar Wig, the way is thrust out into Ramsey Sound by the westernmost promontory on mainland Pembrokeshire. Offshore rocks called 'The Bitches' tear trailers of foam when the tidal race is running—it can reach 6 knots—and there is a real sense of engagement with the elements as you drop almost to sea level, close to the aeons-old interface between ocean and land.

An old quarry and the remains of a small copper mine provide passing interest but in a few hundred metres you are turning east, climbing a little and reaching a major land mark. This is the northern 'horn' of St Bride's bay, a massive bite in the Pembrokeshire seaboard which forms three sides of a square down to Skomer Island and the Marloes peninsula. To the south-east, the distant chimneys of Milford Haven's oil refineries peep incongruously above farmland. The farther south one progresses, the more visually repetitive they become until, like waking to find the nightmare is, after all, reality, one is drawn in beneath steaming pipelines and jetties through a shabby industrial landscape and finally pushed across the Neyland Bridge to Pembroke. But that is another story . . .

Wild thyme, thrift and sea squill impart colour and delicacy to rugged slopes above Mrs Morgan's Cave (no-one, it seems, knows who she was!). Short grass is nibbled by sheep whose pungent odour assaults the nostrils; ponds to the left are used to irrigate early potatoes, for which this area is renowned.

In spring sunshine, the turquoise shallows of Porthlysgi Bay take on a Mediterranean translucency—a vibrating field of colour against yellow gorse. Carreg yr Esgob—Bishop's Rock—sits out in the bay, a natural breakwater, so the shingle beach is safe for bathing (with discretion), but is too rocky and out-of-the-way for most tastes and thus never becomes crowded.

Porth Clais has been St David's port since the fifteenth century, and before then missionaries and saints must have set sail from and returned to this narrow inlet. Limekilns and quaysides have been restored and bear witness to the erstwhile importance of this diminutive harbour; coasters continued to bring in coal for the gasworks (now a car park) up to the 1950s.

Rounding Trwyn Cynddeiriog, you reach St Non's Bay. St Non was the mother of St David, who was born in a cottage on the site of the present chapel ruins during a great storm in about 462. A short distance to the north-east, in the grounds of St Non's Retreat, is the Holy Well of St Non, regarded for centuries as one of Wales's most sacred.

About a mile inland and hardly larger than a village, stands the city of St David's. Its status arises from its fine cathedral; along with the adjacent Bishop's Palace ruins, it is of exceptional interest. Throughout the Middle Ages, pilgrims by the thousand would have travelled from Ireland via St David's, Cornwall and Brittany to Santiago de Compostella in Spain. In modern times, the railway never reached here, ensuring the settlement's obscurity until the advent of motor transport. Even today, St David's is saved from the excesses of tourist exploitation by being well off the beaten track. Set apart from the shops and tea rooms, the eleventh-century cathedral complex lies in a protective hollow formed by the River Alun; from St Non's or Caerfai bay, lanes lead straightforwardly to the 'city' centre.

Stone for constructing the cathedral was quarried from around Caerfai Bay—a popular beach for children, incidentally—and more of the chocolate-purple Cambrian sandstone is evident beyond the spectacular Iron Age promontory fort ranged across the Penpleiddiau headland. Caer Bwdy Bay is next, then the long path over Morfa Common, where the eye will be attracted to a skyline of houses above Solva, and the ear by RAF Brawdy. The high pitched whine of jets taking off and landing is not conducive to peaceful reflection, but mercifully, flying practice is not continuous!

There is a big drop to Porth y Rhaw, with its mill ruins and fine Iron Age fort to the east. High, loose cliffs follow, colonised by rabbits and gorse—rampant species both. Two tugs were wrecked here in the early 1980s, jammed tight between foreshore rocks by tide and storm. A trod was worn by sightseers down the steep, shaley slopes and if conditions are favourable, a descent is worthwhile for a closer inspection. However, each successive year sees a marked deterioration in the wreckage and before long there will be little left to see.

Solva's harbour, despite its awkward, rock-bound entrance, is the best on this sector of St Bride's Bay and is heavily patronised by the boating fraternity. Until the mid-1800s trade was brisk, mainly in agricultural products, and Solva was the principal lime-burning centre for the St David's region. In common with so many picturesque harbours, tourism has supplanted sea trade: here it has diluted the 'Welsh-ness' too, though the village remains delightful and is a fitting end to this magnificent long walk.

Facing page: ***The beach at Dale.***

Walk 6: *Pembrokeshire — Dale to Little Haven*

Map: OS Landranger Sheet 157—St David's and Haverfordwest. **Start:** Dale. **Finish:** Little Haven. **Distance:** 20 miles (32km), or 14 miles (32km) shorter alternative—allow 8 to 9 hours or 6 to 7 hours respectively. **Access:** Dale is at the southern end of the B4327 from Haverfordwest. Little Haven (and nearby Broad Haven) are at the western end of the B4341 from Haverfordwest. Nearest railway stations—Haverfordwest, Johnston and Milford Haven. **Type of Walking:** A clear, undulating cliff path virtually all the way; can be overgrown in places; one or two steep little climbs but mostly easy going. **Features of Interest:** 'Palmerston Follies' fortifications; St Ann's Head lighthouse; Marloes Sands and Gateholm Island; Skomer and Skokholm Island bird reserves (boat trips available); dramatic transitions between rock types. **Accommodation:** Available at Dale, Little Haven and Broad Haven, also at Marloes. Youth hostels at Broad Haven and Runwayskiln near Marloes.

Peninsulas, Beaches, Islands and Cliffs

Tucked into the outer reaches of Milford Haven and sheltered from south-westerly blows by St Ann's Head, Dale is understandably popular with boat-owning holidaymakers. It is said to be Wales's sunniest spot and provided you turn a blind eye to the Esso refinery glinting 3 miles (5km) east, it has all the attributes one would expect from the starting point of a magnificent coastal walk. Mind you, apart from the yacht club, post office, pub and shop, there is little to look at in Dale, which is surprising considering its long seafaring tradition. Among its inhabitants in the mid-nineteenth century were mariners and tradesmen involved in the shipping of mixed cargoes and substantial imports of lime, but that was all long ago and today even fishing is largely given over to trips for visitors.

Before leaving Dale, there is a decision to make regarding the length of this walk; the full 20 miles (32km) is admittedly quite a hike and may be beyond the comfortable range of some walkers. It can be reduced to 14 miles (23km) by short-cutting through Dale Valley to Westdale Bay along the line of the Ritec fault. In pre-glacial times, the St Ann's Head peninsula would have been an offshore island, but the narrow sea channel was plugged by boulders, stones and soil deposited at the end of the last Ice Age. This unconsolidated, low-lying valley is subject to erosion from the elements and in geological terms is quite an unstable feature.

Several variations on this walk are possible, using Marloes as an intermediate base. However, taken in its entirety the route is full of interest and variety, enhanced by frequent changes in direction as you trace the outline of headlands and bays.

From the south end of Dale village, a road is followed through woods for almost a mile to Dale Fort Field Centre which specialises in marine biology. The onward path leaves by an early Iron Age fort and heads south-west through Castlebeach Bay and on round Watwick Point. This powerful shipping beacon, together with the one on West Blockhouse Point and 3 transit markers, assist vast tankers laden with crude oil to navigate the dredged deep-water channel leading to the refinery jetties further up the Haven.

Beyond Watwick Bay stands the abandoned and vaguely sinister West Blockhouse, one of nine forts constructed in the mid-nineteenth century to protect Milford Haven from a feared French invasion. Building costs were enormous but the forts were never used and within a few decades had become obsolete owing to advances in long-range artillery. Coastal and air-defence garrisons were installed during both World Wars, but with one or two exceptions, these so-called 'Palmerston Follies' (after the government of the day) have been left derelict. Care is required when exploring, for although the building fabric is of high quality, floors and fitments are inevitably disintegrating with the passage of time. Just round the headland, Mill Bay is well known as the landing place of Henry Tudor in 1485 on his way from exile in Brittany to defeat Richard III at the battle of Bosworth Field and seize the throne of England.

Above: ***St. Ann's Head.***

Left below: ***Mill Haven and Stack Rocks offshore, on the secluded coast between St. Bride's and Little Haven.***

Right below: ***Musselwick Sands and distant Tower Point (top left).***

I have walked the path in both directions and prefer this approach to St Ann's Head. As you skirt farmland facing into the Haven, there is a real sense of imminent emergence from protected waters to the open sea. Statistics support this impression of increasing exposure: gale force winds are regularly recorded on the headland and severe gusts of up to 90mph (145kph) are not uncommon! Tide races and offshore reefs threaten shipping entering Milford Haven and for centuries a warning light has shone from St Ann's Head. The Haven—a fine example of a 'ria' or drowned river valley—was considered by Nelson to be the best natural harbour in Europe but its potential was not fully realised until the 1880s.

The present lighthouse dates from 1841, having been modernised in 1910 and connected to the electricity supply in 1958. To the rear stands a Coastguard lookout, converted from an earlier lighthouse on the site of fifteenth-century St Ann's chapel. If there's time to spare, this is a premier viewpoint for watching the comings and goings of ships large and small.

Virtually opposite the row of Trinity House cottages, the path branches off left above beetling red and purple-grey cliffs. Past Frenchman's Bay, the National Trust acquired $1\frac{1}{2}$ miles (2.5km) of coastline in 1967 with funds raised by Enterprise Neptune, the land having previously belonged to the MOD as HMS Harrier, a radar and weather school. At my last visit, the cliff edge of soft red sandstone was eroding badly along Welshman's Bay and in such places it is best to keep well back if you can. The unmistakable earth ramparts of an Iron Age fort on Great Castle Head are followed by a steep descent to Westdale Bay. (A 6 mile/9.5km circuit of the St Ann's Head peninsula can be completed here by taking the footpath through fields past Dale Castle to St James's church and continuing by lane to Dale village.)

Back on high, crumbling cliffs, the path is well walked owing to parking on a nearby lane. Flanking the concrete wasteland of Dale Airfield (at one time a Fleet Air Arm station), the going becomes pleasantly level for almost 2 miles (3km). There are good views ahead, but with less to think about underfoot (except to avoid falling over the edge!), this easy stretch allows attention to be lifted to wider horizons. Out in the west lies flat-topped Skokholm Island, composed of the same Old Red Sandstone and, like neighbouring Skomer, a notable sea bird sanctuary. Although the island was farmed between 1750 and 1900 (and even earlier by the Normans, who introduced rabbits), the establishment of Britain's first bird observatory by R M Lockley in 1939 set the precedent for its subsequent use: it is now a West Wales Naturalists' Trust Nature Reserve. Access is on a weekly, full-board basis only, at the converted farmhouse.

A little farther round to the north-west and between Skokholm and Skomer, the low hump of Grassholm Island is visible. Waterless and too inaccessible to have been settled by man,

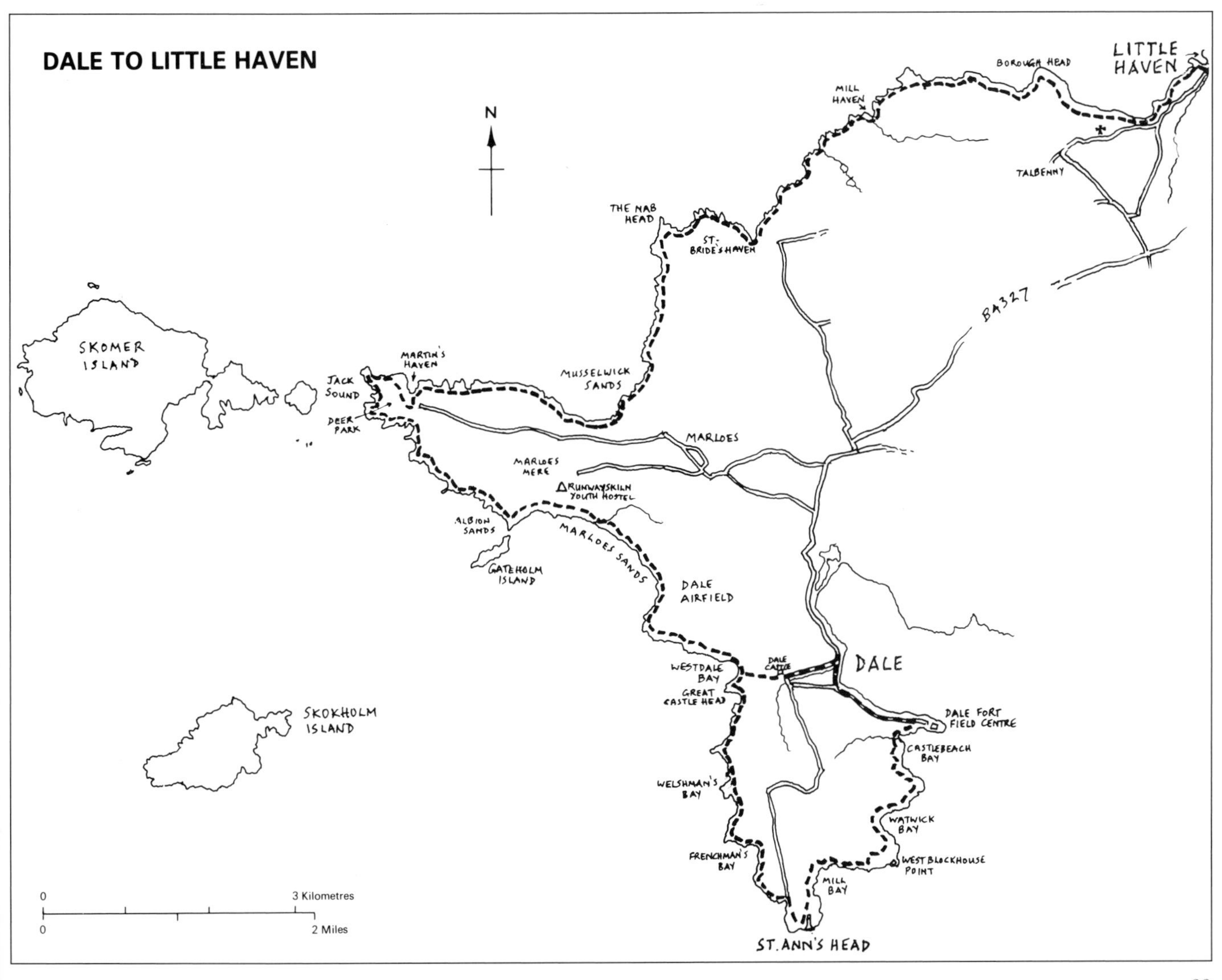

it too is a National Nature Reserve, home to many thousands of gannets. Even farther out to sea are dangerous reefs known as The Smalls and the Hats and Barrels.

As the walk begins, above Marloes Sands, the rocks change from Lower Old Red Sandstone to Silurian shales and mudstone. Down on the beach west of Red Cliff, vertical bedding called the Three Chimneys demonstrates the enormous pressures generated by the Armorican Earth Movements some 240 million years ago. Marloes Sands are reached from a lane west of Marloes village by a sunken path which ends at a stream valley and Mill Beach. Cross this depression to approach Horse Neck, the promontory overlooking Gateholm Island. The island, accessible at low water, has a history of occupation by man. Remains of over 100 hut circles have been found, largely arranged round courtyards and inhabited during the third and sixth centuries. The island may even have been an early Christian monastic settlement.

Before continuing, take a last glance back at the mile-long sweep of Marloes Sands backed by impressive cliffs and thorny vegetation. Good, easy, clifftop walking takes us on past Albion Sands, named after a paddle steamer wrecked here in 1840 and still protruding—just—above low tide sand. On the right above tiny Watery Bay, a path leads to Runwayskiln youth hostel and a National Trust car park. During the eighteenth century, leeches were gathered from nearby Marloes Mere and sent to Harley Street doctors for blood-letting! Rock scenery is truly magnificent, not only along the mainland at such spots as Deadman's Cove, but taking in Skomer Island too.

Skomer, separated from the southern horn of St Bride's Bay by the ferocious tidal race of Jack Sound, is composed mainly of resistant volcanic rock, predating Skokholm by around 40 million years. Its reputation as a sea bird reserve is internationally acknowledged and its colonies of breeding birds include some 30 species, the most famous being the Manx Shearwaters. Once well populated by man (sea birds would have provided abundant meat), Skomer is now leased by the WWNT which R M Lockley helped set up. The waters surrounding these islands are due to become a Marine Nature Reserve. Between April and September you can visit Skomer by boat from Martin's Haven: details from Lockley Lodge Information Centre above the beach.

The pretty, sandy cove of Renny Slip leads on to the Deer Park, which can readily be omitted if time presses by cutting down the valley at its neck. However, in all but the foulest weather a circuit of this most westerly point on the Marloes peninsula is recommended, though don't expect to see any deer! As you come round past the Coastguard lookout on the highest ground (189ft/58m), you enter St Bride's Bay, but because of the coastline's convolutions, this is not immediately apparent. In clear visibility, the St David's peninsula and Ramsey Island hug the northern horizon 8 miles (13km) away as the seagull flies—over 30 miles (48km) by coast path!

Martin's Haven is little more than a shingle and rock inlet, but the cove is ideal for small craft and is popular with fishermen and sub-aqua divers. The path cuts behind four distinct headlands and valleys formed by complex faulting, before arriving high above Musselwick Sands. There is only one way down to the beach, a precariously steep one at that, and the tide comes right in against precipitous cliffs: agility and tide tables seem to be the order of the day if you are bent on a paddle here! Marloes, a stone's throw away up field tracks, offers refreshments, accommodation and a last realistic chance to short-cut back to Dale via Little Marloes Farm and Red Cliff. It is advisable to press on, however, for the remaining leg to Little Haven, though straightforward, is deceptively long.

A confined foreshore and unreachable cliffs beloved of fulmars border a disused MOD bombing range used by the RAF during World War II and before long we have reached The Nab Head. Flints were fashioned into tools and weapons here by Neolithic man some 7000 years ago and finds from an archaeological excavation of the site are on show in Tenby Museum. Old Red Sandstone has replaced black Ordovician shales, its ruddy colouring noticeable in cliffs, fields and on the path itself for several miles. The way shadows a substantial boundary wall in whose secret crevices plants and lichens thrive, then descends gently to St Bride's Haven.

Followers of the fifth-century Irish Saint Bride set up a chapel here, as they did in many other parts of the Celtic world, but it was probably destroyed by a storm; the present medieval church was heavily restored in the mid-nineteenth century. A few metres north of an old lime kiln, two early Christian coffins are appearing in an eroding cliff. The extraordinary Georgian mansion which stands back across elegant gardens and has, perhaps, intrigued you since The Nab Head, was built by Lord Kensington in 1800. When his estate was dissolved, it became a local authority geriatric hospital, later a private rest home and is now converted to luxury holiday flats and known as St Bride's Castle.

Walkers who have persisted with the route this far will be delighted to know that the final $5\frac{1}{2}$ miles (9km) are quietly pastoral in character and not at all strenuous. Nevertheless, because significant landmarks are few, progress always seems difficult to measure and on more than one occasion I have found myself wondering why it was taking so long to reach Little Haven! At first, the soil and low cliffs are Devon-red, but just beyond Mill Haven (a diminutive shingly cove and the only point of access to or from the coast path between St Bride's Haven and Little Haven), there is an abrupt transition from Old Red Sandstone to ancient, dark-grey Pre-Cambrian rocks.

Now facing north, the coast has swung into the sheltered recesses of Goultrop Roads. Bracken, brambles and tall grasses grow chest high in summer unless the path is regularly cleared, but once past Borough Head, quite unexpectedly you find yourself walking through a mile of woodland. Oak, ash, hazel, beech, blackthorn and larch all flourish here, protected from prevailing salt winds. After encountering the minor road from Talbenny, whose church of St Mary the Virgin is well worth a visit, the coast path takes to a short section of clifftop. From down on The Point, it passes the Swan Inn and reaches journey's end in Little Haven, a delightful village at the mouth of a narrow valley. You will find shops and all the usual amenities here and if the tide is low, a stroll along the sands towards Broad Haven will reveal some marvellous examples of cliff folding.

Facing page: ***Landimore Marsh – an expanse of creeks and saltings grazed by horses.***

Walk 7: *The Gower Peninsula*

Map: OS Landranger Sheet 159—Swansea, Gower and area. **Start:** Llanmadoc village. **Finish:** Port-Eynon. **Distance:** 14 miles (23km)—allow 6 to 7 hours (an hour or two longer if visiting Worms Head). **Access:** Llanmadoc is reached by following the B4295 or B4271 from Swansea and the M4 motorway, then country lanes via Llanrhidian, Landimore and Cheriton. Port-Eynon lies at the western end of the A4118 from Swansea. Nearest railway station—Swansea. **Type of Walking:** Extremely varied, from flat saltmarsh, extensive sand-dunes and sandy beaches to rocky foreshore, precipitous headlands and undulating cliffs. Generally well-defined paths, mostly sandy in the first half of the walk, but not always waymarked. **Features of Interest:** Whiteford Burrows and Landimore Marsh in the Loughor estuary; clifftop sand-dunes; Burry Holms island; the vast beach and dunes of Rhossili Bay; Worms Head; marvellous limestone cliffs and coves; Culver Hole and the Old Salt House. **Accommodation:** Available at villages throughout western Gower. Numerous camping and caravan sites. Youth hostel at Port-Eynon.

Saltmarsh, Dunes, Headlands and Limestone Cliffs

The Gower Peninsula thrusts itself like a clenched fist into the Bristol Channel. East to the once busy coal ports of Barry, Penarth and Cardiff, pockets of industry still sour the coastline, but here, on the threshold of open sea, there is seclusion and unspoiled scenery of astonishing variety. More than a dozen miles from the Swansea conurbation and accessible only along narrow, winding roads, this offshoot of the South Wales coast—en route for nowhere—has retained a remoteness and wild grandeur despite looking over its shoulder, so to speak, at the distant factories and docks of Burry Port, Llanelli, Swansea and Neath.

In high summer, roads do get congested and holidaymakers throng to the open spaces—conditions not unique to Gower—yet as this walk will show, the landscape is too expansive, too generously proportioned, to become crowded.

The walk starts at Llanmadoc, tucked behind its hill on the Gower's north-western tip and, along with neighbouring Cheriton, once associated with the infamous Lucas family of local notoriety as smugglers and wreckers. (There is a little roadside parking, and a short-cut to the sands if required by forking right at the tiny thirteenth-century church of St Madog down Cwm Ivy). A hundred metres beyond the Britannia Inn, you turn right into a signposted roadway between houses and into a gated track down past the one-time mortuary and along by Burry Pill ('Pill' meaning watercourse). At the highest spring tides, the marsh and Burry Pill become flooded right upstream to Cheriton. Indeed, during the 1800s before serious silting-up had occurred, ships could navigate these pills to obtain shelter.

Past Pill Cottage, the track narrows to a path alongside Cwm Ivy woods, raucous with crows, and a stile leads you out onto the sea wall embankment. To the east stretches Landimore Marsh, a vast expanse of meandering creeks and grassy saltings grazed by horses. North Hill (locally 'Nottle') Tor rears boldly from the tidal flats; its stone was once quarried and a large cave yielded evidence of occupation by Stone Age man. To your left, reedy marshland ends at a fringe of conifers and where the sea wall meets them you turn left along the plantation. (An interesting diversion, perhaps for another day, would be to turn right here and explore the wild, unfrequented dunes behind Whiteford Sands. Whiteford Point's estuary shore is a nature reserve owned by the National Trust; the elegant, cast-iron lighthouse built in 1865 and still largely intact has been out of service since 1933.)

Turning right for the beach at the Cwm Ivy track, you come round Hills Tor and Prissen's Tor outcrops. The latter possesses a cave high in its limestone face in which ancient human and animal bones were discovered during quarrying in the mid-nineteenth century. Broughton (pronounced 'Bruffton') Bay now unfolds ahead and at most states of the tide you can walk along its firm sands. It is necessary to come inland a little to the caravan park at Broughton Burrows and take a path just above the foreshore to Twlc Point. Although it is possible to beach-walk round to Burry Holms at the lowest spring tides, local advice is that you should be prepared to paddle! Certainly, accurate knowledge of tide times would be essential to avoid getting cut off.

Climbing on a sandy path out towards Foxhole Point, you soon join a broad swath of short-cropped turf across an incongruous coastscape of banks and mounds, tussocks of wire grass and unexpected sandy hollows, all lying atop rocky cliffs. A large signboard above Bluepool Corner (or Bay) leaves you in no doubt about the dangers of sea-bathing hereabouts. The small curve of bay ending in a rock arch takes its name from a 15ft (4.5m) circular pool at the northern end. Gold coins from a 400 year-old Spanish shipwreck were found on the beach.

Many pathways weave tortuously and often indeterminately through the countless acres of Broughton and Llangennith Burrows and it is easy to stray from the coast itself. You should emerge past the remains of a small brick structure overlooking Burry Holms and the impressive sweep of Rhossili Bay culminating in Worms Head. A broad footpath drops towards foreshore rocks over which you can scramble to reach Burry Holms island about 2 hours either side of low water. This 400m long island bears an Iron Age fortification and a modern, automated lighthouse at its western end. Of more immediate interest will be a solitary ruined chapel wall, all that is left of a sizeable ecclesiastical settlement dating back to 1100 and which would have once covered much of the island's surface.

A high tide might force you up along the edge of low dunes, but more likely you will be able to cross Spaniard Rocks (legend has it that the crew of a wrecked seventeenth-century Spanish galleon buried treasure here) and set your sights on reaching Rhossili, some 3 miles (4.8km) distant at the southern end of the bay. Several paths penetrate Llangennith Burrows—a summer haunt of picnickers and sun-worshippers—but refreshments or a road are over a mile away.

In the seventeenth century, lured perhaps by local wreckers, the famous 'Dollar Ship' foundered in the bay and much silver coin was recovered. Shifting sand and an encroaching sea obscured the wreck for over a century until, in 1807, it was once more revealed at a spring ebb tide. Crowds of local people

Above: ***Culver Hole.***

Facing page: ***The Port-Eynon memorial.***

flocked to the scene, staked their claim and took what they could before tide and winds prevented further access. Since 1833, nothing more has been found. George Edmunds, a diver and shipwreck expert (author of *The Gower Coast*, available locally) estimates the wreck site to be midway between Diles Lake and the Old Parsonage, probably well below low water mark and possibly containing a great deal more treasure. Hull timbers visible in the sand belong to the *City of Bristol* and, further south, the *Helvetia*, a coaster wrecked in 1887.

In stark contrast to historical associations with shipwreck and Viking invasion (Sweyne's Howes on Rhossili Down's summit is the burial place of a Danish Viking chieftain), the bay is popular with surfers, sea anglers (casting for bass and flounders) and hang-gliders who launch themselves from the lofty ridge.

A rising track beyond the Old Parsonage, or steps from the beach, take you up to Rhossili, little more than a hamlet at the end of the B4247 but well patronised by visitors bound for Worms Head. Here you can obtain refreshments and view a small exhibition at the National Trust's Visitor Centre near the car park. (Check tide times displayed outside if contemplating a detour out on Worms Head). Walking continues south-west on a motorable track, but tremendous views back to Burry Holms are obtained nearer the grassy cliff edge. During the last century, limestone was quarried from this headland and shipped across the Bristol Channel to sweeten the fields of North Devon. One or two steep paths traversing precipitous outcrops below lead to the fishing inlet of Kitchen Corner and Coonan's Boathouse (after a Swansea angler).

By now, eyes will have become firmly fixed on the sharp-spined grass and rock of Worms Head whose unlikely profile monopolises attention from so many viewpoints. Locally known as 'The Worm', it is Gower's westernmost point, its name a derivation of the Danish *Wurm* or the Viking *Orm*, meaning 'serpent' or 'dragon'. For $2\frac{1}{2}$ hours either side of low water, you can walk down from the Coastguard lookout and cross a natural causeway of grey rock, once a prolific lobster and crabbing ground. The Head consists of two islets connected by a narrow neck of rock called Devil's Bridge. Outer Head has a blowhole and a cave right at the precipitous seaward extremity, once used by wreckers whose lights lured ships into an illusory haven. Crossing the causeway is rough going and the Worm's paths call for a steady head, so allow plenty of time to return safely to the mainland: the tide comes in swiftly and there have been fatalities.

Worms Head is the walk's turning point, both in direction and terrain. Gone are open sands, downland and dunes and in their place a progression of limestone cliffs considered by the Nature Conservancy Council to be of national importance for nature conservation. The path veers east and runs through low gorse outside a matrix of old walled fields above Mewslade Bay, with its fine bathing beach and rock climbing crags. Once past its stream valley, the way trends south-east above a succession of inlets, sometimes back from the cliff line in a world of birdsong and grazing sheep, separated from the coast road by more than a mile's width of fields.

Halfway along but very difficult to reach is Paviland Cove, occupied by man even before the last Ice Age and, in 1823, found to contain a headless skeleton, mammoth bones and flint implements. Rhossili's Life Saving Association gained special recognition for its courageous rescue by breeches buoy of the crew of the *Roche Castle*, wrecked on nearby rocks.

Eventually the clifftop path reaches a bridle track and turns seaward down to Overton Cliff, continuing at low level over brambly, gorsy cliffside. At ebb tide, Overton Mere's acres of grey, water-dappled limestone are exposed, but lack the configuration, flora and fauna necessary for really interesting rock pools. Where the path climbs ahead, you can keep right on a thinner trod and scramble down easy, lichen-covered rocks for a good view of Culver Hole. Mystery surrounds this high, walled-up cleft with window and doorway apertures. Its walls are 10ft (3m) thick and it certainly existed back in the fourteenth century, probably being adopted in more recent times by smugglers and wreckers, including the Lucas family. Whether it was originally a smugglers' retreat, a pigeon house or part of an early clifftop castle, no-one seems to know.

A short-cut will return you to the main cliff path leading to the monolith on Port-Eynon Point in memory of two founder-members of the Gower Society. From the prow-like headland, you walk down through old quarry workings. Limestone was last shipped out 100 years ago, but in its heyday the industry formed a major complement to the local oyster trade. Such traditional activities have long since declined, though a little lobster and crab fishing remain, eclipsed by tourism.

Until 1703, the Salt House was occupied, at one time by the Lucas family. Cottages were put up for the oystermen but had become derelict by the 1870s and marine erosion began to take its toll of the sea wall, leaving adjacent land much more vulnerable. At the time of writing, the Salt House site is undergoing excavation and should soon be well worth visiting.

Heading now towards Port-Eynon, you swing right past the youth hostel and join a stony track to a car park and the road by a café and shop; sheltered Port-Eynon Bay stretches away east to Oxwich point. Just up in the village churchyard stands a memorial 'To the memory of Billy Gibbs Coxwain, William Eynon 2nd Coxwain and George Harry Lifeboatman, drowned off Pwlldu Head 1st January 1916, when Port-Eynon's lifeboat *Janet* twice capsized in an endeavour to render assistance to the SS *Dunvegan*'. It was a tragic incident indeed, involving 20 hours of duty in heavy seas and ending in the loss of *Janet*'s mast and most of her oars. She drifted with wind and waves to The Mumbles, where the surviving crew, exhausted and suffering from exposure, were brought ashore.

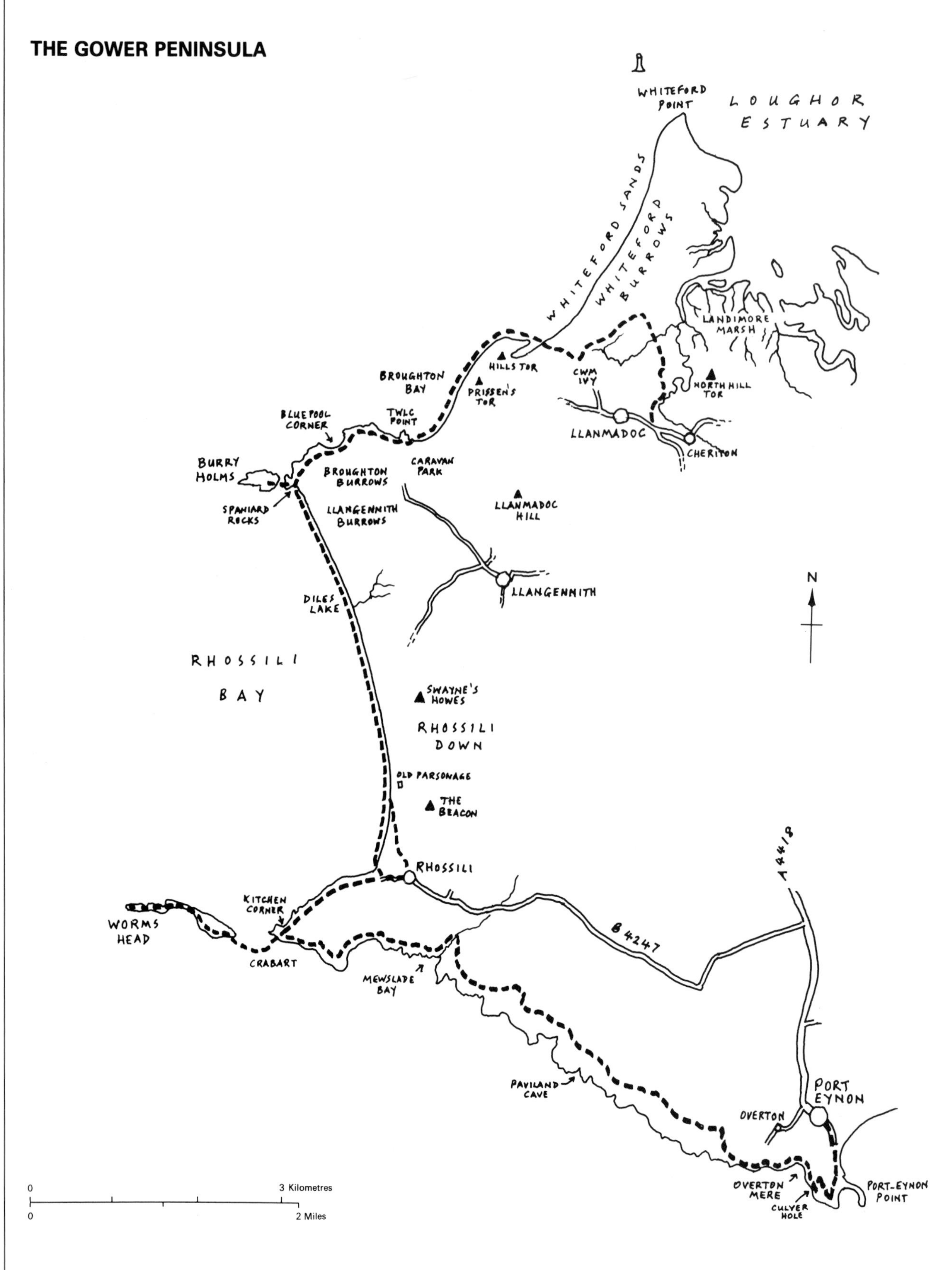
THE GOWER PENINSULA
WHITEFORD POINT
LOUGHOR ESTUARY
WHITEFORD SANDS
WHITEFORD BURROWS
LANDIMORE MARSH
HILLS TOR
CWM IVY
NORTH HILL TOR
BROUGHTON BAY
PRISSEN'S TOR
BLUEPOOL CORNER
TWLC POINT
LLANMADOC
CHERITON
BURRY HOLMS
BROUGHTON BURROWS
CARAVAN PARK
SPANIARD ROCKS
LLANGENNITH BURROWS
LLANMADOC HILL
LLANGENNITH
DILES LAKE
N
RHOSSILI BAY
SWAYNE'S HOWES
RHOSSILI DOWN
OLD PARSONAGE
THE BEACON
RHOSSILI
A 4118
KITCHEN CORNER
WORMS HEAD
B 4247
CRABART
MEWSLADE BAY
PAVILAND CAVE
PORT EYNON
OVERTON
OVERTON MERE
CULVER HOLE
PORT-EYNON POINT
0
3 Kilometres
0
2 Miles

A view back from the path near Highveer Point on Devon's north coast.

Walk 8: *Exmoor National Park — Lynmouth to Combe Martin*

Map: OS Landranger Sheet 180—Barnstaple and Ilfracombe. **Start:** Lynmouth harbour. **Finish:** Combe Martin. **Distance:** 13 miles (21km)—allow 6 to 7 hours **Access:** Lynmouth (and adjacent Lynton) are just off the A39 which runs through Combe Martin farther west. Nearest railway station—Barnstaple. **Type of Walking:** Woodland paths, rough cliffside and high moorland; modest gradients except for a couple of steep ascents, both involving around 1000ft (300m) of climbing; good waymarking generally. **Features of Interest:** Lynmouth, Lynton and their cliff railway; Valley of the Rocks; Heddon's Mouth Cleave and Hunter's Inn; the Great Hangman and Little Hangman; fine coastal views throughout. **Accommodation:** Widely available at Lynmouth/Lynton and Combe Martin, also to a limited extent at Hunter's Inn. Youth hostel at Lynton.

Where Exmoor meets the sea

Lynmouth holds a special place in my memory. As a child I was taken to see the aftermath of the great flood disaster of August 1952. The impression this left of the frailty of buildings and the unimaginable forcefulness of nature has faded little over the years. Massive summer storms over Exmoor following a protracted spell of wet weather had produced almost 10in. (254mm) of rainfall in 24 hours and an unprecedented volume of water had drained into the upper reaches of the East and West Lyn rivers. The consequences were disastrous. A wall of water, rock debris and mud washed away entire houses complete with their occupants, killing 34 people. I recall boulders, tree trunks and heavy silt choking the river bed, either side of which those houses still standing were torn open and strewn with masonry.

Thirty-eight years have elapsed and the incident recedes into history. Extensive engineering work on the bed of the 'rivers' ensured the town's safety from flooding and it has grown into a resort of considerable popularity. It is not the easiest of places to reach, being tightly confined at the confluence of two hill-girt valleys and even the main A39 plummets down a 1 in 4 gradient on the infamous Countisbury Hill, scene of many a stall and runaway!

If you start the walk from Lynmouth's seafront, a steep pedestrian way leaves through an arch just past the National Park Information Centre, zig-zagging up through gardens to the more sedate, higher town of Lynton (the Exmoor Museum is well worth a visit). En route you will have passed 3 times over the cliff railway—an alternative method of ascent. Its motive power is gravity and its system ingenious. To each of the two cars is attached a 700-gallon water tank; when the top tank is filled and the bottom one emptied, gravity does the rest for both cars are fixed to a continuous cable. Opened in 1890 under the patronage of the publisher Sir George Newnes, the railway rises some 500ft (174m) and has a 100 per cent safety record.

Just below the top station, you turn right into North Walk, a broad and favoured tarmac pathway 400ft (122m) above the sea. A Mr Sanford had this path cut in 1817, prompting one to reflect on the enterprise shown by individuals in the nineteenth century. Despite its tameness, this easy walk traverses impressive—even romantic—terrain and was a favourite haunt of the poet Percy Bysshe Shelley who stayed with his young bride in the village for nine weeks during 1812, avoiding the girl's outraged parents! Wordsworth, Coleridge and Southey had already patronised Lynmouth, but Shelley's exploits finally put it on the map and from the humblest of origins as a little fishing community, the town became known as the 'Switzerland of England'.

Beyond striking Castle Rock (which can be scrambled over), the path descends to grassy levels in Valley of the Rocks. On fine summer weekends it can get like Blackpool Sands, humanity mingling with a thriving herd of feral goats which are best kept downwind! The landscape is a curious one, probably formed 10,000 years ago during the last Ice Age when the ice sheet encasing the south-west coast forced the Riven Lyn to excavate a drainage channel parallel to the sea instead of directly into it. Resulting geological features include caves and eroded limestone pinnacles which have been christened with names such as Ragged Jack and the Devil's Cheesewring.

After passing a small roundabout, you can avoid the road by taking the second path on the right, looping round to the Lee Abbey estate fence and climbing back to the one-time toll house. It is a great shame that access problems prevent a circuit of Duty Point, but private landowners are notorious for their intransigence. In fact, Lee Abbey is a church conference and holiday centre, originally built as a private residence despite its name. Directly opposite, a clear track branches off left and provides a short woodland interlude, interrupting true coastal walking but infinitely better than the onward road past Lee Bay. The way is marked and crosses Bonhill Top to rejoin the toll road which is followed along to Woody Bay Hotel, there being no space for a path as well on the precipitous cliffside.

Majestic oaks sweep down to Woody Bay, but its secluded ambience was very nearly lost in the late 1800s when a Colonel Lake initiated its development as a rival resort to Lynmouth. A beach bathing pool, a golf course on higher ground and a carriage drive to Hunter's Inn were duly installed and a massive iron pier built to receive the Bristol Channel fleet of paddle steamers which plied the coast in those days. Within a short time the pier had been demolished by storms and Colonel Lake's grandiose plans were scuttled. He was later declared a bankrupt and eventually jailed for misappropriating trust funds.

From here to Combe Martin you will

Devastation at Lynmouth following the 1952 flood disaster.

experience a transition to wilder country, with Hunter's Inn the only refreshment point in 9 miles (14km) of rough walking. Just before the Woody Bay Hotel, you turn right through a gate, signposted for the beach, and emerge at a lane, turning up left. Where it swings sharp left, you cross a stile on the right and fork left up a steep track past gnarled trees. These woods above Wringapeak are recovering from a ferocious blizzard in December 1981 which decimated the tree population. Soon the path leads you round past a spectacular little waterfall in Hollow Brook, issuing from rocks 30ft

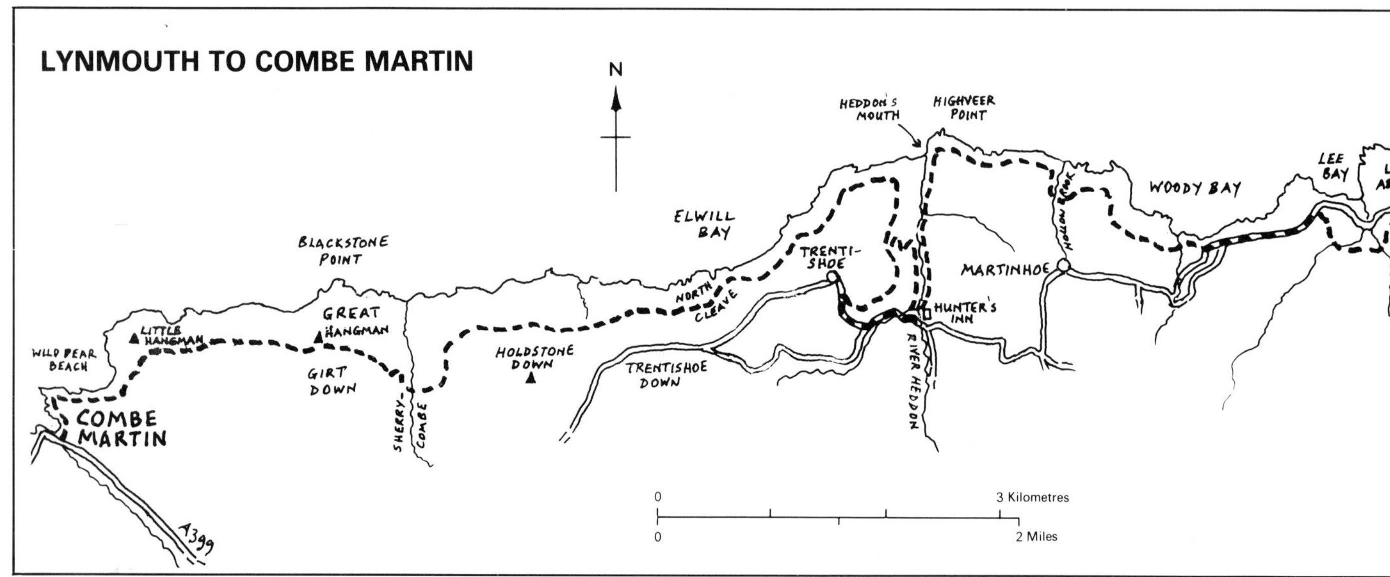

The aptly named Castle Rock on North Walk.

(9m) above. Continuing across scree, you reach an exhilarating rocky corner with wide cliff views extending back east. Many species of sea bird breed on Woody Bay's cliffs, including guillemots, kittewakes, auks, shags, razorbills, fulmars and gulls.

For the first time on this walk you can relate to the scenery without the interposition of man-made features, whether tarmac, buildings or the proximity of traffic. I walked this section shortly after it was opened as an alternative to the old carriage drive which loops round hillsides a couple of hundred feet higher up. What struck me was the greater sense of intimacy with the coastline gained by the lower path. These northern fringes of Exmoor often swoop to the sea in great convex hog's-backs which force path-makers relatively high to avoid unmanageably steep ground. Whenever this occurs, the foreshore is hidden and the sea remote, sometimes for several miles.

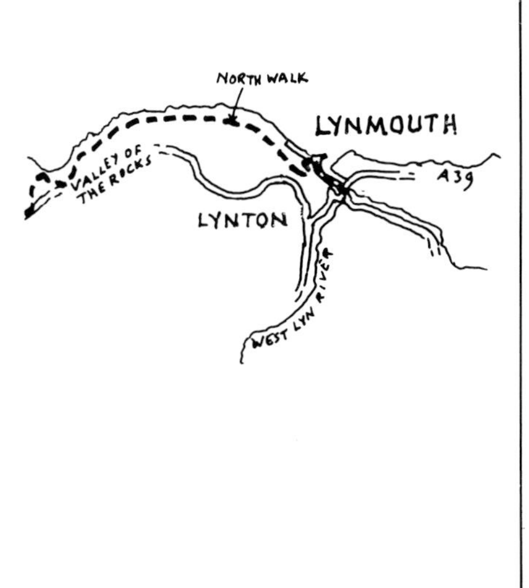

Walking uphill then contouring along rugged, heather-clad hillside directly above the sea for less than a mile, you reach Highveer Point and the dramatic bastion of land at Heddon's Mouth. Jutting proud of the general cliff line, this is a wonderful vantage point in clear weather, Widmouth Head near Ilfracombe visible to the west, Foreland Point to the east. To quote Ward, writing in 1895, 'we look down upon the trout stream flashing seaward towards the bar of shingle which the sea has piled across its mouth. An abandoned limekiln perched on the rocky bank . . . is worn by age and weather to picturesqueness, like some old castle guarding the pass inland.'

Descending steadily, you join a broad path along the heavily wooded valley floor and follow it inland to Hunter's Inn. (If in no need of refreshment, simply by crossing the first bridge over the River Heddon you can tackle an almost alpine zig-zag path opposite that takes you seaward to the ongoing route at the top of the Cleave.) The hospitable and popular Hunter's Inn stands near the confluence of the River Heddon's two arms in one of Devon's deepest and most poetic combes. With its complement of peacocks and a surrounding landscape held, it seems, in suspension from the last century, Hunter's Inn is one of those places you earmark for a future stay, preferably out of the high season. Meals and drinks are available and if the hour is right, many walkers will take on fuel for the ensuing 8 miles (13km) of strenuous going to Combe Martin.

A footpath leaves the Combe Martin road after 180m and follows the river's west bank to the start of the zig-zags, waymarked 'Trentishoe only. Steep Path'. More often than not, coast paths are squeezed into a margin of land between fields and the sea, with insufficient space to do other than mount gradients in a direct, uncompromising way, to the frequent discomfiture of walkers. On this occasion, however, well graded hairpin bends take you up over bracken and widening views add to the pleasure of gaining height so effortlessly. From just over half way up, a new path created by the National Trust loops seaward round Peter Rock and rejoins the old routing on East Cleave: either way is a treat!

Outside an old field wall, you come round above Elwill Bay whose cliffs suffer badly from erosion. The path has vanished at Bosley Gut, necessitating a diversion and underlining the need for caution whenever you approach the edge. At a particularly steep and Stygian chasm, you veer inland to a marker post on North Cleave then, at a fork junction, keep up to the next post, climbing gently above Neck Wood Gut. A broad track through rough heather branches off right across the wild flanks of Holdstone Down. Inland of the path it rises to 1145ft (349m) and on this unlikely summit, a late nineteenth-century landowner-turned-property speculator hatched a plan for housing development, even clearing still usable tracks named Seaview Road and Beach Road before the scheme was aborted.

Moorland vegetation prevails—a mixture of heather, western gorse and bracken, with sheep grazing more grassy areas—and the call of sea birds has been replaced by that of skylarks, wheatears, stonechats and members of the crow family. True upland country this, and as

Woody Bay from the woods above Wringapeak.

bleak as moors anywhere in hostile weather.

Further on, a white acorn symbol—universal logo for Britain's official long-distance footpaths—denotes a swing left into the sizeable Sherrycombe valley. Boggy and lacking the textural variety of woodland, I have always found it a rather dour place, overshadowed as it is by the intimidating bulk of the Great Hangman. Some way inland from the coast, you squelch steeply down to the stream footbridge and set about climbing the best part of 1000ft (305m).

At first, abrupt zig-zags attack the stony slopes of Girt Down, then as you gain altitude, the way trends left by a bench and on up alongside a wall. At its top corner, you can divert to the right on an old miners' track to the shoulder of Blackstone Point and an exciting clifftop situation. The Combe Martin district has a long history of mining, silver, lead, copper, iron and manganese all being extracted from the workings in sight here. The main path continues straight up to a sprawling cairn.

The Great Hangman (1043ft/318m) retains a certain mountain-like aloofness by virtue of its height (exceeded nowhere else on the entire south-west peninsula coast) and its relative remoteness a mile north of the nearest road. Each time I have climbed it, mist or rain has obscured any views, but I understand they are exceptionally wide-ranging, taking in Exmoor, a glimpse of Ilfracombe, Lundy Island, the Welsh coast and even far-away Dartmoor. Nevertheless, from such altitudes there is a flattening of perspective and you would need good clear visibility to reveal theoretically possible panoramas. The hill's macabre name may indeed have derived from the siting of a fifteenth-century gallows, but a more popular story involves a thief who stole a neighbour's sheep, binding its legs together round his neck to carry it and choking to death when the animal struggled backwards, strangling him as effectively as a noose! A more scientific explanation may be a corruption of *An Maen* meaning 'hill of stone'.

Leaving the cairn slightly left and crossing a stile, you walk gently downhill through gorse, veering right to stay outside a field fence. Ever more conspicuous now is the Little Hangman's pointed eminence, more often visited and reached by a spur path to the right. You are soon descending over grass in sight of Combe Martin's 2-mile (3km) straggle in the valley of the River Umber. After a long section of superb open country, the undulating path is now drawn narrowly towards impending civilisation between a field fence and clifftop hedge above Wild Pear Beach. From a pre-war promenade shelter on Lester Cliff, the more visually rewarding route swings round to the optimistically named Sandy Bay and the A399.

Workers from as far afield as Wales and Derbyshire were employed by Combe Martin's prosperous silver and lead mines during the Middle Ages. In the nineteenth century, a number of schemes were mooted to construct a protected harbour and bring in the railway, but they never materialised owing to lack of capital. The unusually long main street contains all shops and amenities of value to the walker, as well as an Exmoor National Park Information Centre. This is the western perimeter of the Park and the end of 36 miles (58km) of conscientiously maintained coast path, some of the very best of which has just been savoured.

Facing page: **Clovelly harbour.**

WALK 9: *North Devon — Westward Ho! to Clovelly*

Maps: OS Landranger Sheets 180 (Barnstaple and Ilfracombe) and 190 (Bude and Clovelly). **Start:** Westward Ho! seafront. **Finish:** Clovelly harbour. **Distance:** 12 miles (19km)—allow about 6 hours. **Access:** Westward Ho! lies north-west of Bideford on the B3236. Clovelly is reached by taking the B3237 off the main A39 coast road. Nearest railway station—Barnstaple. **Type of Walking:** Fairly rough terrain with considerable ups and downs, at first on open coast then through woods. Easy walking for the last 3 miles (5km). **Features of Interest:** Westward Ho! shingle bank; Buck's Mills hamlet; the Hobby Drive; Clovelly village and harbour; wild shoreline and beautiful, deciduous woodland. **Accommodation:** Widely available at Westward Ho! and nearby Appledore/Bideford. Portledge Hotel just off-route; some B & B at Buck's Mills and Clovelly. Youth hostel at Instow (by ferry from Appledore).

A Walk around Bideford Bay

Westward Ho! was a bit of a disappointment. The site was chosen for development in 1863 and named in response to public acclamation for Charles Kingsley's Elizabethan seafaring tale, *Westward Ho!*. As the first foundation stones were laid, there was every prospect of success and future prosperity, but both Charles Kingsley himself and a public who saw few advantages in forsaking established Devon esorts for this windswept and stony spot gave it the thumbs down. Nevertheless, by the 1870s a 500ft (152m) pier had been erected, though seas on this brutally exposed eastern end of Bideford Bay had destroyed it within a decade. In 1874, the United Services College was set up as an alternative to traditional public school for aspiring young officers (it subsequently moved nearer to London 30 years later and the building is now a terrace of flats). Rudyard Kipling attended for 4 years and was later to adapt his schoolday experiences in *Stalky and Co*.

After many miles tramping a disused railway trackbed round the big Taw estuary via Barnstaple, Westward Ho! represents a resumption of true coastal walking for those travelling south on the long-distance South-West Way. In that context, the town provides a chance to top up supplies and arrange

accommodation for the much less populous coast ahead. However, divested of this particular function, and despite its auspicious literary connections, Westward Ho! might strike you as rather brash, dedicated as it is to fast food and entertainment. (The contrast with Clovelly, where this walk ends, could hardly be greater.) Extensive sands to the north are backed by a 2-mile (3km) pebble ridge and the Royal North Devon golf links, but are covered by high tides, while to the west a discouragingly rocky foreshore runs along beneath the promenade. Relics from the Middle Stone Age were uncovered from a preserving layer of peat offshore, among them flint tools, animal bones and deer antlers; 7500 years ago, the site would have been above high water mark.

As you walk west, seafront chalets line the exit from Westward Ho!, each one customised to its owner's taste and given such names as *'Jis the Job'* and *'It'll du'*! Beyond, the way keeps straight ahead and for a few hundred metres joins the trackbed of the old Bideford to Appledore railway. Completed by 1908 but never connected to the main rail network, the line closed down 9 years later during World War I when its rolling stock was shipped to France for war service.

Before long, the railway embankment swings away inland at a fence and the coast path begins a foray into much wilder country. In no time at all, seaside crowds are but a memory, for it seems we British rarely stray far from our cars or the reassuring crush of humanity. The truth is that resorts, however large, are mere punctuation marks in the unfolding poetry of cliffs, bays and estuaries—a notion that only the coastal walker can fully appreciate.

Rising and dipping along low, Carboniferous sandstone and shale cliffs above spectacular rock beds known locally as 'ranes', you will be able to make out the pale specks of Buck's Mills and Clovelly far ahead on the great, wooded sweep of Bideford Bay. I have always found the sighting of journey's end—often a feature of coastal walks—to be double edged, for while measuring progress can be an absorbing exercise, it always takes longer that you imagine to get there! Near the second of two well-used footpaths inland to Abbotsham are the remains of Greencliff lime kiln, in which limestone brought ashore from small vessels was burned using local anthracite and carted away to sweeten the fields of Devon farms. Wreckage from the Cypriot coaster *Eva V* which drifted onto the beach in March 1981 on her way to the scrapyard, can be seen below, though each year it is reduced by storms.

Above: ***Storm over Bideford Bay.***

Facing page: ***Majestic woods along the Hobby Drive.***

Legwork now begins in earnest as you climb Cockington Cliff (108ft/33m) and drop right back to sea level to cross a stream. Driftwood and jetsam litter this remote bouldery beach, but what was once an awkward scramble back onto the cliffside has thankfully been provided with timber steps; proposals for a footbridge to span the little ravine were dropped for economy reasons. Once over Babbacombe Mouth and another watercourse, there is more climbing to do as the path weaves up over rough, broken ground onto open cliff at Higher Rowden and down to secluded Portledge Mouth. A track up to the left leads to the Portledge Hotel, but the mansion itself, home to the Coffin family for some 800 years, is obscured by trees.

The landscape ahead now changes in two respects: not only are the cliffs between here

and Peppercombe deep red from an isolated outcrop of that same Permian sandstone which characterises the South Devon coast, but as Bideford Bay curves towards the north-east facing lee of Hartland Point, it is fringed with 6 miles (9.5km) of luxuriant woods.

The next 800m can be taken along the beach at low tide, or by path, to Peppercombe. Beyond a stile by a large copper beech, you cross the stream and a lane to Peppercombe Farm, climbing sharp left directly opposite the entrance to Castle Bungalow into woodland, which dominates the remainder of this walk and is an utter delight, especially in May when bluebells are in flower.

You pass momentarily through a field containing Peppercombe Castle; marked on OS maps, this is an Iron Age hill fort, but a difficult one to discern beneath the scrub. Sloo Wood is too good to be rushed! The path undulates through sessile oak and birch, and on sunny spring days the dappled ground is richly embroidered with wildflowers such as primroses, campions, foxgloves and numerous ferns.

At Gauter Pool there is an abrupt left turn inland over double stiles into a green track and over two more stiles to Worthygate; here a hedged farm track to the right leads you along a ridge before narrowing to a path which winds downhill past a Coastguard lookout to emerge at the hamlet of Buck's Mills.

Between May and September, walkers can obtain welcome pots of tea at the little General Stores-cum-café here, run by Grenville Braund. Curiously, the settlement seems to have once been the exclusive domain of the Braund family—dark, swarthy folk quite unlike other Devonians and traditionally thought to have descended from survivors of a Spanish Armada galleon. According to a nineteenth-century journalist, Captain James Braund, King of Buck's Mills, would recite a poem about the villagers while accompanying himself on the fiddle. Two of the thirty verses go thus:

The Braunds of Bucks, The Braunds of Bucks!
A race of hardy Men!
So full of courage, that their pluck—
Eternally remain.

No haven have they! not a pier!
Wherein to moor their Craft,
But up and down the rocks, with care,
They haul them fore and aft . . ..

Limestone from Caldy Island in Pembrokeshire was burned here and the ivy-clad kilns, with buttresses and a circular 'keep' could be mistaken for a small fort. Buck's Mills remains unspoiled and charming principally because car parking is non-existent; its population dwindles with the winter exodus of holidaymakers and second-home owners.

Seaward of the shop, the coast path climbs determinedly through old established woods, then follows field edges inland to Bideford Bay Holiday Village, once the house of Welland Cary. Keeping left in front of its off-licence, you come round past a noxious rubbish dump but are soon returned to more pleasant surroundings. A stile is crossed and a left turn taken at the field top ahead where dramatic views unfold towards the precipitous wooded headlands west of Clovelly. Having negotiated another stile, you angle down left, cross a stream footbridge, mount steps and arrive at the Hobby Drive.

Construction of this scenic toll road—whether by Napoleonic prisoners of war or by Clovelly fishermen during hard times—was the 'hobby' of Sir James Hamlyn-Williams, owner of the Clovelly Estate in the early 1800s. A newer section, by-passing landslips, is marked by a bench inscribed: 'The new portion of road measuring 833 yards was added to the Hobby by Frederick and Christine Hamlyn in the year of our Lord God 1901.' Opinions differ as to

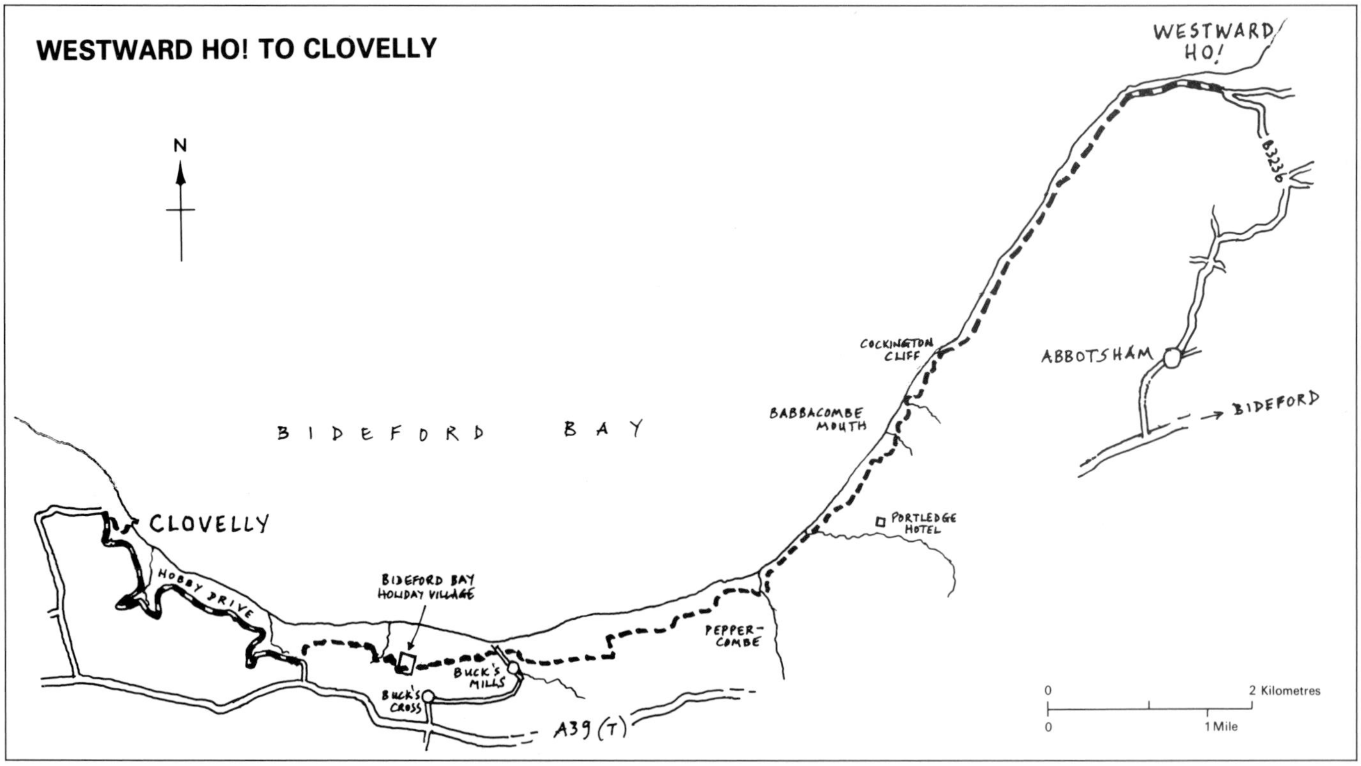

WESTWARD HO! TO CLOVELLY

N
WESTWARD HO!
B3236
ABBOTSHAM
BIDEFORD
COCKINGTON CLIFF
BABBACOMBE MOUTH
BIDEFORD BAY
PORTLEDGE HOTEL
CLOVELLY
HOBBY DRIVE
BIDEFORD BAY HOLIDAY VILLAGE
PEPPERCOMBE
BUCK'S MILLS
BUCK'S CROSS
A39 (T)
0 2 Kilometres
0 1 Mile

the Hobby's walking qualities, some claiming that lack of open sea views and the occasional passage of motor vehicles from a toll house on the A39 diminishes its attractiveness. Yet the surface is firm, the encompassing mature woods majestic, and when, after almost 3 miles (5km) of dog-leg loops round a series of combes, you glimpse Clovelly below, you are assured of approaching the village with foreknowledge of its coastal location and freedom from the merry-go-round of traffic queues and parking.

During the main holiday periods, countless thousands of visitors risk twisted ankles as a diurnal tide of humanity flows down the main street at 10 am and ebbs with the departure of coaches and day-trippers around 5 pm. Exposed to a public hunger for the picturesque, the inhabitants of Clovelly lead strangely unprivate lives. They have had time to adjust, however, for Clovelly's importance as a herring fishing port was already giving way to tourism by 1880, its reputation fuelled by the writings of Charles Kingsley and Charles Dickens. That the village has not succumbed to gross commercial exploitation is due in large part to the stewardship of the Hamlyns, a London banking family who acquired the estate in 1730, and especially to Christine Hamlyn who devoted her life to the village's restoration.

Visitor Centre and car parks are situated at the top of the village, wheeled transport never having penetrated the stepped and cobbled High Street (or 'Up-a-long' and 'Down-a-long' as it is known). Goods are transported by sledge or donkey, or by 4-wheel-drive to the quayside area near the private back road. Walk down to the harbour and you will appreciate the gradient on which some of the houses are built. The original jetty forming Quay Pool was constructed around 1600 by the Carys of Clovelly Court, Lords of the Manor for 4 centuries, and extended in 1826 to accommodate a then large fishing fleet.

Moored offshore, Clovelly's powerful lifeboat awaits the call to service on a coast renowned for ferocious weather. In 1821, 24 local boats sank in a gale, with 31 lives lost; 17 years later a similar disaster claimed 21 lives. On a lighter note, you could end the walk by staying in Clovelly or at least enjoying a well-earned drink at the Red Lion Hotel, right on the harbour quayside.

On the coast path round Bideford Bay.

Descending to Marsland Mouth at North Devon's rugged border with Cornwall.

WALK 10: *North Devon / Cornwall—Hartland Quay to Bude*

Map: OS Landranger Sheet 190—Bude and Clovelly. **Start:** Hartland Quay. **Finish:** Bude. **Distance:** 13 miles (21km)—allow at least 7 hours. **Access:** Hartland Quay lies just over 2 miles (3km) west of Hartland and is reached by taking the B3248 off the main A39 coast road. Bude lies west of the A39 at Stratton and connects by bus with British Rail at Taunton and Exeter. **Type of Walking:** Not for the faint hearted! A switchback of deep combes with some long and hefty gradients; very few refreshment points; good but rugged path, exposed to bad weather. **Features of Interest:** Speke's Mill Mouth waterfall; Marsland Mouth—the Devon/Cornwall border; Morwenstow village and Coombe Valley Nature Trail (both off route); unsurpassed, wild cliff scenery throughout the walk. **Accommodation:** Hotel at Hartland Quay; limited accommodation at Hartland; possible farm B & B near Morwenstow; all types of accommodation at Bude; youth hostel at Elmscott, 2 miles (3km) from the start.

A Walk on the Wild Side

For rugged terrain, sustained climbs and descents, remoteness from amenities and exposure to the elements, Hartland Quay to Bude takes some beating! In my view there is no more challenging a hike on any of Britain's official long-distance footpaths and this might surprise some readers who associate coastal walking with strolls on beaches or manicured cliff walkways near holiday resorts. Masochism, however, is not the name of the game and for a walk to be worth undertaking—especially if, like this one, it requires thoughtful preparation—there must be an appropriate pay-off.

Pay-off there is, for on this almost ruler-straight span of west-facing coast, the primeval margin where ocean meets land is experienced at close quarters. Unlike protected shores which encourage quiet contemplation and allow us to remain masters of our own actions, this savage, elemental boundary imposes conditions upon those who seek to explore it: treat it with carelessness or disdain and you risk uncomfortable consequences. Frankly, it is not a walk for stormy days, unless you relish a protracted struggle; even a bracing headwind will sap your resolve at times. For all that, there are few places on our shores which guarantee such rich rewards for the effort involved. This is some of the grandest and least frequented, yet accessible, ocean seaboard anywhere in Europe, containing an abundance of wildlife and spirit-lifting cliff scenery.

Hartland Quay stands at the road-end west of Bideford, no great distance from the dramatic corner turned by Hartland Point, the Roman 'Promontory of Hercules'. Wrecks litter this unforgiving and desolate coast, so it is with no surprise that we learn of Hartland Quay's demise as a trading community. A small harbour was built here, financed by none other than Sir Francis Drake, Sir Walter Raleigh and Sir John Hawkins in the late sixteenth century, but trade was destined to decline when the railway came to Bideford in 1855; by 1896, storms had completely demolished the quay and pierhead. A row of buildings was converted into the Hartland Quay Hotel, opposite which are a small museum and a gift shop. Before starting the walk, it's as well to obtain a weather forecast, to check you are carrying food, drink and suitable clothing and to verify that you have plenty of time in hand.

The path begins at a stile off the lane above Hartland Quay and enters a Devon Trust Nature Reserve before dropping round the truncated profile of St Catherine's Tor. No remains exist, but it is believed to have once borne a fourteenth-century chapel. Stepping stones lead on over Wargery Water in a flowery little valley, whereafter a sharp but short climb takes you over to Speke's Mill Mouth. Cascading onto rocks below is one of the best waterfalls on the south-west coast, but you need to scramble to beach level at low tide to appreciate its full 52ft (16m) drop. A motorable track penetrates this valley and on sunny days you will certainly have company for a while. In fact, the coast path follows the track inland a short distance then, by way of a footbridge, angles back and makes directly for the cliff crest on Swansford Hill. Here is a situation to savour—one of many on this walk. Damehole Point to the north is a pyramid of perfect symmetry, while to the south it is possible to see as far as Tintagel.

On the crumbling perimeter of flat fields 400ft (122m) above the sea, spare a thought for the 136-odd ships that have come to grief on this hostile coast over the past 200 years, and for the tragic loss of life this represents. Most recent was the Royal Fleet Auxiliary tanker *Green Ranger* which parted her tow in a November gale in 1962 and was wrecked on the Longpeak rocks; her crew of 7 was rescued by breeches buoy and pieces of rusty winching gear can still be found on the clifftop.

Not far beyond the path off to Elmscott youth hostel, you are pounding the tarmac of a country lane for half a mile before a field track restores the status quo. Rising gently above Sandhole Farm, a mile or so of open walking brings you to Embury Beacon, a sheepy, gorse-scattered hilltop bearing what is left of an Iron Age promontory fort. In 1973 an emergency excavation of the site was thought necessary owing to the alarming rate of cliff erosion; timbers and domestic pottery from ancient dwelling huts and cattle enclosures were found.

Once dangerously steep and loose, the descent to the valley of Strawberry Water has been provided with timber steps which will doubtless annoy purists to whom such 'taming' measures are anathema, but will at least reduce further serious erosion. Popular for its rough beach and picnic spots, Welcombe Mouth is accessible to vehicles by dirt road—a mixed blessing! Having pitched a lightweight tent here one Spring Bank Holiday after long miles on the coast path, my companion and I were kept awake by rowdy youngsters who arrived on motorcycles and proceeded to set fire to dry undergrowth. Why is it, we mused, that the coast seems to encourage anarchy; we reflected on all the illegal dumping, the running battles between mods and rockers, the litter and the pollution and got ourselves thoroughly depressed!

Approaching Stanbury Mouth and Lower Sharpnose Point.

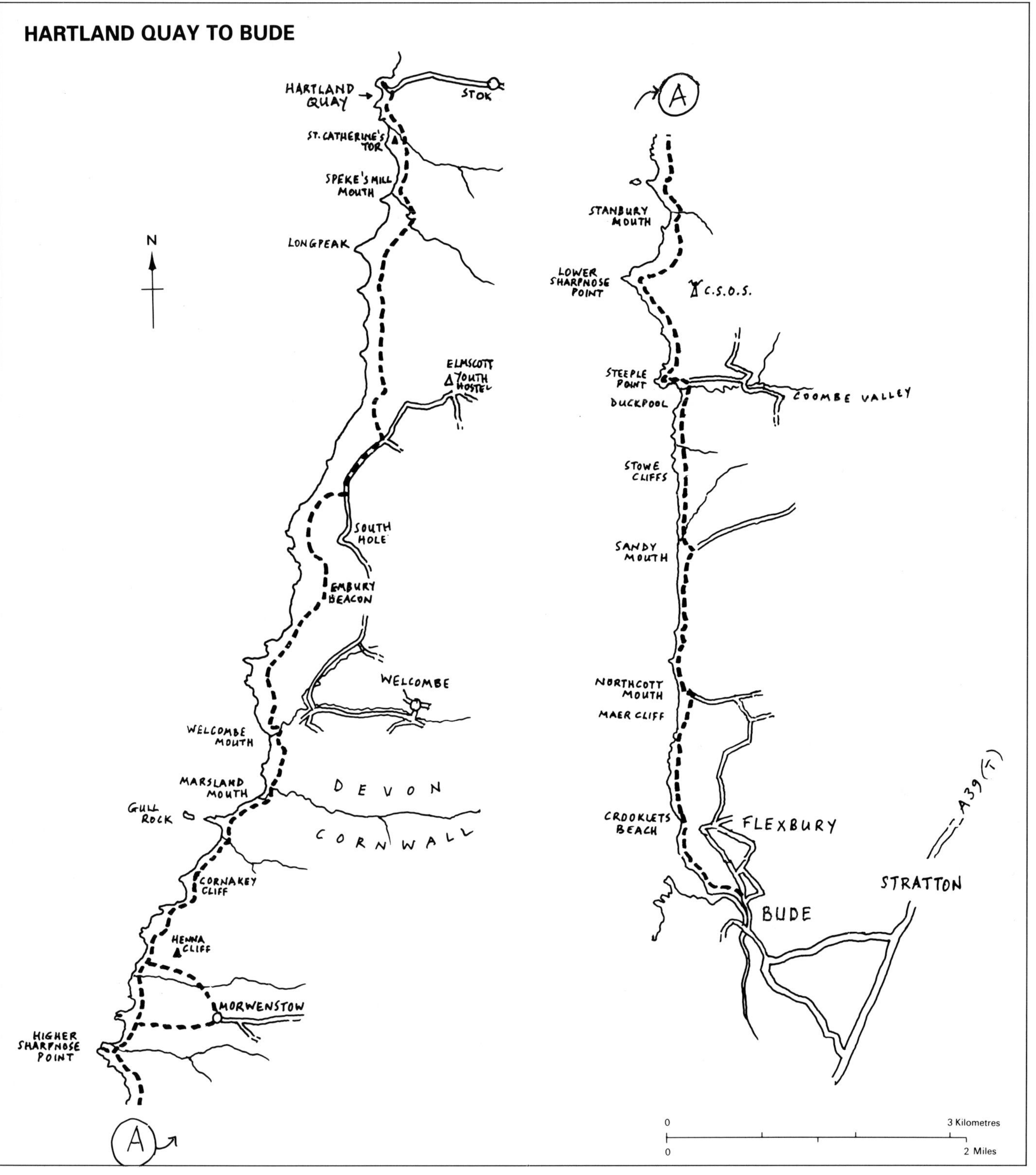
HARTLAND QUAY TO BUDE
N
HARTLAND QUAY
STOK
ST. CATHERINE'S TOR
SPEKE'S MILL MOUTH
LONGPEAK
ELMSCOTT YOUTH HOSTEL
SOUTH HOLE
EMBURY BEACON
WELCOMBE
WELCOMBE MOUTH
MARSLAND MOUTH
DEVON
CORNWALL
GULL ROCK
CORNAKEY CLIFF
HENNA CLIFF
MORWENSTOW
HIGHER SHARPNOSE POINT
A
A
STANBURY MOUTH
LOWER SHARPNOSE POINT
C.S.O.S.
STEEPLE POINT
DUCKPOOL
COOMBE VALLEY
STOWE CLIFFS
SANDY MOUTH
NORTHCOTT MOUTH
MAER CLIFF
CROOKLETS BEACH
FLEXBURY
A39(T)
STRATTON
BUDE
0
3 Kilometres
0
2 Miles

The pub in Welcombe village is a 3 mile (5km) round trip—not much of a proposition so early in the walk! More pertinent is to steel mind and body against the strenuous legwork about to begin. Once over Strawberry Water, there are 5 big combes to negotiate in relentless succession. The first ascent, to a hilltop field with massive railway-sleeper stiles, is countered by a steep drop past a tiny stone cabin that once belonged to the poet-playwright Ronald Duncan. Below you lies Marsland Mouth, county boundary between North Devon and Cornwall. As the way zig-zags down, growing noticeably less well walked, you may be reminded of lines from Charles Kingsley's *Westward Ho!*, 'To landward all richness, softness and peace; to seaward, a waste and howling wilderness of rock and roller, barren to the fisherman and hopeless to the shipwrecked mariner . . .'

Remote and gloriously expansive, Cornwall beckons. Crossing Marsland Water downstream from a miniature gorge, you take a track east then double back on the path to the level summit of Marsland Cliff. Almost immediately you are losing height again down a long series of steps into the next deep combe. Litter Water ends in a 70ft (21m) waterfall to the beach, but you see little of this, concentrating instead on the 2 telegraph poles laid side by side which constitute footbridges on these less frequented stretches of path: in windy conditions, crossing calls for steady footwork.

Looking back from Stowe Cliffs above Sandy Mouth.

The switchback continues with a hefty pull up to 400ft (122m) on Cornakey Cliff, but take a backward look at the extraordinary folded arch of Gull Rock running offshore. One of this walk's great attractions is the continuing revelation it provides of geological structures and rock architecture. As the sea erodes away the softer shales, harder sandstones are uncovered, contorted and folded by those same apocalyptic movements in the earth's crust that threw up mountain ranges. Laid before you is a stage upon which the irresistible forces of nature are acting out their role in shaping the earth's surface; never is this more apparent than when Atlantic swells vent their fury on the raw, broken edge of *terra firma.*

Next to jar the knees is Yeol Water combe and next to exercise the lungs Henna Cliff, at 450ft (137m) the English coast's second highest sheer cliff, after Beachy Head. Before descending from this magnificent viewpoint, there is an opportunity to turn inland and break the walk by visiting Morwenstow village. At about half way, its pub and tea room are considerable inducements and the Norman church is worth seeing. The writer and Reverend extraordinaire R S Hawker was priest to this and neighbouring Welcombe parish in the mid-1800s. He is remembered for instituting Harvest Festival and for writing *Song of the Western Men*, as well as for his eccentricity. He would sit in a driftwood cabin just below Vicarage Cliff (it is still there, in the hands of the National Trust), smoking opium and writing in solitude. His rectory chimneys are said to resemble church towers from previous incumbencies.

Higher Sharpnose Point follows Tidna Water's combe and a narrow spur just off the path gives thrilling, airy views, though it is not recommended in high winds. Along the lofty clifftops, stiles here and there have slipped away, underlining the shoreline's instability. Stanbury Water is crossed at an awkward little gully, followed by the now familiar 400ft (122m) climb out. Already seen from afar, a clutch of enormous aerial dishes looms ahead. They belong to the Composite Signals Organisation Station (an outpost of GCHQ) and, graceful or sinister depending on your point of view, their presence strikes a note of extreme contrast with the primordial landscape being walked through.

One hundred metres along the station's access road, you turn your back on all that technology and soon reach Steeple Point. Be sure to go right out under its sharp apex before slanting down inland to the car park and summertime ice creams at Duckpool. The Forestry Commission has laid out a nature trail on the south side of wooded Coombe Valley and if there's time to spare, the mile detour will make a refreshing interlude to the exposed coast path. Crossing the river mouth here during flood or storm was impossible until a footbridge was installed in 1981.

Yet another tough climb is required to reach Warren Gutter and Stowe Cliffs, but kinder gradients await! Grassy cornices hang out over space like their snowy mountain counterparts and one has some sympathy for farmers who plough and fence as near to the edge of their diminishing land as they dare. However, I can recall dozens of locations where this practice puts walkers in jeopardy and I'm afraid I have no compunction about hopping into fields on the basis that technical trespass is preferable to falling from a great height!

A track leads down to Sandy Mouth (good National Trust café during the season), then you are on lower cliffs, passing a conspicuous Bronze Age barrow and descending steps to Northcott Mouth. It is feasible to walk all the way from Sandy Mouth to Bude along the sands but this is the only point of escape should the tide look like beating you to it. It is gently downhill now over short-cropped turf to Crooklets Beach—the Bondi of Bude—where Britain's first Surf Lifesaving Club was set up and oversees the belly-board and Malibu experts out in the usually impressive surf. With plentiful amenities and good public transport links, Bude not only assures your return to the bosom of civilisation but makes a good base for exploring the superb coast to the south.

Cliff strata north of Bude.

WALK 11: *North Cornwall — Boscastle to Trebarwith Strand*

Maps: OS Landranger Sheets 190 (Bude and Clovelly) and 200 (Newquay, Bodmin & area). **Start:** Boscastle harbour. **Finish:** Trebarwith Strand. **Distance:** 7 miles (11km)—allow about 4 hours. **Access:** Boscastle is on the B3263 some 4 miles (6.5km) west of the main A39 coast road. Trebarwith Strand is reached on country lanes south of Tintagel which is also on the B3263. Nearest railway station—Bodmin Parkway. **Type of Walking:** Undulating clifftop, the well-walked path often rocky or stony; a few steep but short climbs. **Features of Interest:** Boscastle village and harbour; Rocky Valley and St Nectan's Kieve; Tintagel Castle; old slate quarries; dramatic cliffs. **Accommodation:** Widely available at Boscastle and Tintagel; an hotel at Trebarwith Strand. Youth hostels at Boscastle and Tintagel.

King Arthur Country

From Padstow Bar to Lundy Light
Is a sailor's grave by day or night.

Thus goes a local saying from the days of sail when mariners were at the mercy of storms along this formidably hostile north Cornish coast. Other than Bude and Port Isaac, Boscastle is the only natural haven for shipping north of Padstow; right from Elizabeth I's reign during which the legendary Sir Richard Grenville had the inner jetty rebuilt, the port thrived, reaching its heyday in the nineteenth century when an outer breakwater had been added to facilitate the export of slate.

Picturesque though this tortuous channel at the mouth of the River Valency may look to a modern visitor, Boscastle harbour was never easy to negotiate. Its entrance, complicated by the rock island of Meachard, is perilously narrow and in rough seas would have been a nightmare to manoeuvre into. Indeed, ships

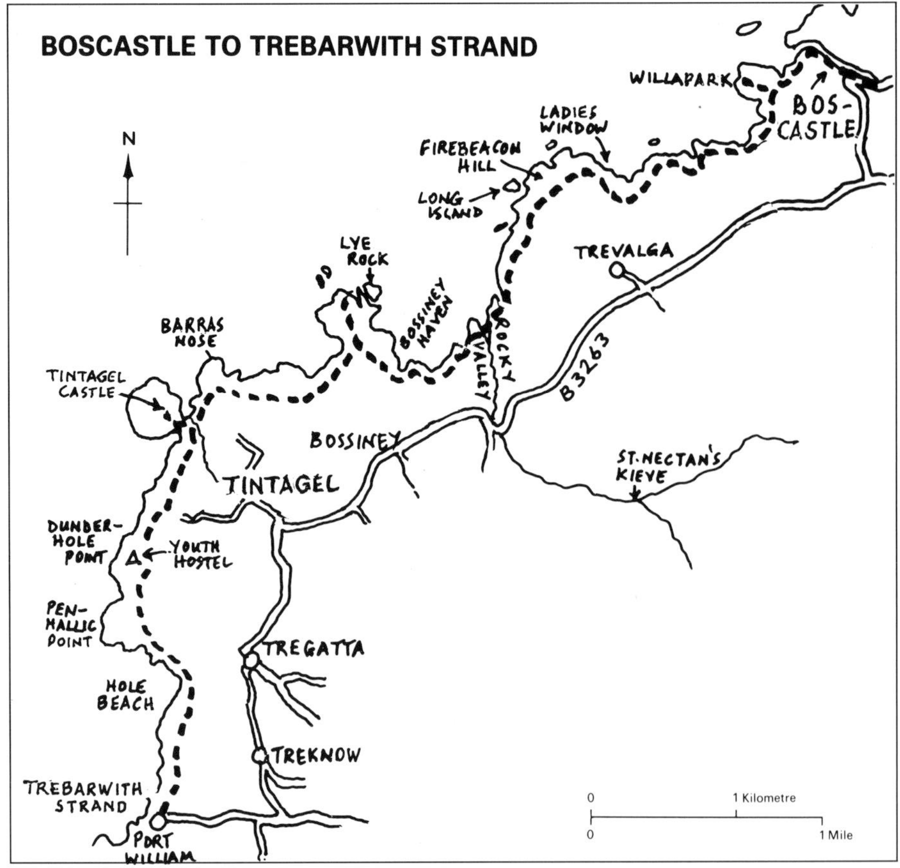

Previous page: ***Firebeacon Hill and Short Island (top right) from Willapark headland above Boscastle.***

Below ***Tintagel's Old Post Office.***

were often towed in by eight-oared boats called 'hobblers' and steered by teams of men hauling on ropes from ashore. It is testimony to the scarcity of shelter on this exposed coast that the port was commercially active for so long. Its decline began when the railway came to Camelford and heavy goods no longer needed to be shifted by sea. Today, tourism plays a significant part in Boscastle's economy but there is some fishing too.

Before starting the walk, a stroll round the village is worthwhile. The original twelfth-century castle, built by the de Bottreaux family, followers of William the Conqueror, has long since disappeared, but its name has corrupted to Boscastle. Steep streets lined with thatched cottages lead to the quieter upper village with its sixteenth-century pub, The Napoleon, while shops and eating places below attract large numbers of holidaymakers in the high season. Most of the surrounding land is owned by the National Trust which has a shop and Information Centre on the quay near the Palace Stables, now a youth hostel.

Crossing the River Valency, the route follows the southern quayside to the outer breakwater, constructed in the late 1700s. During World War II it was severely damaged by a stray mine and was rebuilt by the National Trust in 1962 using granite from Plymouth's old Laira Bridge, brought to the site by a light railway specially installed along the harbour's north side. Walking along the inlet onto open coast gives a sense of emergence, of relinquishing shelter, not dissimilar to that experienced by the crews of ketches and schooners that plied between here and Bristol or South Wales. Like us, they were never sure of wind and sea conditions until out from the protection of dark, quartz-seamed walls flanking the channel. I vividly recall the unexpected buffeting my companion and I received one chill and stormy Easter when we set off for Port Isaac from a quiet Boscastle harbour, only to walk into the teeth of a westerly gale as we crested the first rise; perhaps we should have been forewarned by the sight of huge seas crashing over the outer rocks!

Willapark (meaning 'lookout') rises to 317ft (97m) and is crowned by a whitewashed tower. Used for many years by customs officers to combat smuggling and later as a Coastguard lookout, it may have begun life as an observatory. Walk out to the tower—it's a superb local viewpoint—or continue along the coast path across the isthmus near the ditch and bank of an Iron Age promontory fortification. Inland lies Forrabury Common, divided into 42 strips, or 'stitches', a rare form of Celtic land use in which individual plots are cultivated from March to September then given over to common grazing. Were it not for the National Trust, this agricultural antiquity might well have been lost to the plough.

Keeping to the cliff edge, the path undulates on, dropping steeply over Grower Gut and climbing past the top workings of California Slate Quarry. Over a stile and bank ahead is a 'curzyway' wall, characteristic of the region and built by laying slate slabs on the diagonal to form a distinctive herringbone, or chevron, pattern. Rugged but straightforward progress is made towards Trevalga church and manor on cliffs ahead, before contouring round to Firebeacon Hill. Below is an extraordinary aperture in the cliffs known as the Ladies Window and just round the headland stands Long Island, a 200ft (61m) high stack topped by a rock climbers' cairn.

Still entertaining, the way continues past a camp site and descends inland to Rocky Valley. As natural features go, it is not large—a stream tumbling over rocky steps in a miniature gorge—but the valley's chief interest lies in its Bronze Age maze carvings on a rock near a ruined mill. These and a summer tea room at the restored Trevillet Mill tempt many walkers to make a diversion up the luxuriantly wooded footpath alongside the stream. Even further up the ivy-clad glen, beyond the B3263 road in fact, St Nectan's Kieve cascades 40ft (12m) through a little circular rock arch, but to see it allow an extra half-hour each way from the coast path.

Steps provide an exit from Rocky Valley and the path curves round above Bossiney Haven, dropping over the beach path and climbing to another Willapark, also an Iron Age cliff-castle site. Lye Rock, almost but not quite an island, presents the most incredible sliced-off profile from this angle. It is likely to be surrounded by swooping sea birds, as its sheer faces are breeding grounds for fulmars, puffins, cormorants, razorbills and other cliff-nesting species.

More prominent even than adjacent headlands, King Arthur's Castle Hotel proclaims its proud—some might say vulgar—Victorian origins. Built at the turn of the century and a product of early exploitation of the Arthurian legend by the astute directors of the London and South Western Railway Company, it pinpoints Tintagel's position on the coast from great distances. I have spotted its square profile from as far afield as the Devon/Cornwall border to the north and Pentire Point to the south. By keeping seaward of the hotel, a National Trust sign for Barras Nose is passed (the promontory was the National Trust's second acquisition, back in 1896) and soon Tintagel Castle and Merlin's Cave appear across the tiny cove of Tintagel Haven.

There is little firm evidence for linking the King Arthur legend with historical fact. His depiction as a medieval knight is probably attributable to romantic distortion following the publication of Tennyson's *Morte d'Arthur* and *Idylls of the King*, and to the revival of chivalry instigated by the writings of Sir Walter Scott. Even the village itself, originally Trevena, changed its name to Tintagel in order to exploit burgeoning public imagination at the time. There can be no denying that the island castle conjures up visions of knights and derring-do, however fanciful they may be!

Thought to have been built over a third century Celtic monastery, the castle was put up in the twelfth century by Reginald de Cornwall, illegitimate son of Henry I, and extended 200 years later by the Black Prince. It served as a prison for some time but had become ruinous by the 1500s and only fragments of the original structure remain today. The castle's inner and outer wards have become separated by the ravages of marine erosion, yet the ruins are still impressive, enhanced considerably by a wild and inspiring coastline.

It must be said—the picture will seem less rosy during busy holiday periods when a motor shuttle service from the village adds its complement of trippers to those who have come down on foot. At such times the castle and its surroundings are overrun with sightseers. Disappointingly, much the same goes for Tintagel. Set back 300ft (91m) above the sea and a kilometre off the coast path, a detour is only recommended to view the old Post Office in a curious medieval manor house owned by the National Trust, or to make use of amenities.

Eschewing Tintagel's fleshpots, the onward path forks right off the castle access track, passes near the interesting Norman Church of St Materiana and emerges onto a broad track over open ground adjacent to the village outskirts. Crowds and vehicles are soon left behind as the way dips seaward on Glebe Cliff past Tintagel's youth hostel. Converted from old slate quarry buildings on Dunderhole Point, its location must rank as one of the most spectacular in the UK. Offshore, Gull Rock pierces the sea's surface like a shark's fin as the walk contours along grassy cliffs above Penhallic Point.

Turning left up shaley slopes towards the houses of Tregatta and Treknow hamlets, disused slate quarries are revealed below, behind Hole Beach. Some say the conspicuous 80ft (24m) high pinnacle was deliberately left by the quarrymen as a shelter from wind and weather, others that it is simply of inferior quality slate. Relics of slate quarrying between Tintagel and Trebarwith Strand, along with the interpretations of industrial archaeologists, paint dramatic pictures of an industry which remained active until the 1930s. As well as 'hole-in-the-ground' extraction, slate was also won from smaller cliff-face quarries, men scrambling down flights of ladders or lowered on ropes to drill the beds—rusty railings and stanchions can still be seen in Long Grass Quarry below the youth hostel. Ingenious winching systems, powered by a blindfolded horse or donkey operating a 'whim', enabled slate to be taken up for splitting and cargoes to be lowered into sailing vessels moored against specially trimmed cliff berths.

The slate-quarry pinnacle behind Hole Beach.

Soon after passing a cliff rescue rope box, the path descends to Trebarwith Strand. Here, from diminutive Port William, locally finished slates were shipped out, with reciprocal cargoes of coal and lime arriving mainly from Bideford and Appledore. Landing or berthing anywhere along this treacherously rocky stretch of coast was not without considerable risk to the ketches and their crews and such precarious anchorages as Port William were only operational in quiet or moderate sea conditions. Complete with pub and restaurant, Trebarwith Strand is a pleasant place at which to finish this fascinating itinerary, which manages to combine splendid scenery with glimpses into our cultural and industrial past.

St. Ives at Eastertide, from Porthminster Point.

WALK 12: *West Cornwall — St Ives to Lamorna Cove*

Map: OS Landranger Sheet 203—Land's End, The Lizard and Isles of Scilly. **Start:** St Ives harbour. **Finish:** Lamorna Cove. **Distance:** 33 miles (53km)—3 days suggested. **Access:** St Ives is on the A3074, north west of the A30 at Hayle. Lamorna Cove is reached from the B3315 west of Newlyn. Nearest railway stations—St Ives and Penzance. **Type of Walking:** Rugged cliff —most of the way: boggy and rocky in many places, with repetitive ups and downs, especially between St Ives and Pendeen Watch, which is also fairly remote. Few refreshment places until Sennen Cove. **Features of Interest:** Some of the most spectacular and unspoiled coastal scenery in Europe; the resort of St Ives; Zennor village; old mine buildings; Land's End; Porthcurno's Minack open-air theatre; the Logan Rock; Lamorna Cove. **Accommodation:** Widely available in St Ives, Pendeen, St Just and Sennen; also at Land's End, Porthcurno, Treen and Lamorna. Farms and hamlets everywhere tend to offer B & B or camping during the summer. Youth hostels at Phillack, near Hayle; Bosavern, near St Just; and at Penzance.

Round the Magnificent Land's End Peninsula

We had arrived in the middle of April expecting blustery showers: instead, St Ives glowed with Aegean colour and the sky held no more cloud than sparse arabesques of cirrus. The two of us intended to use a lightweight tent on the trek around this delectable western tip of Britain, but after a train journey which, beyond Plymouth, had slowed from Inter-City haste to a branch-line dawdle, we opted for bed and breakfast and a chance to orientate ourselves to new surroundings.

St Ives is named after St Ia, missionary daughter of an Irish chieftain said to have arrived by coracle from Ireland in the sixth century. Since then, through an often turbulent history, the town has seen profound changes, none more cataclysmic than the rapid decline of its pilchard fishing in the 1890s after 500 years as the mainstay of its economy. Before the pilchards disappeared—due, some say, to climatic changes—St Ives's fishing fleet was the most productive in Cornwall. Much of the east-facing harbour's stonework was constructed in the 1770s by John Smeaton, using audacious new techniques pioneered during his design of the third Eddystone lighthouse 20 years earlier.

Three generations ago, West Penwith experienced an eruption of artistic activity of all kinds and once this creative movement had begun, artists flocked here, renting fish lofts overlooking the harbour and beaches, finding inspiration in the special qualities of light and lifestyle. Many famous names are associated with St Ives and Newlyn, among them Barbara Hepworth, Ben Nicholson and the potter Bernard Leach. Fashions change, and the excitement generated by this far-flung corner of Britain gradually became diluted by easy travel and tourists' demands for cheaper kitsch rather than the real thing. Nevertheless, something of a genuine Celtic revival in craftwork also took place and the tradition lives on in numerous workshops.

For many holiday visitors, St Ives epitomises Cornwall and during the brief summer season its quaysides and narrow, winding streets are overrun. And yet at other times of the year—another profound change but on an annual cycle—the place can seem deserted. In this it has much in common with other Cornish resorts which suffer a kind of off-season fossilisation. A shrinking indigenous population is being replaced by a new influx of retired folk from 'up country' seeking tranquillity and revitalisation, as well as by absentee second home owners. There is little doubt that the town is at its best in spring and autumn.

Day 1: St Ives to Pendeen Watch (13 miles/21km)

Day dawned like the realisation of a dream—the sort of weather that elevates walking to the pinnacle of carefree enjoyment. Even so, it is necessary to develop some advance strategy for dealing with the 22 miles (35km) of rugged and largely empty coastline to Sennen Cove. Obtaining food and drink and deciding where to sleep could pose problems for the unprepared: it is a stretch of rough walking to be reckoned with in every sense, a potentially serious undertaking in heavy wind and rain.

With well stocked rucksacks, we climbed to St Nicholas's chapel on the 'Island', an elevated little isthmus between Porthmeor beach and the harbour, for a last look at Eastertide St Ives. The metalled, westward path from Porthmeor beach takes you past putting and bowling greens towards Clodgy Point, where paving slabs laid over bog signal your departure from civilisation.

Reversing the expected order, headlands on the first part of this walk are descended to—often quite steeply—while inlets and stream valleys lie back in higher ground. We found the path rocky, tortuous and spasmodically boggy, imposing a speed limit on progress. Crossing several streams, we rounded Pen Enys Point and gazed down into Polgassick Cove. Badger setts had disturbed the path here, but the next kilometre gave superb high-level walking above a sea which on that day heaved and sighed lazily against the cliffs.

To a crescendo of expanding views, we reached Carn Naun Point, its OS pillar (318ft/97m) pin-pointing our position; its greatest value would be in poor visibility. Gorse-covered moorland scattered with boulders reaches inland to the granite spine of West Penwith. Hills rise to over 700ft (220m) but appear more mountainous than that, their

The harbour, St. Ives.

slopes bearing a profusion of Iron Age fortifications, standing stones, burial mounds, stone circles and ancient village sites. Strange how often early man chose to settle on land we reject as remote and unyielding . . .

The two Carracks rocks offshore are reputedly the haunt of seals, while farther on the great bastions of Zennor Head and Gurnard Head thrust proud of the general cliff line. In exceptionally clear air, it is possible to see as far north-east as Trevose Head, a major turning point back between Padstow and Newquay but views forward are restricted by the coast's south-curving trend.

Had the hour been later, we might have pitched our tent above River Cove, for it offers a waterfall and seclusion. Good 'wild' pitches are hard to come by on this steep, uninhabited coastline. Not only is it essential to seek permission before camping on farmland, but fresh water and shelter from an often boisterous wind have also to be found. Streams running off pasture may look clear but can be contaminated by stock or fertiliser run-off, so considerable discretion should be exercised before drinking it.

Beyond the climb out from River Cove and a succession of small rocky inlets traced by the path, we dropped to Mussel Point through flora more characteristic of a rock garden than exposed clifftop. The path was living up to its reputation as hard and fairly unremitting, though foul weather would add a whole dimension of misery by swelling streams and bog and lubricating the already ankle-twisting terrain!

During rough seas and high tides you would get a drenching from spray behind Wicca Pool, for the way falls close to sea level. Soon, evidence of granite is encountered in the form of castellated rock, a distinctive and recurrent feature for much of this walk. Tremedda Cliff is sheer and riven with indentations, the climb out to Zennor Head all the more exhilarating. The headland was donated to the National Trust in 1953 by 'A.B.'—'in memory of the friends who have sustained me'. It is a marvellous spot and we scrambled out beyond the plaque for a well-earned picnic lunch high above Pendour Cove.

Zennor village lies just inland along a public footpath and lane. A few metres south of the Tinners Arms pub, Cornish life is captured in models and exhibits in the little Wayside Museum. If you're detouring to the village (perhaps in search of accommodation), make a point of seeing the church of St Senara, dating from the twelfth century. Its best known feature is a medieval carved Mermaid bench-end in a side chapel, though there are also interesting memorials and ancient Cornish crosses in the churchyard. D H Lawrence and his German wife Frieda lived in Zennor for two years from 1915 while the novelist was writing *Women in Love*. Surrounding the village, an archaic landscape anchored by granite walls of prodigious mass, seems held by an ageless silence.

Resuming our hike—Pendeen Watch was still a rugged 6 miles (9.5km) away—we crossed the luxuriant stream valley above Pendour Cove and joined the by-now familiar switch-back over promontory and hollow. Veering inland round a dramatic cleft and waterfall behind Porthglaze Cove, we climbed past an impressive mine engine house ruin to the neck of Gurnard's Head. A clear path leads out onto the rocky headland with its Iron Age fort and splendid views; for some, a more compelling detour may well be the Gurnard's Head Hotel 750 metres inland at Treen—one of precious few refreshment places accessible to the walker.

Pendeen Watch lighthouse did seem closer now, but, as with so much coastal walking,

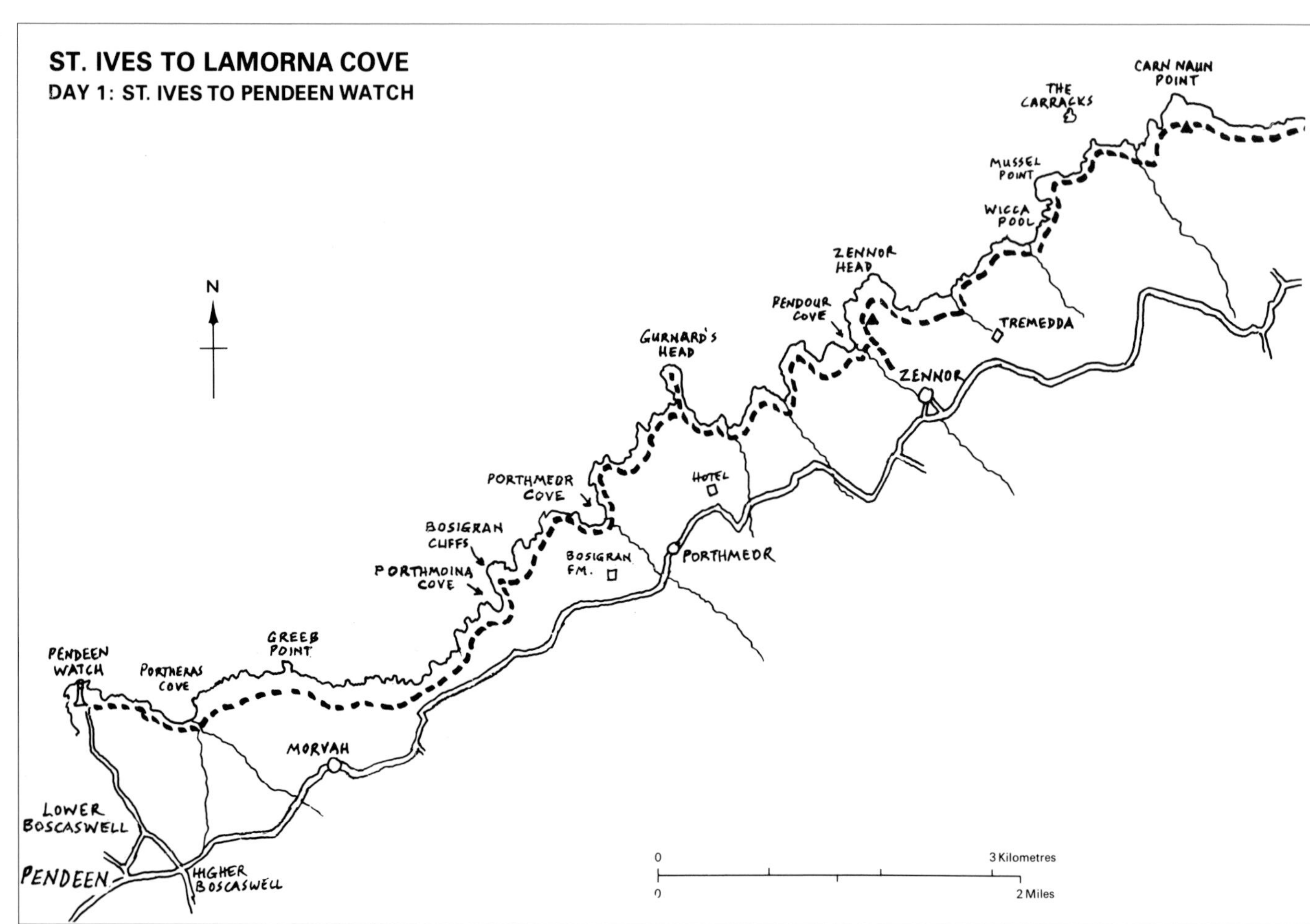

linear progress was slowed by endless convolutions in the path. Slopes above Porthmeor Cove—with no features to set a scale—appeared high and almost alpine in character, granite pinnacles outcropping to the north. Beyond the stream (and a summer diversion left up to Bosigran Farm for cream teas!), there is a bog to negotiate and for a time the way is indeterminate. After Carn Moyle, however, you climb steeply back onto granite above Great Zawn—a vertiginous drop—and on over Halldrine Cliff's shattered rock to the slabby summit of Bosigran Cliff.

We dropped to Porthmoina Cove and drank the last of our water with a snack. Though only April, the unseasonal heatwave was warming the afternoon to almost summer values, a reminder of how sunshine, welcome though it is, can pose its own exposure problems, in extreme cases producing hyperthermia, a dangerous raising of blood temperature.

The bold granite architecture around Bosigran has attracted rock climbers for many years (inland on the B3306 there is a regional Climbers' Club hut and a rescue post). There was time now to watch their painstaking moves, the inching upwards, the waiting on stances, and to acknowledge that it is not everyone's cup of tea!

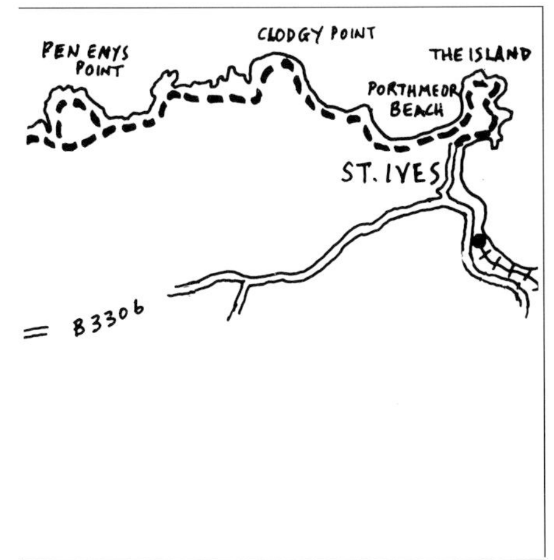

This little enclave of activity was rapidly left behind for unfettered walking which, for a while, was level; boginess persisted, exacerbated by brooks and grazing cattle. Eventually, a wider path is joined down to Portheras Cove, still plagued it seems by razor-sharp metal fragments from a wreck blown up to improve the environment: walking barefoot here is to court disaster! Once over the last stream, we ambled up the slipway track to the immaculate black and white lighthouse at Pendeen Watch. During the 1800s, when shipping was used extensively to shift ores and coal, wrecks occurred with unacceptable frequency on this exposed coast fringed with treacherous offshore reefs; even the St Ives lifeboat was lost in January 1939. Something had to be done and this light was opened in 1900.

A mile up a lane to the left are the almost contiguous villages of Boscaswell and Pendeen containing shops and amenities. With thirsts to assuage, we called it a day and pitched on a small camp site at Trewellard. Just off the coast road here at Geevor Mine, you can trace the history of tin mining—that most hazardous of occupations—in a fascinating museum. During the summer season, there are guided tours of the surface workings and refreshments are available.

Day 2: Pendeen Watch to Sennen Cove (9 miles/14.5km)

We cut down a lane to the coast path at Trewellard Zawn, having missed no more than a kilometre of the path from the road above Pendeen Watch. Ahead, the natural landscape is overlaid with a patina of derelict buildings, for mining activity in this area throughout the last century was intense.

During the Carboniferous period, molten granite rose into already folded and contorted sedimentary rocks—the so-called Cornish 'killas'—cooling slowly and allowing the formation of its constituent crystals (quartz, felspar and mica). Under intense pressure and heat, other liquids and gaseous materials were produced, giving rise to metal ores. Although tin and copper occurred in commercially viable quantities, other metals such as gold, silver, nickel, cobalt, zinc and iron also exist.

Mines were located where valuable deposits were most accessible, often on or near the coast. As you walk through the desecration of Levant Mine, spare a thought for the men who risked their lives daily in appalling conditions to earn a meagre wage. Levant was a major producer of tin and copper ore for over a hundred years until the beam engine failed in October 1919, killing 31 men in the shaft and injuring many more. It was Cornwall's worst mining disaster and sounded the death knell for an industry already threatened by cheaper foreign imports. Nearby Geevor is exploiting reclaimed reserves in Levant and Boscaswell mines.

Broad and stony, the onward path passes more chimneys and ruined buildings. Over to the right stands the OS pillar on Botallack Head and soon you are above the restored engine houses of Old Crowns Mine, dramatically—one is tempted to say romantically—situated on a rocky ledge above the waves. It is much photographed and was visited by the Prince and Princess of Wales in 1865.

I have never been offended by nineteenth century industrial ruins, however 'untidy' they appear to be. Variety is the spice of walking, to coin a phrase, and an unrelieved diet of virgin clifftop would eventually pall. Besides, these relics provide an experienced connection with our industrial heritage, a window into the past through which imagination is free to roam. Really objectionable were graffiti-daubed concrete walls and picnic litter near the road from Botallack village.

Overgrown heaps of stone and old winding houses led us onwards. A large adder slithered across the track and off into the heather scrub, then we were walking on grass once more and at a corner were confronted by the Kenidjack valley and a distant sighting of the Longships lighthouse off Land's End. You can cross the stream on boulders at its mouth, but we followed the coast path line, down from the well-defined Iron Age fort, past great banks of dead bracken and heard our first cuckoo of the year. The little footbridge is hidden in luxuriant vegetation; a few weeks later and the steep zig-zags beyond would have taken us through drifts of bluebells. Within a few minutes we had reached Cape Cornwall.

As the day had settled quiet and cloudless, we bought cups of tea from the car park refreshment kiosk and wandered out onto the cape. Thought to be England's most westerly point for many centuries (it only misses this distinction by a thousand metres or so), Cape Cornwall lacks the razzmatazz of Land's End, some might add mercifully! Its almost futuristic summit beacon is, in fact, a tin mine chimney, disused since 1878, while the seaward tip is occupied by yet another of the Iron Age defensive positions with which this coast abounds.

A rough track leads up past cottages to clifftop level where you turn down right, opposite the OS pillar on Carn Gloose. Before continuing, we gazed south to the buildings at Land's End, now clearly visible beyond Whitesand Bay and Sennen. A kilometre offshore lie the Brisons upon which many a ship has foundered. Taking you inland a little at first (there is a youth hostel up the lane), the way returns to the shore at Porth Nanven, notable for its raised beach. We crossed the stream there, climbed through rocks past dangerous mineshafts to the clifftops again and angled down grassy slopes to the next watercourse. Thereafter, the path undulates along sloping cliffside and has you scrambling through two granite spurs in quick succession nearing Aire Point.

At this end of Whitesand Bay, exposed to south westerly storms, we found the cliff edge in an unstable, eroded condition and were glad to reach the first little sandy beach. Had the tide been out, we could have walked along the sands to Sennen Cove, but high water forced us onto a sinuous, awkward path to an area of dunes and thence to the road.

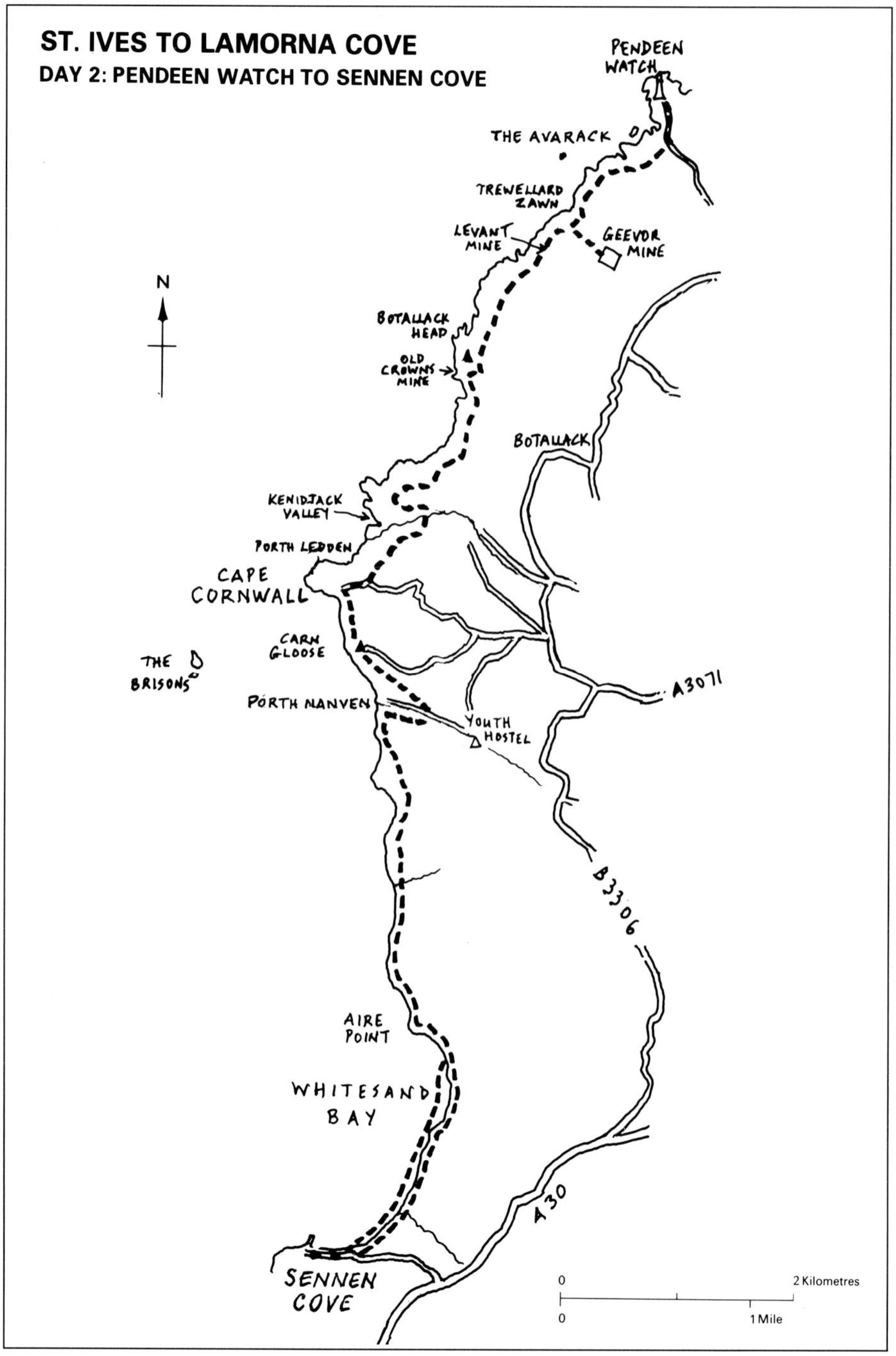

Sennen Cove faces north but fails to escape the onslaught of Atlantic swells. Perhaps its lack of elevation above sea level, or the village's position huddled into a corner of the bay generates a sense of vulnerability to the elements as you walk towards the harbour. There are shops, pubs and eating places here, so we took a late lunch and joined throngs of Easter trippers exploring the cove. As you would expect, Sennen lifeboat plays a crucial role in sea rescue off this cruel shore. Special tribute was paid by the Prime Minister to the crew's heroic 9-hour mission in August 1979, when they helped pick up survivors of the Fastnet Race in exceptionally severe weather.

We could easily have continued walking, but chose instead to watch the surfers in Whitesand Bay and find a leisurely pitch on one of the farm camp sites just inland.

Day 3: Sennen Cove to Lamorna Cove (11 miles/17.5km)

Britain, the weathermen said, was warmer than Corfu and we should expect temperatures to stay in the 70s. The night had been airlessly still, itself remarkable on this south-western extremity of Britain. Ocean swells poured into Whitesand Bay and already surfers were out, riding 10ft waves which peaked green over unseen reefs.

We walked back to Sennen Lifeboat Station above the old circular Capstan House and took the coast path up past the battlemented Coastguard Station and onto Mayon Cliff. The way soon bifurcates—paths take a heavy pounding from thousands of feet each year—but you are recommended to keep right, past the National Trust's Iron Age Maen Castle to Dr Syntax's Head. This is the UK's most westerly mainland point and is named after a fictional character from a late nineteenth-century book by William Coombes entitled *Dr Syntax in Search of the Picturesque etc.*, a copy of which I have as yet been unable to find!

Although coastal walkers can pass Land's End without charge, you are as likely to be drawn into its commercial clutches as we were. Within the last few years the site has undergone a £4 million facelift, extending amenities and rationalising the rather ad hoc development which existed before and which always seemed in danger of pandering to the lowest common denominator of public taste. If nothing else, you can obtain a coffee here, as we did, or a meal and accommodation.

ST. IVES TO LAMORNA COVE
DAY 2: PENDEEN WATCH TO SENNEN COVE

Despite the inevitable presence of other people—possibly in considerable numbers—there is a great deal to look at besides man-made attractions. From Dr Johnson's Head, generally assumed to be the true 'land's end', broken rocks spilling westwards continue to defy the ocean's attempts at total domination. The Longships, and even Wolf Rock lighthouse, can be made out with the naked eye, while any dark, low smudge on the south-western horizon is likely to be the Isles of Scilly, 28 miles (45km) away.

Nothing but open ocean separates you from America and this uninterrupted fetch endows Atlantic waves with awesome power. I have known flat calms here, but they are very much the exception and in rough weather salt spray is carried far inland. Sea level is accessible here and there with a little scrambling in quiet conditions, but it is generally considered unwise to linger owing to the incidence of freak waves. Tragically, lives are lost from time to time through ignorance of how the ocean behaves.

After miles of walking unfrequented cliffs and gaining a kind of psychological momentum towards reaching Land's End, we felt oddly cheated by the exploitation—as if the place is tamed rather than enhanced by all the hype. Little matter—within a few minutes on one of the southbound paths it was all a

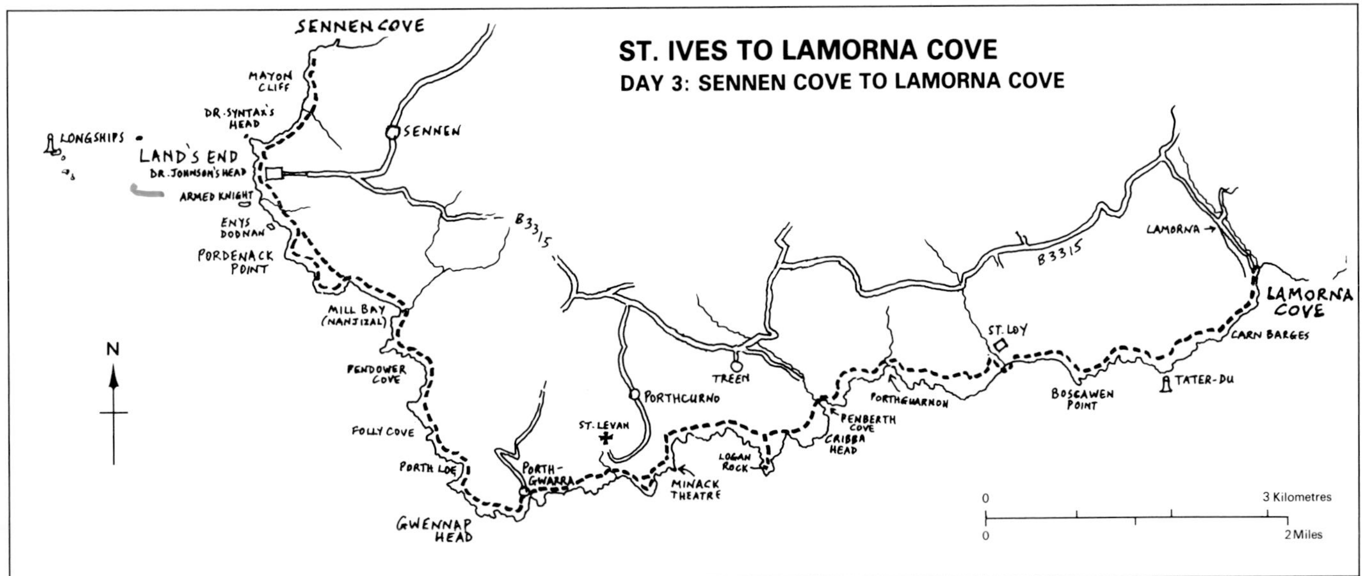

memory and from a walker's standpoint the best, as the saying goes, was yet to come! Indeed, in retrospect, what follows is unsurpassed in drama and natural beauty, not only on the South-West Way but, I would assert, anywhere on the British coast.

We passed the castellated 'Armed Knight' and the arched 'Enys Dodman' rock islands and followed the cliffs past cove and headland. Around Pordenack Point, rock structures are infinitely varied—an ordered chaos of boulder perched upon boulder, pinnacled ridges, stepped slabs and soaring towers of granite. Monolithic rocks mottled with lichen stand by the path preceding Mill Bay (or Nanzijal). It was good to be at sea level legitimately, on a proper beach where we could cool hot feet in pools left by the tide. We chatted to an American couple 'doing' Penzance to Land's End and returning by bus, before deciding it was high time to put a few miles behind us after a morning's leisurely stroll.

The way undulates above Pendower, Folly and Porth Loe coves to the Coastguard Station on the great buttressed mass of Gwennap Head, or *Tol-Pedn-Penwith*—'The Holed Headland of Penwith'—so named from the collapsed sea cave at its apex. Its sea cliffs have several fine rock climbs. Red and black-and-white daymarks warn shipping of the Runnel Stone reef a mile offshore, also marked by a whistling buoy. On October 8th 1923, the 6173-ton *City of Westminster* struck the rock and broke off its top 20ft (6m) or so, rendering it a significantly lesser hazard than hitherto!

We ducked through the tiny fishing hamlet of Porthgwarra with its curious rock tunnel and turned up by Cove Cottage to regain the clifftops round Carne Scathe. Sometimes the little path wound through secluded beds of humid vegetation, at others it loped across granite hillside fringed with gorse and hawthorn above a Mediterranean-azure sea. We came across adders and many more people out walking the cliffs than was normal for Easter, both attracted by the glorious sunshine.

St Levan's Norman church stands about 400m inland from the white sands of Porthchapel, but is worth visiting for some unusual features and details. Otherwise, be content as we were with St Levan's Holy Well in a little pathside enclosure. This is a deep valley to walk through and the climb out reminded us of gradients on the first leg of the trip.

You can either make a loop round the National Trust's Pedn-mên-an-mere headland or simply cut across the back to arrive above Porthcurno's famous Minack open-air theatre. A play was in progress and we had mistaken the actors' voices for a transistor radio being played close by. Founded in 1935 by Rowena Cade, the almost Grecian auditorium was refined from a natural amphitheatre high in the cliffs. During the main holiday periods, productions are put on, weather permitting, and at other times you can view the theatre for a small charge.

The coast path drops very abruptly on rock steps; vertically below us, boats seemed suspended in air, so clear was the water. We ate a picnic lunch on Porthcurno's beach of tiny shells then climbed past a pyramidal daymark which both aids navigation for shipping and commemorates the laying of the first transatlantic cable, via Brest to Nova Scotia in 1880. A decade before that, the first link with India incorporating submarine cables was routed ashore here.

We soon found ourselves walking between hedges—a long-forgotten experience—with views extending ahead to the Lizard at the far end of Mount's Bay. Once past a track to Treen village, many walkers will take a short path out to the Logan Rock. Logan is Cornish for 'moving' or 'rocking', but the stone in question, perched atop a jumble of granite boulders, is, alas, immovable. In April 1824, it was dislodged as a prank by young seamen from HMS *Nimble* under Lt. Goldsmith RN, nephew of the poet Oliver. So strongly did the local populace object to this act of vandalism that the Admiralty was obliged to order the repositioning of the 80-ton rock, using teams of men and lifting gear, but its rocking movement was never regained.

We strode on over Cribba Head, descended to unspoilt Penberth Cove and continued along the undulating path above small fields once used to cultivate daffodils. Porthguarnon, a substantial combe with waterfall and bouldery beach, presages a wilder passage of coastline compared to much-walked Land's End and the sheltered intimacy of coves and hamlets where the cliffs turn east.

St Loy, a couple of houses submerged in idyllic woodland (the first since St Ives), pushes the path out onto a beach of large, rounded boulders. This isolated settlement is reputed to enjoy one of Britain's warmest micro-climates. We hopped over baulks of timber washed up by storms and attacked the rough, boggy climb to Bosacawen Point. Tater-du lighthouse stands low down on the next headland. Built in 1965 following the loss of 11 crew from the Spanish vessel *Juan Ferrer*, the automatic light has ended a long series of wrecks on this unforgiving section of coast. That day, the sea was at its most benign, its glittering surface criss-crossed by the wakes of pleasure cruisers and fishing boats.

From Carn Barges to Lamorna Cove, eyes were treated to a visual feast of early springtime blooms. Wild garlic, daffodils, drifts of white narcissi and bushes of starry hawthorn blossom overflowed from neglected little enclosures where flowers were once profitably cultivated. Underfoot was a different story—a procession of stony steps, twists and turns until the path suddenly swung north and we had arrived at Lamorna Cove.

Frequented these days by sub-aqua divers and holidaymakers, Lamorna once exported high quality granite; quarry waste can still be seen spilling down the cove's enclosing hillsides. Lamorna village, just up inland, is associated with artists, who mount summer exhibitions, and with sites of archaeological interest in the vicinity, notably the Bronze Age Merry Maidens stone circle about a mile north-west. After a meal in the quayside café, we pitched on a site near the B3315 coast road in preparation for a return home from Penzance next morning.

Time for reflection: eclipsing all had been the constantly moving, radiant, mysterious infinity of ocean, an all-encompassing presence which, after weeks without storm, had settled into crystal clarity. Bordering the path, gorse, wild flowers, blossoms and the luminous green of new growth had provided a frieze of brilliant colour, possibly as unseasonally early as the warm weather itself had been. Conditions may not have been representative of Britain's south-west peninsula, but they raised an already exquisite walk into the realms of the unforgettable.

On the path above Penberth Cove.

Facing page: ***The Lizard lighthouse above Polpeor Cove (photo Gill Thallon).***

WALK 13: *West Cornwall — Porthleven to The Lizard*

Map: OS Landranger Sheet 203—Land's End, The Lizard and Isles of Scilly. **Start:** Porthleven harbour. **Finish:** The Lizard (Polpeor Cove). **Distance:** 13 miles (21km)—allow 6 to 7 hours. **Access:** Porthleven is on the B3304 from Helston or off the A394 from Penzance. Lizard village lies at the end of the A3083. Nearest railway station—Penzance. **Type of Walking:** Mostly clifftop paths, exposed to wind and weather; numerous ups and downs but on generally moderate gradients. The path can be boggy in places. **Features of Interest:** Loe Pool and Loe Bar; St Winwalloe church; the Marconi Monument; Mullion Cove; Lizard Nature Reserve; Kynance Cove; Lizard Point; outstanding rugged cliffs and marvellous coastal views. **Accommodation:** Widely available throughout the area. Nearest youth hostels—Penzance and Coverack.

A Walk round Mount's Bay in Southernmost Britain

Porthleven lies 3 miles (5km) south-west from the market town of Helston, midway round the great arc of Mount's Bay. Its granite mole and quays appear imposing enough, yet surprisingly the port was never a financial success. In 1855, 44 years after work on it had begun, Harvey and Co., a mining concern, took over the port installations and added an inner breakwater with flood gates and sluices.

Even for experienced mariners, however, the lee shore of Mount's Bay, caught as it were in the jaws of Land's End and the Lizard, is a hazardous place. Nineteenth-century sailing ships, outbound with copper, china-clay and soapstone, or arriving with mining machinery, would often face dangerous conditions at the harbour entrance and in the seaway beyond.

Although fishing continued to thrive as it had done for over 500 years, general cargo dwindled when Cornwall was connected to the country's railway network. Today the town relies on a combination of fishing, fish-canning, boat building and tourism, focused on the busy harbour and streets leading off.

This walk (part of the long-distance South-West Way) begins on Cliff Road, seaward of the Bickford-Smith Institute clock tower, and leads you past a Coastguard lookout above Porthleven Sands. The erstwhile coast road, undermined by storm damage, is only reliably passable to walkers before it continues south-

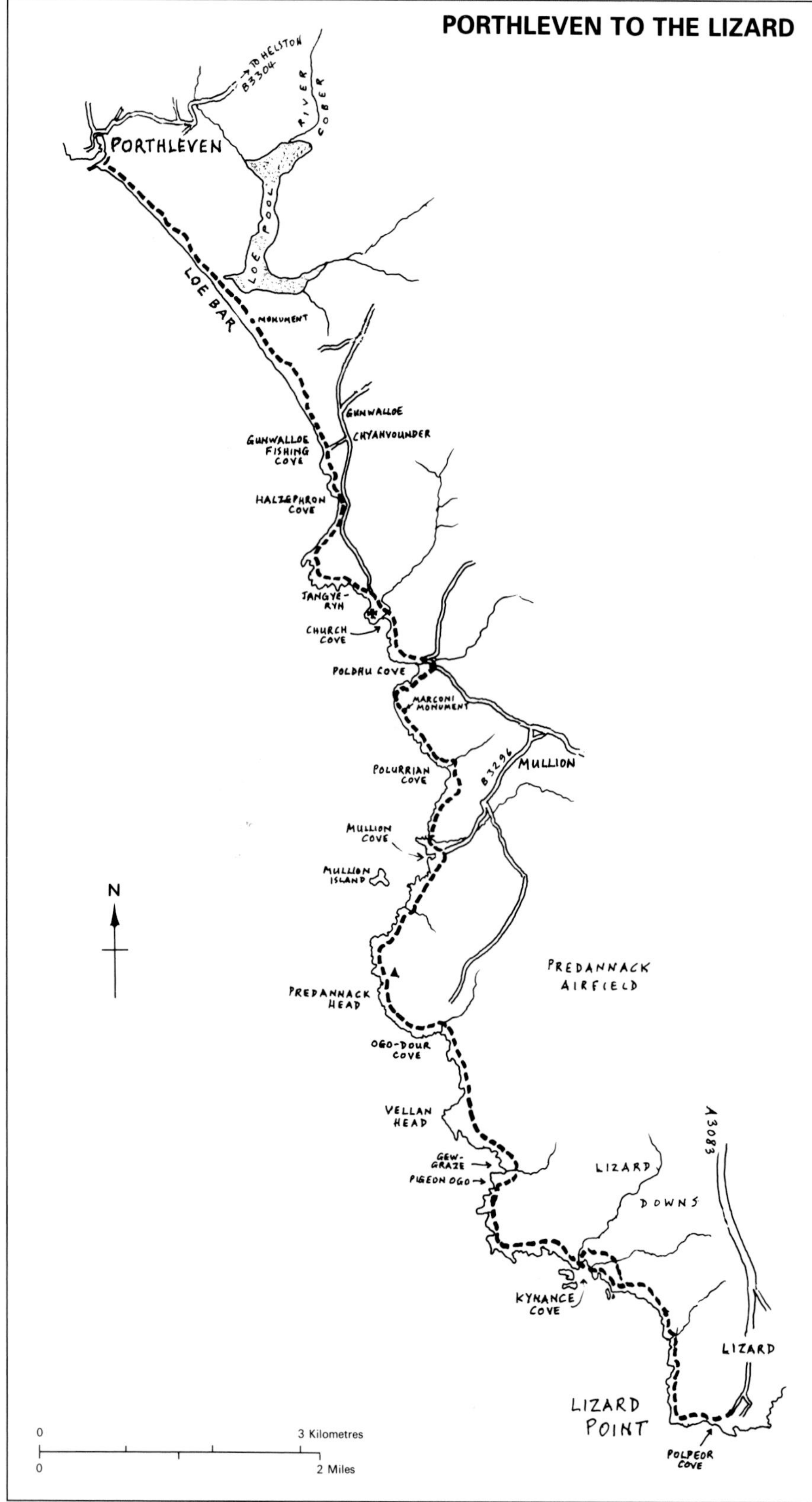

east past the ancient Wheal Penrose lead mine which closed in 1844.

Ahead lies Loe Pool, Cornwall's largest lake and a centrepiece to the National Trust's 1600-acre Penrose Estate. Designated as a Site of Special Scientific Interest, Loe Pool is celebrated for its water fowl, trout and water lilies. Its luxuriantly wooded shores are open during daylight hours and can be walked round (if you have the time) in about 2 hours. Should you find yourself here on a quiet evening, claims will seem well founded that this mile-long arm of brackish water is associated with the legendary Excalibur from Tennyson's *The Passing of Arthur.*

A trudge ensues along the finely graded flint shingle of Loe Bar, a natural feature which finally blocked the River Cober's mouth during the thirteenth century and formed Loe Pool. Following heavy rainfall, Helston's mills just upstream suffered repeated flooding, to alleviate which local men would dig a channel through Loe Bar. Only recently has a permanent flow-controlling culvert been installed beneath the shingle.

A pathside memorial cross east of the Bar remembers Henry Trengrouse, son of a Helston cabinet maker, who developed the rocket-fired lifeline after witnessing the tragic loss of HMS *Anson* in December 1807. The frigate was wrecked only yards from shore but 120 lives were lost, watched by a crowd of helpless onlookers.

Waymarking is part of the local authority's work in maintaining a safe coastal path, but incessant erosion, here as in countless other locations, leads to periodic re-routing. Climbing diagonally away from the unstable edge, you enter a lane between fields and turn right at a disused quarry before regaining the cliff path and descending to Gunwalloe Fishing Cove.

From behind a bungalow there, a stiff pull up ensues to 200ft (60m) above Halzephron Cove and round a field edge near Winnianton Farm, detouring onto Jangye-ryn cliffs above Dollar Cove, scene of two early shipwrecks. The second, in 1785, involved an unnamed Spanish vessel laden with $2\frac{1}{2}$ tons of gold and silver coin which spilled into an inaccessible gully. Spurred by the prospect of instant wealth, many salvage operations were mounted, employing pumping, sieving and tunnelling techniques. Even so, just a mere fraction of the treasure was recovered, due, it is thought, to massive sand movements on the sea bed.

In the days of sail, ships entering Mount's Bay in south-westerly gales were frequently doomed to founder on the inhospitable coast. Floating wreckage and corpses strewn amongst the rocks would receive the attention of local bounty hunters if the Coastguards were not first on the scene. Lest they were heathen, bodies were interred unceremoniously in mass graves near the wreck, until, under an Act of 1808 initiated by a Reverend Gryll, proper burial in consecrated ground was allowed for.

A wall leads down to St Winwalloe church, huddled behind a rock mass on the edge of Church Cove. Founded in the sixth century, by Brittany monks, the present church building dates mainly from the fifteenth century, though its unusual, detached bell tower is probably earlier. It is a perilous location for any structure, prone to drifting sand and eventual inundation by the sea as its protective cliff disintegrates.

Following the broad track uphill past Mullion Golf Course, you drop down the country road to Poldhu Cove. Deeper than most bites in the south Cornish coastline, it offers seductive surf and golden sand at low tide and is justifiably popular in summer.

Beyond a road bridge over the stream, you turn right up a private drive towards a residential home, once an hotel, but cut down steps on the right before reaching the building. A short walk round Poldhu Point brings you to the Marconi Monument on Angrouse Cliff. Erected in 1937 on the site of a former wireless telegraphy station, the granite pillar commemorates Guglielmo Marconi's momentous invention of the 'wireless', from which all modern telecommunications derive. From this spot, the first transatlantic signal—a repeated Morse 'S'—was transmitted on December 12th 1901 to the young Italian engineer almost 3000 miles away in St John's, Newfoundland. Interestingly, the first transatlantic television pictures were received at nearby Goonhilly Earth Station in July 1962.

Accompanied by spectacular coastal views, the path dips through Polurrian Cove and climbs a stony track, veering right in front of clifftop houses to reach the road by Mullion Cove Hotel. Here a path goes seaward down steps which give a definitive glimpse of Mullion Cove, quickly reached.

Porth Mellin—to give it its real name—is a tiny, cliff-bound inlet; until the greenstone breakwater was built in 1895, fishing boats ran the gauntlet of wind and swell to reach safety. Today, like Blackpool Tower or the white cliffs of Dover, Mullion Cove has become a kind of British institution, the quintessential Cornish fishing harbour stamped onto our collective memory by countless publicity photographs. It is a dubious honour, however—one shared with Polperro farther east and Clovelly in North Devon—and results in overcrowding during the high summer. In dismal weather out of season, it loses much of its appeal.

Mullion village lies a mile inland but is well worth earmarking for a visit, particularly to see its fifteenth-century church containing carved pew-ends, some very old glass in the east window and an ancient oak south door thought to be Norman.

A short way inland, the onward path leaves from behind houses to attack Mullion Cliff. It is a good idea to pause on the climb and admire the cove, with Mullion Island just offshore—darkly beautiful, guano-streaked, of volcanic origin and a sanctuary for seabirds. As you enter the Lizard National Nature Reserve, surroundings typify Lizard peninsula country: magnificent cliff scenery fringing a level plateau at around 300ft (91m) above the sea. Serpentine becomes the dominant rock type, an uncommon one and named after its resemblance to snakeskin. Local workshops fashion ornaments and knick-knacks from the green or reddish mottled stone, sold widely as souvenirs.

Porthleven harbour.

Descending to Kynance Cove on a stormy winter's day, Lizard Point in the distance.

The Lizard is also of special botanical interest, with many rare grasses, plants and flowers in evidence on the thin heathland soil.

Crossing a stream valley by a white house, you continue outside a field fence round Predannack Head with Mount's Bay unfolding behind you in a sweeping panorama. Underfoot it is flat and delightfully grassy, though the peace is occasionally shattered by helicopters from nearby RNAS Culdrose, one of Europe's largest naval air stations.

From a rocky viewpoint, the way angles down over the next stream above Ogo-dour Cove and resumes straightforward clifftop progress. Almost imperceptibly, the landscape has grown less hospitable and in miserable weather can evoke a bleak Pennine moor! Soon you cut across Vellan Head and descend abrupt, rugged slopes through Gew-graze, also known as Soapy Cove. Here is the best known of several local quarries whose soapstone—or 'steatite'—was worked from about 1750 to 1800 and used in the manufacture of Wedgewood and Worcester porcelain.

Though the path becomes indistinct, keep to seaward on the climb out for glimpes of beetling precipices and Pigeon Ogo ('ogo' means cave). Unless bullied by a southwesterly, walking will call for little effort as you pass small rocky outcrops on a meandering trod. Before long you drop to the right, following marker posts down to the stream footbridge at Kynance Cove.

A renowned beauty spot since the mid-1800s when it was a fashionable destination for 'excursionists', artists and writers, Kynance Cove holds a number of dramatic, serpentine islets which rear menacingly from low-tide sands. Their names—such as Devil's Bellows, The Ladies Bathing Pool and The Drawing Room—refer to a fascinating variety of rock profiles, while to the west of the cove are exciting, interconnected caves and sensational blowholes.

If the tide is low enough, you cross the stony beach and climb back to clifftop level; should waves or high water prevent this, a path between the beach café and a cottage climbs the valley side to a broad track. Off to the right, a stepped and popular path will be seen rising towards the National Trust car park and refreshment hut.

Keeping outside the car park wall, you engage the final lap of this southbound walk, the Lizard lighthouse now appreciably closer. The path is easy to follow, undulating along above the Holestrow landslip, crossing a pair of streams and reaching a jutting prow of rock at Lizard point. Britain's most southerly mainland spot is marginally further ahead at Polpeor Cove, but here you gain a vivid sense of arrival, of turning east, of rounding an ocean-bound extremity of land.

Beyond the disused Coastguard lookout and another stream valley stand the Lizard's seasonal cafés (try their delicious fresh crab sandwiches!), serpentine shops and the large lighthouse complex. Its resistant rock mass protruding far into shipping lanes, the Lizard has caused more shipwrecks than anywhere else on the south coast. A continuous warning light has burned here since 1640, fired by wood and coal before the advent of oil lamps in 1812 and electric arc lights in 1878. Today's 4 million candle power beam plays a vital role in shipping safety.

Polpeor Cove has a long history as a lifeboat station. Its first craft was housed on the clifftop lane and would often be launched at Mullion or Cadgwith when conditions dictated. By 1892 a new house was provided to seaward, replaced again in 1913 with the arrival of a motor powered vessel, by which time Cadgwith too had its own lifeboat. Both were closed down in 1961 and a new, larger boat now operates from Kilkobben Cove just round the headland.

The walk ends here, but a busy mile of lane leads to the fleshpots of Lizard village; it is more agreeably reached by continuing on the coast path for about 800 metres to Housel Bay and turning left.

Facing page: ***St. Anthony-in-Roseland, near the start of the walk.***

WALK 14: *South Cornwall — Place to Mevagissey*

Map: OS Landranger Sheet 204—Truro, Falmouth and area. **Start:** Place Manor. **Finish:** Mevagissey harbour. **Distance:** 23 miles (37km)—2 days suggested. **Access:** Place is reached by car from Falmouth or Truro via the King Harry Ferry, then the B3289, A3078 and country lanes south. Parking at Porth Farm and Zone Point. Mevagissey is at the end of the B3273 south of St Austell. Nearest railway stations—Falmouth and St Austell. (NB. There is no direct passenger ferry from Falmouth to Place, but private arrangements can sometimes be made at Prince of Wales Pier. The same situation applies at St Mawes, which is connected to Falmouth by a regular passenger ferry.) **Type of Walking:** Undulating clifftops on good paths, with bigger climbs to headlands and more frequent gradients in the middle section of the walk. A few short stretches on minor roads. **Features of Interest:** St Anthony-in-Roseland church; superb views over Carrick Roads to Falmouth and St Mawes; Zone Point lighthouse and old wartime bunker; the small harbour resorts of Portscatho, Portloe, Portholland, Gorran Head and Mevagissey; Caerhays Castle; numerous magnificent headland viewpoints and quiet beaches. **Accommodation:** Available at Place Manor Hotel, Porthscatho, Pendower Beach, Portloe, Gorran Haven, Portmellon and Mevagissey. Youth hostels at Falmouth and Boswinger.

Off the Beaten Track in Quieter Cornwall

It is a long drive on country roads to Place, whether from the Falmouth/Truro area or from St Austell. The A3078 loops round St Mawes, its southern terminus, but the countryside on either side is convoluted and withdrawn—not at all the Cornwall we associate with holidays, traffic jams and cream teas! Minor roads sparsely penetrate this folded, secret landscape which, to the east of Truro, is cut through by tributaries of the River Fal. With none of West Penwith's high drama or the north coast's elemental struggle against the Atlantic, this south-east facing span of lesser known Cornwall offers a succession of lofty headlands, broad sandy beaches and modest resorts. Walking is in a slightly lower key, the wild and exposed hinterland of the peninsula's north coast supplanted by farmland rolling uninterrupted across the inland horizon. Even so, the going is rough and demanding in places, with amenities few and far between out of the holiday season.

Day 1: Place to Portloe (13 miles/21km)

Having arrived at Place—a slipway on a secluded creek of the Percuil river—you can hardly miss the imposing Place Manor Hotel. Put up in 1840 for the Spry family on the site of a thirteenth-century monastic building, its vast lawns were once the pond for a tidal-power mill which served the local community for some 3 centuries before being filled in during the mid-1800s.

You have to walk up the lane from the slipway for about 300m to find a signpost for the start of this walk. Old tombstones lead to the parish church of St Anthony-in-Roseland which Sir Nikolaus Pevsner considers 'the best example in the county of what a parish church was like in the twelfth and thirteenth centuries . . . although much restored in 1850'. Passing its Norman doorway, you walk up left to a wide track which will return you to the shady Percuil river foreshore. From a little river beach, there are tranquil views out to yachts off St Mawes' east headland, but instead of continuing on the track to Amsterdam Point, you turn left up a field to emerge at a breathtaking panorama over Carrick Roads, taking in the great castles at St Mawes and Pendennis, Falmouth Docks and a wealth of shipping activity.

Walking towards Carricknath Point, you can either aim down between Scots pines and the sea (the true coast path) or take a higher line over the hilly field ahead. Both paths soon converge to cross a stream footbridge on the approach to St Anthony Head. Keep right here, past the one-time paraffin store and, if time and weather are favourable, it is well worth asking the keeper to show you round the lighthouse. Completed in 1835, it marks the entrance to Carrick Roads, one of Britain's premier natural anchorages; its 225,000 candlepower beam is filtered red when seen from the treacherous Manacles reef sector to the south-west. In mid-channel can be seen the beacon atop Black Rock, another navigational hazard.

Steps lead back to the clifftop and a right turn from the car park there past cottages brings you to the old St Anthony Battery. Along with those at Pendennis and St Mawes, this defended Falmouth for 60 years and as recently as 1956—just 3 years before it was acquired by the National Trust—the battery was still fully operational. A topograph helps identify views, then you are rounding Zone Point, swinging north-east on open, gorsey cliffs, immediately sampling the delights of this gloriously unspoiled and pastoral coastline.

Remote from the hustle and bustle of Cornwall's main resort areas, you are skirting the boundary of large grain fields high above Porthbeor Beach, on past dramatic Elwinick Cove and over Porthmellin Head. The distinctive bulk of Nare Head—our next major landmark—has already grown nearer as a shallow bay curves inward from Kiligerran Head past a rocket post to Towan Beach. There is a National Trust car park 5 minutes inland at Porth Farm, but with a complete absence of amenities, the coarse sand-and-shingle beach backed by dunes and low cliffs rarely receives more than a thin scattering of visitors. A marvellous 5 mile (8km) circuit of the Roseland peninsula can be made by following the creekside path from Porth Farm along to Place then picking up this itinerary, returning to Porth Farm from Towan Beach.

Some care is needed on dangerously overhanging cliff edges, but as soon as Greeb Point is reached, the way leads straight to a tarmac path and the buildings of Portscatho. Originally a fishing village, with typically narrow streets running down to the harbour, Portscatho has become a quiet holiday retreat. It is not without life, however, the seventeenth-century Plume of Feathers pub and a café/restaurant admirably attending to the inner man, a handful of guesthouses offering accommodation, a beach full of boats and windsurfers, all overseen by the pointed spire of Gerrans church.

The onward coast path is picked up from a street heading north and you soon drop to the private Porthcurnick Beach. Pednvadan headland with its Coastguard lookout and fine views back over Portscatho gives way to modest cliffs backed by less modest hotels and a brief descent to Porthbean Beach. Low trees and bushes precede the next drop to a stream and Creek Stephen Point. For those interested in archaeology and with time to spare, the site of Dingerein Castle, reputedly once belonging to Geraint, the eighth-century Cornish king and saint, stands near the main road half a mile up inland.

Two kilometres farther along the coast, you are brought up behind the Pendower Hotel (to avoid walking through its grounds!) and onto a lane down to popular Pendower Beach. The hotel here offers coffees, light lunches, cream teas and a beer garden. If refreshments are needed, I would advise taking them, for soon the going becomes noticeably more strenuous and fast progress is less easy to maintain on the tortuous path.

Pendower Beach was spared commercial exploitation by the fund-raising efforts of the local community, enabling them to present it to the National Trust in 1961. Thanks to that organisation, a good deal of the coastline traversed by this walk has retained its original character and only limited concessions have been made in providing motor access and public facilities. Long may it be so! From a little country road at the far end of the beach, you cross a stile and walk above the safe bathing sands of Carne Beach, passing tennis courts at Nare Hotel and turning right onto a lane.

Within 50m you have entered rough pasture, meandering easily at first, then feeling the pull of gravity as you cross the stream valley above Pradda Cove and climb steeply to a waymark post (especially useful in poor visibility). Aiming now for the crest of Nare Head (350ft/100m above the sea and a prehistoric promontory fort), it is worth pausing, perhaps at the impeccably placed bench beneath a rock outcrop, to gaze back along Gerrans Bay and far beyond to the Helford river mouth and even Black Head on the Lizard peninsula. Inspiring stuff, and typical of coastal walking where headlands like this are equivalent to cols or saddles in mountain country, each one providing wide retrospective views and surprising vistas of fresh territory ahead.

It is important to veer left of the gorse, despite no obvious path, and you will soon pick up a farm track leading to a National Trust car park. I once thrashed around through chest-high gorse in a vain attempt to find a path on the cliff edge: there were good views of Gull Rock and its sea bird colonies, but enjoyment was nullified by frustration and copious scratches! From the car park, you head for a stile in the far clifftop corner from where Veryan Bay is dramatically revealed, ending in the Dodman, notorious wrecker of ships. Inland, heaps of china-clay waste—the so-called 'Cornish Alps'—rise surrealistically from workings near St Austell: this industrial enclave signifies the dislocation of unspoiled coast, though things improve swiftly beyond Par.

An elegant scoop of valley behind Kiberick Cove should not, notices request, be cut across by walkers. Field edges lead on past Parc Caragloose where a new section of path bypasses the old flight of 70-odd steep steps to sea level and back. The rocky cliff line is closely hugged round Manare and Jacka points and quite suddenly you have arrived at Portloe.

Day 2: Portloe to Mevagissey (11 miles/18km)

Past the seventeenth-century Lugger Hotel, steps lead up to a Coastguard lookout and for a while the path is close to the edge of sheer drops. In half a mile you have passed Caragloose Point, with Shag Rock offshore, and will be attacking a sharp little climb past

Portloe.

an isolated house onto easier ground with fine views ahead to Dodman Point. Downhill to the track from Tregenna, you pass a steep path to Portlay Beach, cross a stream and climb again inland to cut Perbargus Point and reach the country road at West Portholland by the old Methodist chapel. The road is prone to subsidence, but in 300m you are over to East Portholland, a quiet, sandy cove with a post office/stores selling ice cream and Cornish pasties during the season.

A tarmac pathway zig-zags up to the clifftops but fizzles out at a field whose seaward perimeter you skirt to emerge on a shady lane leading down to Porthluney Cove. Behind walls and amidst impressive gardens and trees stands the romantic, almost medieval-looking Caerhays Castle. It was actually constructed in 1808 on the site of an old manor house by none other than the great Regency architect John Nash, better known for his design of London's Marble Arch and the Brighton Pavilion.

From this popular little beach with its grassy car park and excellent café, the coast path veers right up round field edges and it is from here that the best views of Caerhays Castle are obtained. Once the climbing is done, the way takes you along bushy hilltop. Lambsowden Cove near Greeb Point is virtually inaccessible and signals the start of an unexpectedly remote stretch, winding rockily and sinuously through low scrub. Eventually, Hemmick Beach appears, right on the eastern rim of Veryan Bay, and is descended to over grassy fields. Tall Reed grass grows here, as does the rare dittander plant, a relative of pepperworts and once cultivated as a condiment. Twenty-five metres up the road ahead, you turn right onto the Dodman and after an initially stiff climb, the path eases off pleasantly through bracken and gorse. A second climb brings you to the massive ditch and bank of an Iron Age fortification and a level walk to Dodman Point. On the way up you may have spotted ling, bell heather, golden rod and yellow toadflax, while birds commonly seen include fulmars, shags, herring gulls, kestrels and jackdaws.

National Trust ownership of this major Cornish landmark began in 1919 and has extended to 276 acres. The name means 'dead man', a reference to the grim reputation this promontory holds as a wrecker of ships. Particularly vulnerable were vessels which missed Falmouth in pre-radar days, but as recently as July 1966, the pleasure boat *Darlwin* sank here with no survivors. The huge granite cross right on the point, 373ft (114m) above the sea, was erected in 1896 at the instigation of a local clergyman. Its primary function was to act as a sea-mark following the collision and grounding of the destroyers *Thrasher* and *Lynx* in thick fog earlier that year. There can be no doubting its symbolic significance, however, and it is said that the clergyman involved—the Rector of St Michael Caerhays—spent the night of the cross's dedication praying for shipwrecked souls.

In clear weather there is no finer viewpoint on the entire south coast and binoculars will extend the range of vision even further. As you swing north round the cliff edge, the conical profile of Rame Head at the entrance to Plymouth Sound can often be seen, with Bodmin Moor prominent inland. Nearer to hand, the red-and-white striped daymark on Gribbin Head marks the far extremity of St Austell Bay.

Field edges are followed round the long shingle strand of Bow (or Vault) Beach and a modest scramble over Pen-a-maen Point brings you down to Gorran Haven. Swelled by new building, the village seems uncomfortably squeezed into its valley and I can't recommend the sandy beach as particularly attractive, even though it gets crowded in summer. However,

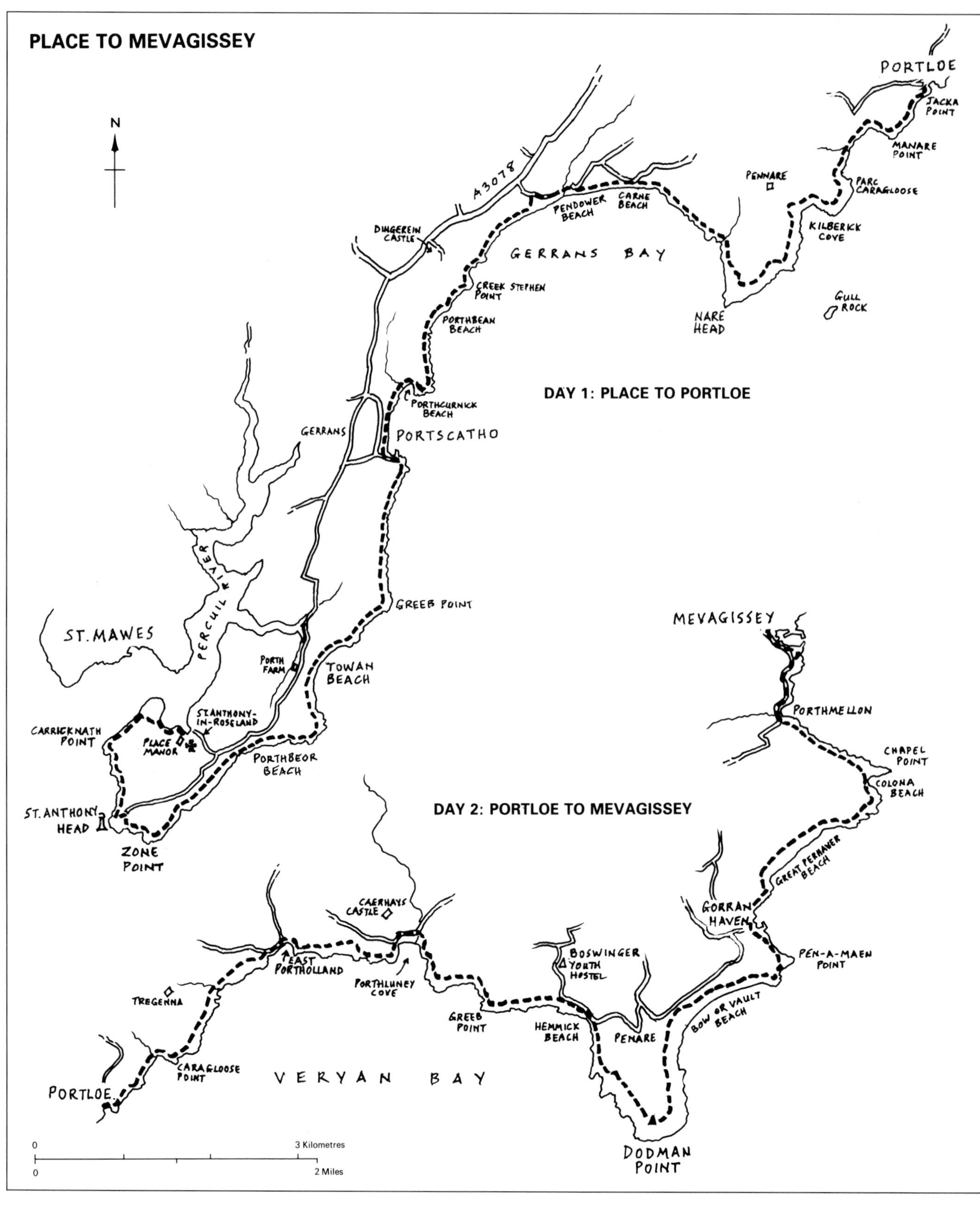
PLACE TO MEVAGISSEY
N
PORTLOE
JACKA POINT
MANARE POINT
PENNARE
PARC CARAGLOOSE
KILBERICK COVE
A3078
PENDOWER BEACH
CARNE BEACH
DINGEREIN CASTLE
GERRANS BAY
CREEK STEPHEN POINT
PORTHBEAN BEACH
NARE HEAD
GULL ROCK
DAY 1: PLACE TO PORTLOE
PORTHCURNICK BEACH
GERRANS
PORTSCATHO
PERCUIL RIVER
GREEB POINT
ST. MAWES
MEVAGISSEY
PORTH FARM
TOWAN BEACH
ST. ANTHONY-IN-ROSELAND
CARRICKNATH POINT
PLACE MANOR
PORTHBEOR BEACH
PORTHMELLON
CHAPEL POINT
COLONA BEACH
DAY 2: PORTLOE TO MEVAGISSEY
ST. ANTHONY HEAD
ZONE POINT
GREAT PERHAVER BEACH
CAERHAYS CASTLE
GORRAN HAVEN
EAST PORTHOLLAND
BOSWINGER YOUTH HOSTEL
PEN-A-MAEN POINT
PORTHLUNEY COVE
TREGENNA
GREEB POINT
HEMMICK BEACH
PENARE
BOW OR VAULT BEACH
CARAGLOOSE POINT
VERYAN BAY
PORTLOE
0
3 Kilometres
0
2 Miles
DODMAN POINT

amenities there certainly are, and old narrow streets take you up from the harbour past the tiny St Just chapel and along Cliff Road to where a stile provides access to the cliff path above Great Perhaver Beach. A mile offshore lie the Gwineas Rocks, responsible for many shipwrecks but now equipped with a bell buoy.

After a mile or so, you descend to Turbot Point and cross a stream issuing onto Colona Beach; houses on nearby Chapel Point, put up speculatively in the 1930s, have a surprisingly continental appearance. By following a field round west, you will reach a private road down to Portmellon. Before being overwhelmed by building development and becoming virtually a suburb of Mevagissey, this cluster of houses, seasonal pub and a boat repair yard was a delightful little settlement. However, owing to the funnelling effect of its narrow, rock-clasped bay, waves are pushed up higher than normal by an incoming tide. The result, as road signs warn, is frequent flooding and I well recall a summer holiday spent in one of the seafront houses when only stout window shutters and 3ft-thick walls prevented high seas from crashing into our rooms!

Unfortunately, the final kilometre of this walk is confined to the coast road, but you can walk through a small park with comprehensive views over Mevagissey's complex double harbour before descending to the town itself. Established in the Middle Ages and a favourite haunt of smugglers, Mevagissey's heyday was probably around the end of the nineteenth century when its inner and outer breakwaters sheltered a large fleet of fishing boats whose main catch was pilchards. When the shoals declined, owing, it is thought, to climatic changes, fishing throughout the south-west suffered drastic recession, but in places such as Mevagissey the down-turn was far from terminal and many working boats still use the harbour alongside a plethora of pleasure craft.

The harbour, Mevagissey.

WALK 15: *South Cornwall — Fowey to Looe*

Maps: OS Landranger Sheets 200 (Newquay, Bodmin and area) and 201 (Plymouth and Launceston area). **Start:** Fowey or Polruan (connected by passenger ferry across the River Fowey). **Finish:** Looe harbour. **Distance:** 11 miles (18km)—allow about 5 hours. **Access:** Fowey lies at the end of the A3082 east of St Austell. Looe lies on the A387 due south of Liskeard. Nearest railway stations—Par and Looe. **Type of Walking:** Rugged and remote clifftops with frequent gradients at first, becoming much easier beyond Polperro. A clear path throughout but narrow in places. **Features of Interest:** The historic river mouth ports of Fowey and smaller Polruan; glorious, unspoiled cliff scenery with several major viewpoints; the showpiece fishing village of Polperro; the old twin towns of East and West Looe. **Accommodation:** Widely available at Fowey/Polruan, East and West Looe and to a lesser extent at Polperro. Youth hostel at Golant, north of Fowey.

Unfrequented Coast between Fishing Harbours

Holidaymakers flocking to Cornwall's 'riviera' resorts seldom appreciate what lies beyond the towns they frequent. Touring by car to places on the coast endowed with road access may sketch in part of the picture; however, only those who set out along coast paths prepared to face the elements and a modicum of exertion will discover the essential character of the cliffs and coves, headlands and beaches which separate human settlements and which, happily, remain inaccessible to motor vehicles.

Large sections of Cornwall's north coast are wild and uninhabited, but the south coast is more densely populated. It therefore comes as a surprise to find magnificent and unfrequented coastal walking between the holiday centres of Fowey, Polperro and Looe. The first half of this walk, in particular, is quite remote and devoid of habitation or refreshments points: off season you will have it to yourself.

Fowey's maritime history is long and illustrious. A thriving port since the Middle Ages, its naturally sheltered anchorage fostered generations of spirited sailors who gained a reputation as 'Fowey Gallants'. Such men took part in numerous medieval campaigns, including the Siege of Calais in 1346, turning their hand also to smuggling and piracy in the English Channel. In 1380, Fowey was attacked by a large Spanish fleet and, as a deterrent to future would-be raiders, stretched a heavy chain between two blockhouses at the harbour entrance; remains of the Polruan one still survive and even grooves worked in the rocks by the chain can be discerned.

During the nineteenth century, the export of mineral ores and china-clay vied with ship building as the port's main revenue earner and as recently as World War II Fowey's harbour maintained its strategic importance by acting as a base for rescue services and American forces on D-Day. Today, ocean-going ships of up to 15,000 tons mingle with pleasure craft on their way to and from English China Clays' dock just upstream. It is connected to the works at Par by a private road to avoid pollution of the town and exports some 1.6 million tonnes each year to all parts of the world.

Fowey is a popular centre for yachtsmen and holidaymakers. Several hours can be spent browsing rounds its narrow shopping streets, its museum and aquarium or enjoying boat trips. However, this walk begins from Polruan on the other side of the river. The passenger ferry runs every 10 or 15 minutes from early in the day till late and leaves from a jetty just south-west of the town centre, reached down an alleyway off the main street.

Polruan is almost a miniature Fowey, with a few pubs, shops and cafés of its own and a tradition of shipbuilding which lives to this day.

Facing page: ***In the Fowey River.***

Below: ***Walkers awaiting the ferry from Polruan to Fowey (photos C. W. Footer).***

During the holiday season cars are barred from entering the steep, narrow streets—a considerable blessing for the village could not possibly accommodate them. Fowey's vernacular architecture is seen to best effect from here as you walk along above Polruan's waterfront towards the cliffs.

The lane closes in to path width and breaks out into the open by a Coastguard lookout. Two miles (3km) away to the south-west, a red-and-white striped daymark crowns Gribbin Head, built in the days of sail by Trinity House to demarcate the eastern extremity of St Austell Bay. If you are lucky with the visibility, you might spot Dodman Point some 15 miles (24km) further afield in the same general direction.

The path soon levels off past the stump of an old tower and touches the top road by a school before veering sharp right towards Lantivet Bay. Passing two derelict Coastguard lookouts in quick succession might prompt you to reflect on the early days of the service when customs officers patrolled the cliffs in their constant battle against the importation of contraband. By the time this law-enforcing role had shifted to one of surveillance and rescue, paths we now use for recreation had already been etched into the turf by the passage of countless official boots. Monitoring the safety of shipping no longer relies exclusively upon visual sightings, although some important lookouts are manned, either permanently or during bad weather.

At a National Trust sign for Blackbottle Rock—a smuggling name if ever there was one—the coast ahead unfolds, perhaps to Rame Head near Plymouth. You are now winding round the back of Lantic Bay past gorse, bracken and blackberry bushes. The low-tide sands and exceptionally clear water promise the best prospect of enjoyable bathing on this strip of coast, though the way down is steep. From a stile at the far end, the path drops right and takes you out over Pencarrow Head almost 450ft (137m) above the sea and another fabulous viewpoint. In clear air it is reckoned you can span over 70 miles (113km) from the Lizard to Bolt Tail in Devon.

Entering Lantivet Bay, only Lansallos hamlet on its hillside ahead interrupts a sweep of wild coastline virtually unsullied by the hand of man. Stiles and vegetated undulations lead on past a path up West Combe; 15 minutes away stands Lansallo's fourteenth-century church, worth visiting if you have the time and inclination. Its features include a medieval bell reputed to have been broken by drunken villagers in the 1800s and a gravestone near the gate commemorating John Perry, a local mariner killed in 1779, and magnanimously inscribed thus:

I, by a shot, which rapid flew
Was instantly struck dead.
Lord pardon the offender who
My precious blood did shed.

You soon cross a small footbridge and climb past a white beacon which, together with a bell buoy, marks the position of the dangerous

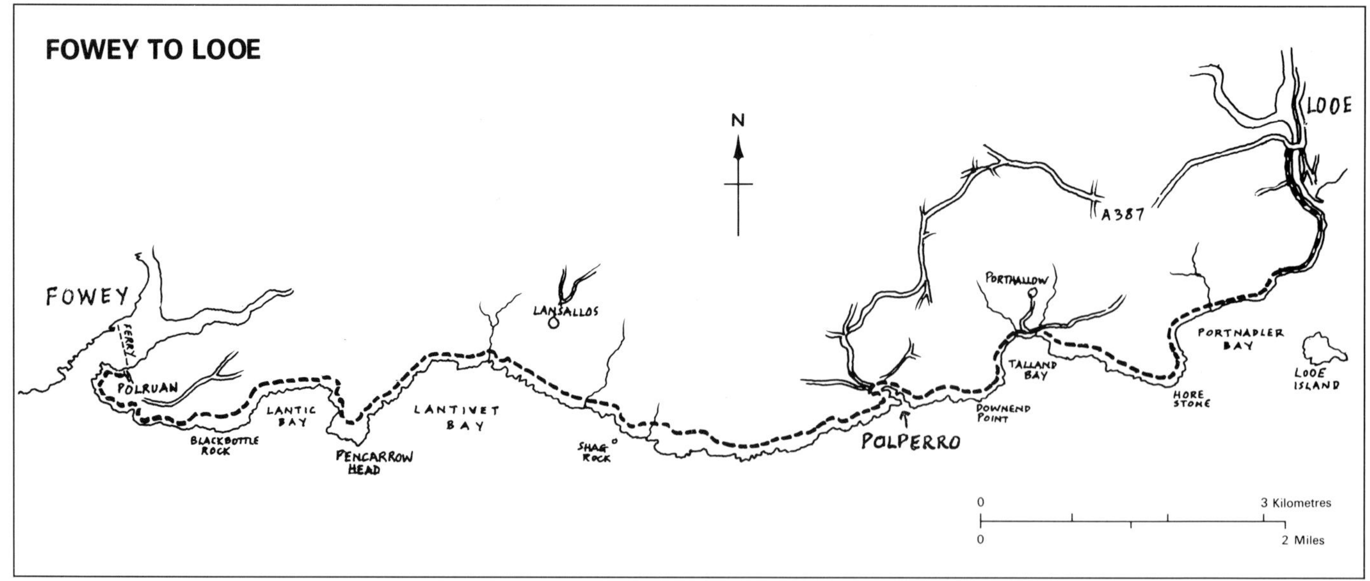

Udder Rock a mile offshore. To regain the 400ft (122m) contour calls for a burst of energy, then almost immediately the path dives steeply down and up over a stream valley. Unexpectedly you pass a superb rocky viewpoint followed by another sharp and slippery descent to a little headland above Shag Rock. When I was here last, the unstable edge had become perilously close to the path: you either scramble round behind or, as I did, hold your breath and say a little prayer!

Beyond the next combe, rocky ledges climb to a well-walked path, increasingly enclosed by greenery and furnished with a shelter and benches—signs of impending civilisation! Sure enough, at Chapel Cliff you swing left and enter one of Cornwall's celebrated tourist showpieces.

Polperro occupies scarcely more than a crevice in the cliffs and its daily influx of summer sightseers must park well away from the village and walk down. Though less spoiled than most, Polperro's picture-postcard charm is exploited to the full during the season, just like its North Devon counterpart, Clovelly. Arriving here on foot is greatly advantageous, leaving you free to stroll, take refreshment or move on—all in your own time. Our concept of the picturesque brings forth 'oohs' and 'aahs' at the prettiness of it all, but the narrow streets of colour-washed cottages tossed together with such artful nonchalance evolved not from any sense of aesthetic but from the need for accommodation near the harbour in a cramped and awkward valley site. The village's very existence was threatened by a great storm in 1824 which swept away several buildings, wrecked the breakwaters and sank some 50 boats. Whatever your thoughts may be, it is a pleasant place in which to linger before heading back to the cliffs.

Climbing past a row of benches at the seaward end of the harbour, you fork up left at a path junction by a National Trust sign for The Warren, thereafter contouring easily until you come to a World War I memorial cross on Downend Point, a marvellous spot. There is a gradual descent to a lane at Talland Bay with its seasonal café, beach shop and clifftop car parks.

With the more strenuous stage behind you, there could be no more agreeable a conclusion to this walk than the meandering line now followed on grassy hillsides round to Portnadler Bay. On the way you might notice a pair of black-and-white beacons on high ground inland which, in conjunction with another pair on the headland above Looe Island, are used by the Admiralty to measure an exact nautical mile during speed trials at sea. The delightful path continues round Hore Stone, a vertical slate stack best seen from offshore, and from the top of a flight of steps the first buildings of Looe are sighted.

Reached by launch from Looe harbour, Looe Island is privately owned and a haven for sea birds. It bears the remains of a medieval chapel and, under that, the foundations of a Celtic hermitage. A curious incident took place during World War II when enemy aircraft mistook the island for a British warship and proceeded to bomb it!

At the eastern end of Portnadler Bay, the going is flat and grassy and leads onto Marine Drive, a promenade lined with salubrious residences and hotels. When the road begins to drop, steps on the right will take you to the quayside in West Looe; a summer ferry or a walk upstream to the road bridge provides access to East Looe. Two wooded valleys merge here, forming a broader and deeper inlet than on adjacent stretches of coast. Until 1832 when they amalgamated, West and East Looe had been separate communities and important centres for trade and fishing. For 500 years each had returned its own member of Parliament and worshipped at its own churches. Although the excellent harbour dries out at low tide, it has always supported a fishing fleet and is the present base for the Shark-fishing Club of Great Britain, a sport with a considerable following.

Looe, like many Cornish resorts, can seem uncomfortably full during the main holiday season, but its double-sided configuration tends to dissipate any oppressive sense of overcrowding. In fact, with a wide range of amenities including a branch railway line and the attraction of boating and quayside activity within the harbour, Looe makes an entertaining stopover just short of a deterioration in the quality of coastal walking towards the great conurbation of Plymouth on the Devon/Cornwall border.

Facing page: ***Salcombe.***

WALK 16: *South Devon — Salcombe to Torcross*

Map: OS Landranger Sheet 202—Torbay and South Dartmoor area. **Start:** Salcombe or East Portlemouth (connected by ferry). **Finish:** Torcross. **Distance:** 11 miles (18km)—allow about 6 hours. **Access:** Salcombe lies at the end of the A381 south of Totnes. Torcross is on the A379 coast road between Kingsbridge and Torbay. Nearest railway station—Totnes. **Type of Walking:** Rocky, tortuous and undulating for most of the way, but easier walking to end with. Virtually no amenities. **Places of Interest:** Salcombe estuary and yachting centre; Prawle Point, most southerly in Devon; wave-cut platforms; birds, flowers and insects on remote, unspoiled cliffs; Start Point lighthouse; Hallsands ruined village; Slapton Ley Nature Reserve. **Accommodation:** Widely available at Salcombe, some at Torcross. Youth hostels at Salcombe and Strete.

Headlands and Shingle in Southernmost Devon

Situated on a tree-lined estuary providing one of the west country's best natural harbours, Salcombe has long been a premier centre for yachting. Nearly 2000 acres of tidal creeks upstream to Kingsbridge are available for exploration by small boats and this sheltered, southerly reach of Devon's shoreline enjoys a mild climate all year round.

More than anywhere else that springs to mind, Salcombe's olde-worlde streets and quaysides are the domain of navy-blue sweaters, caps and smocks worn by the well heeled who congregate here in large numbers to participate in regattas, fishing competitions and other events in the town's busy calendar. Dyed-in-the-wool walkers might feel a trifle out of place amidst such dedication to matters maritime, much as a yachtsman might in the Pen-y-Ghent café or a Scottish climbers' bothy. Yet

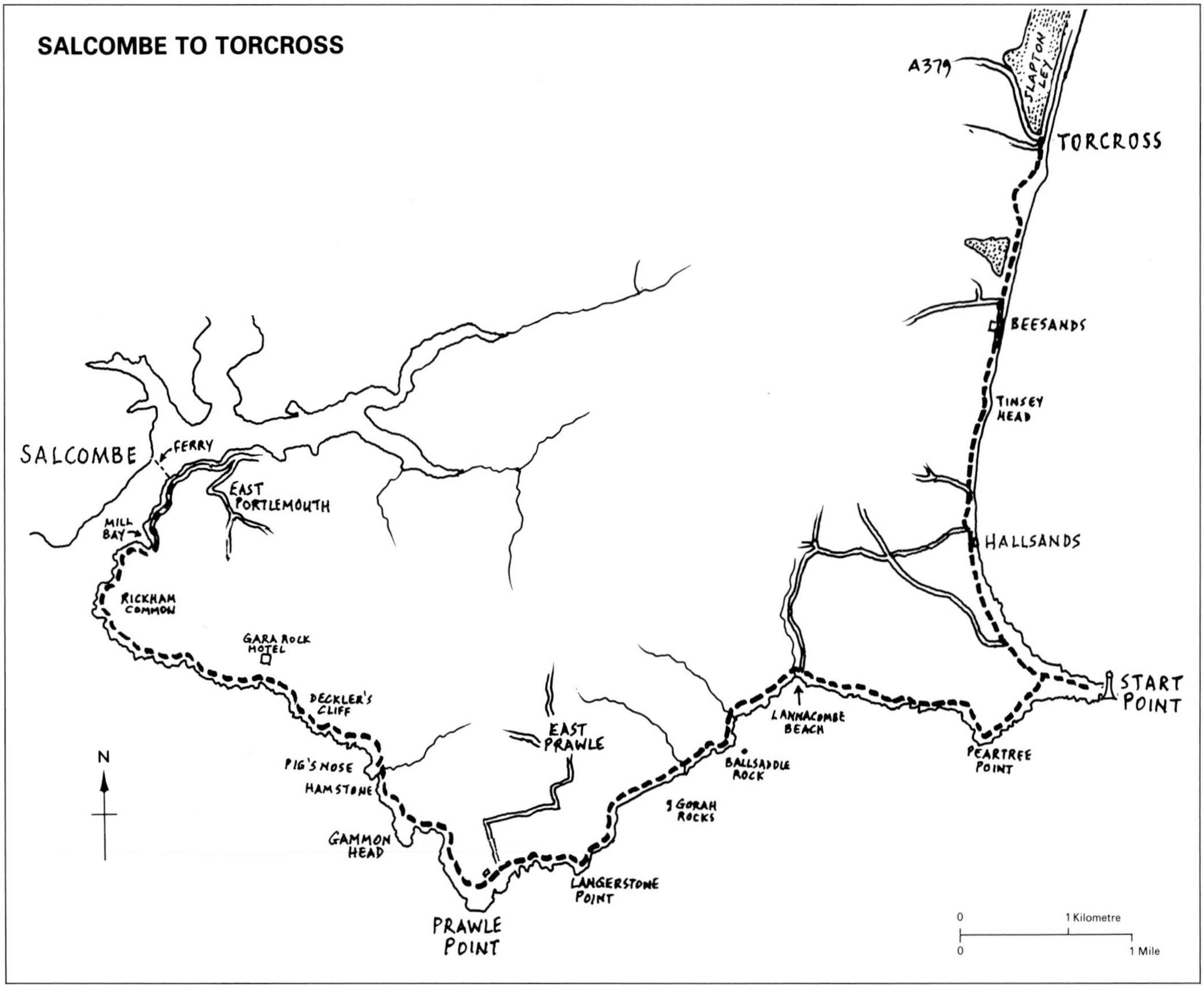

SALCOMBE TO TORCROSS

The ruined village of Hallsands in 1988.

several pleasant hours can be whiled away browsing through the intimate shopping streets or visiting the art gallery and museum.

Considering its proximity to Torbay and Plymouth, this walk is astonishingly unfrequented: there are no amenities whatever in the 10 miles (16km) to Hallsands unless a detour is made to the pub in East Prawle village. Indeed, for rugged terrain and a sense of real remoteness it has no equal anywhere on the South Devon coast. This should not deter you, for it is an exceptionally beautiful and varied stretch of shoreline to traverse and gloriously free of holiday crowds whatever the season. Provided you carry refreshments and are blessed with reasonable weather, a splendid day's hike is guaranteed!

A river crossing to East Portlemouth is easily achieved by taking the frequent ferry from steps at the side of the Midland Bank in Fore Street. Once across, the route climbs steps and turns right along a lane to sandy Mill Bay.

Where the onward path bifurcates, I recommend the lower, right-hand branch leading to open, low cliffs below Rickham Common. Between here and Sharp Tor across the estuary lies The Bar, a sandbank which has always suppressed Salcombe's potential as a port. In southerly gales it presents a serious hazard and caused Devon's worst lifeboat tragedy when, in 1916, 13 crewmen were drowned after their boat, the *William and Emma*, capsized.

A change of direction heralds increasingly rugged terrain, characterised by outcrops of hornblende and mica-schists and frequent ups and downs. Beyond the Gara Rock Hotel converted from Coastguard cottages up left, tortuous progress is made round Deckler's Cliff and behind Pig's Nose, Ham Stone and Gammon Head, a curiously porcine section! Fairly recently acquired by the National Trust, Gammon Head has featured prominently in views since the Salcombe estuary, its thrusting profile typifying the robust grandeur of this coast.

Rock-slab steps drop steeply past a path inland to East Prawle village, the only hope of sustenance for many a mile, though more quickly reached from further along the coastal path. Facing south, sunny banks and hollows support large populations of butterflies, other insects and wild plants. Keeping on the seaward path along rocky hillside and over a wall stile, the Coastguard station on Prawle Point is aimed for.

This is Devon's most southerly headland and a good spot for birdwatching, though of equal interest to the east is a marvellous view—almost a textbook illustration—of wave-cut platforms, or raised beaches. These were formed by wave action when sea levels were higher than today's; the old cliff line, up to 300ft (90m) high, lies a field-width back from the shore and the intervening cultivated land is weathered material called 'head' which has slumped down from higher ground behind.

Past a row of Coastguard cottages and a stile, the path skirts the seaward edge of the field shelf round Langerstone Point, with good retrospective views of Prawle Point's rock arch. The cliff edge is chronically unstable and minor falls could occur anywhere and at any time, so vigilance is advised. Minor deviations (including a path to nearby East Prawle) lead on past Horsley Cove, once used by Prawle fishermen, and Maelcombe House where the rocky path swings inland through gorse, over a stream valley above Ballsaddle Rock and widens to a grassy track to reach Lannacombe Beach. If you were expecting a return to civilisation you will be disappointed! There are no amenities and precious little parking space, so the little sandy cove is often deserted, free for the delectation of passing coastal walkers!

Once across the stream, crumbling cliffs are followed closely a little further along field boundaries before marshy ground gives way to sheep pasture above The Narrows. Swinging round a little cove, the path continues, springy underfoot, until hemmed in by crags at Peartree Point. Clambering round rocky slopes which demand sure footwork in a strong wind, even the use of hands in places, the spiney crest of Start Point is revealed ahead, its great jagged buttresses supporting a dramatic ridge of pinnacles. It is rock architecture of the most memorable kind, embodying the elemental forces generated where tide and swell meet the land's unyielding foundations. Gentle, bracken-clad slopes lead to the headland's ridge top—the nearest thing to an alpine mountain pass on the entire South West Way! A breathtaking new vista is spread out before you round the vast, shallow curve of Start Bay, culminating in the distant Dart Estuary and Scabbacombe Head.

Start Point lighthouse, a short detour to the right, was built in 1836. With a range of 20.8 miles (33km), its beam warns shipping off this particularly evil coastline which has claimed many lives. One incident alone—the great blizzard of 1891—caused four ships to founder; their crews stood little chance of survival in the freezing conditions and fifty-two men died. Back at the road car parking, our route turns off right and begins a long, ambling descent over vegetated hillside to Trouts Hotel and the remains of Hallsands village down a steep lane opposite.

The fate of this tiny coastal community, both fascinating and poignant, has been well documented in early photographs and records (see *Hallsands—a Pictorial History* by Kathy Tanner and Peter Walsh, available locally). A detailed account lies outside the scope of this book, but the following résumé might prompt interested readers to obtain the full story.

In the mid-nineteenth century, Hallsands comprised some 40 dwellings huddled on a rock ledge above a shingle beach upon which its fishing and crabbing boats were hauled. During the late 1800s, a decision was made to extend Devonport Dockyard, not far to the west, and to use dredged shingle from Start Bay instead of expensive crushed rock in the project's concrete. Sixteen hundred tons of shingle were removed daily off Hallsands but it was not replaced naturally by tidal currents as had been expected. Winter storm waves in 1900–1, their power no longer absorbed by the now drastically lowered shingle beach, destroyed the sea wall and several houses. Following a Board of Trade inspection, dredging was stopped in 1902 and new sea defences constructed. Thirteen years passed safely, but on 26th January 1917 huge seas from a severe easterly gale once again breached the hamlet's sea wall and this time all but one of its dwellings were washed away or irreparably damaged. Re-housing was carried out—a grudging admission of guilt by the authorities—and the ruined settlement continued to succumb to the elements, its gaunt gable-ends and broken foundations now a sobering and intensely moving sight.

A recent diversion behind the Hallsands Hotel and the installation of massive breakwater blocks below bear witness to the alarming rate of marine erosion here: guidebooks and even OS maps will certainly require amendment! At the far end of Greenstraight Beach, a short climb over Tinsey Head brings us to Beesands, a row of seafront houses which escaped Hallsands' fate but were unfortunately bombed in 1943. Its caravan site, a rather tatty and uncomfortably exposed example situated on scrubby grass and shingle, is walked through, then beyond Widdecombe Ley the coast path turns sharp left to circumvent an old slate quarry, climbing over to a waymarked descent past hotels onto the seafront at Torcross.

Once a small fishing village surrounded by rough cattle pasture and with no coast road, Torcross now plays host to a plethora of holiday visitors, many of whom will have come to see Slapton Ley nature reserve. Rich in aquatic flora and numerous insect species, this largest of Devon's freshwater lakes encourages birds to rest on migrations, to overwinter and to breed here. Habitats can be explored by joining one of the guided rambles offered by the Field Study Centre at Slapton village during the summer months.

The seafront promenade at Torcross was smashed by storm waves in 1951 and even the reinforced sea walls subsequently erected were broached in 1979, causing half a million pounds' worth of damage to properties inundated by water, rocks and shingle. Questions remain as to whether the Start Bay dredging operations at the turn of the century affected the coast here as well as farther south at Hallsands.

Springtime in the Undercliff.

WALK 17: *South Devon/Dorset — Seaton to Lyme Regis*

Map: OS Landranger Sheet 193—Taunton and Lyme Regis. **Start:** River Axe, Seaton. **Finish:** Lyme Regis seafront. **Distance:** 6 miles (9.5km)—allow 3 to 4 hours. **Access:** Seaton lies at the mouth of the River Axe just south of the A3052 from Lyme Regis. Nearest railway station—Axminster. **Type of Walking:** Unique on the British coast! A tortuous and hilly path through woodland, moderately strenuous and can be muddy in wet weather. Sheltered from wind and sun but no amenities or alternative paths en route. **Features of Interest:** The geology of a vast nineteenth-century landslip; colonisation by plants, animals and birds; unspoiled and luxuriant vegetation; the historic seaside town of Lyme Regis. **Accommodation:** Widely available at Seaton and Lyme Regis. Youth hostel at Beer, west of Seaton.

Through the Famous Dowlands Landslip

This walk will appeal strongly to students of botany and geology, but also offers those of us uninitiated in either the chance to experience a uniquely interesting coastal land form. Sea views are definitely not on the menu! Instead, you are treated to an intimate vision of land recolonised over a century and a half by a profusion of flora and fauna. This is the nearest thing to virgin forest in Britain and the whole undercliff area between Axmouth and Lyme Regis has been a designated National Nature Reserve since 1955-6.

Because the walk's main fascination lies within one homogeneous environment, rather than in the more usual progression from one coastal feature to the next, a little background information will help set the scene. It is an extraordinary story of natural events on a par with earthquake or avalanche and culminating in Britain's biggest recorded landslide, but we must turn the clock back 150 years for its beginning.

The present undercliff measures some 5 miles (8km) in length by about 800m in width and comprises five main slippage sites. The three more westerly ones occurred during the early 1800s and, as luck would have it, two of them—Dowlands and Whitlands—were witnessed by the then president of the Geological Society who happened to be staying at Lyme Regis over Christmas 1839 when the subsidence took place.

An excessively wet autumn's rainfall had, it seems, permeated the clifftop layers of porous chalk and greensand which lay on clay tilted about five degrees towards the sea. Thus lubricated, 8 million tons of waterlogged chalk and 20 acres of fields slipped forward, forming gaping chasms, isolated rock stacks and even offshore reefs which were eventually levelled by wave action. Local residents must have had a nose for disaster, for cottages near the cliffs had already been evacuated the previous day. During the event, onlookers recount seeing the beach buck and lurch like the deck of a ship in rough seas.

The entire area has recovered and developed without man's intervention and has done so over a known time scale, thus providing valuable data on the growth cycles of plant and animal species. Ash woodland is especially common, so too is thorny, bushy scrub. Birds

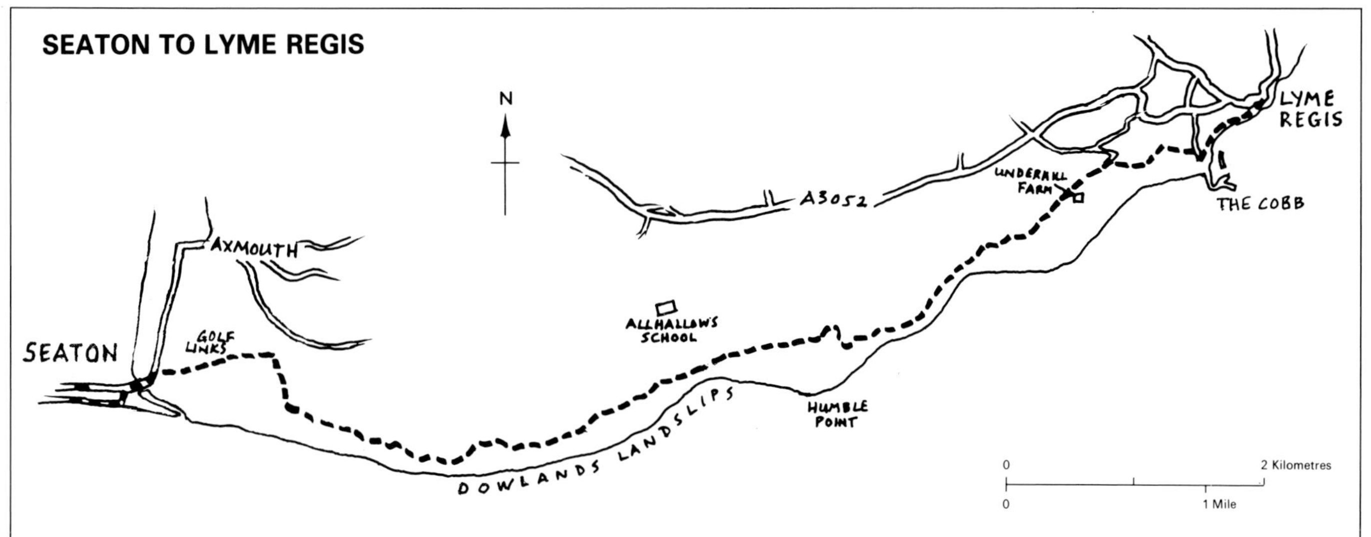

to be watched out for are too numerous to list, while mammals include roe deer, foxes, badgers, rabbits and many other rodents. Fungi, mosses, ferns and insects also thrive in these habitats and the observant naturalist will find the walk thoroughly absorbing. (It should be noted that permits are required to venture off the path; these are obtainable from The Nature Conservancy Council at Roughmoor, Bishops Hull, Taunton).

The walk starts from the eastern outskirts of Seaton—not, I fear, a favourite town of mine, despite its smuggling associations and ample modern amenities. You cross the River Axe road bridge and walk inland for 150m before turning right up a lane to the Axe Cliff Golf Club. From the top of a fairway, a stile leads you onto a farm track where soon a notice and coast path sign are encountered setting out a sensible warning about the nature of the undercliff path. Experienced walkers will wonder what all the fuss is about, but the terrain and distances from habitation involved could lead unprepared strollers into all kinds of difficulties.

A field path is taken seawards, reaching a clifftop stile and a Nature Conservancy signboard. Here you drop down a flight of steps and engage the first of countless gradients as the way rises and falls, twists and turns through an almost continuous, exotic tangle of trees, creepers and ferns. Up to the left and about 500m back stands the 'new' cliff line. In due course, Humble Point is glimpsed through the screen of vegetation and you reach a motorable track from Allhallows School near a tall, brick chimney. Fossil hunters might consider diverting to the foreshore here: given favourable tide and weather conditions, the beach can be walked all the way to Lyme Regis, but progress will be slow over the rockier sections.

Twenty metres up the track you fork off right up a long sequence of steps. These and general maintenance of the path are provided by Conservation Corps volunteers, who sometimes have difficulty keeping up with the clearing of obstructions such as fallen trees. Although you have reached the approximate halfway point, some of the toughest walking is still to come. The up and down work intensifies and a slow, steady rhythm will be needed if attention is to be given to the surroundings. A main road lies a mere mile to the north, yet within the bowels of this chaotic landscape you are deprived of reference points against which to measure progress or direction. Even the OS map has little to contribute! Some find the ambience oppressive and claustrophobic, but there are others—myself among them—whose response echoes the exuberance of nature so that intimidation is replaced by wonder at all that burgeoning growth and the untouched, secret places inhabited by creatures other than ourselves.

At a large tree by a gate, another track is joined and followed downhill to an electricity sub-station—a harbinger of civilisation! Sure enough, there is a metalled lane and up it you walk until it begins to fall gently to a waymark post. Forking right here, the path continues its meandering course, eventually leading out to an access road above Underhill Farm. By threading through gates towards the distant low wedge of Portland Bill, you will cross from Devon into Dorset. Suddenly the Cobb is in sight below and from the top of a scrubby copse, steps lead right down past chalets to the Bowling Club car park where you either walk out on the old harbour Cobb itself (of *The French Lieutenant's Woman* fame) or along the seafront into Lyme Regis.

Lyme was an important Middle Ages' sea port—one of Britain's truly 'loyal and ancient boroughs', but suffered periods of intense privation too. In the eighteenth century under George III, trade diminished, smuggling was rife and within 100 years the population had fallen from 3000 to fewer than 1000. The town's fortunes have always centred upon the Cobb, for without its protection against gale lashed seas, vessels could not be accommodated. Indeed, records of a breakwater date back to 1372 and its repair after storm damage became a recurrent and expensive necessity.

An oar-and-sail powered lifeboat was stationed at Lyme during the nineteenth century and the shipping out of limestone from adjacent cliff quarries in exchange for coal became an important source of revenue. Jane Austen often came here, and to nearby Charmouth, for her summer vacation, writing *Persuasion* while staying in a cottage in Broad Street. Needless to say, there is more to Lyme's history than this sketchy outline, but it falls outside the scope of this book. Today, Lyme's steep, narrow streets of colour-washed houses have the ready charm of a picture postcard and there is no shortage of admiring visitors. I have always found it an endearing place, easy to explore (discounting the hills!) and it certainly forms a most pleasant conclusion to this walk.

On the Chesil Bank.

WALK 18: *Dorset — Charmouth to Abbotsbury*

Maps: OS Landranger Sheets 193 (Taunton & Lyme Regis) and 194 (Dorchester & Weymouth). **Start:** Lower Sea Lane, Charmouth. **Finish:** Abbotsbury village. **Distance:** 17 miles (27km)—allow 7 to 8 hours. **Access:** Charmouth is on the A35 between Bridport and Axminster. Abbotsbury is on the B3157 coast road from Weymouth to Bridport. Nearest railway stations—Axminster and Weymouth. **Type of Walking:** Substantial ups and downs to begin with, but virtually flat for the last 6 miles (10km). Good paths and tracks throughout. **Features of Interest:** Golden Cap, highest cliff on the Channel coast; West Bay harbour; the Chesil Bank; Abbotsbury swannery, sub-tropical gardens and old village. **Accommodation:** Available at Charmouth, Chideock (inland from Seatown), West Bay, Burton Bradstock, West Bexington and Abbotsbury—in greater or lesser amounts. Youth hostels at Bridport and Litton Cheney, both inland.

High Cliffs and a Unique Shingle Bank

Charmouth has a reputation for fossils. In the early nineteenth century, a 12-year-old local girl, Mary Anning, unearthed the first complete fossilised skeleton of an ichthyosaurus, a 21ft (6.4m) long specimen now in the British Natural History Museum. She went on to discover other fossil remains in the landslipped cliffs of Black Ven which constitutes a 161 acre nature reserve to the west of the town (not open to the general public) and new cliff falls continue to expose fresh fossil-bearing rocks. Great care is needed when exploring the beach beneath landslips, many of which are loose and muddy in consistency.

The town has all the usual shops and services and is on a bus route. The Queen's Armes is of historical interest, having offered Charles II refuge in 1651 following his defeat by Cromwell at the Battle of Worcester. Suspicious Roundhead sympathisers forced him to flee Charmouth on horseback rather than sail to France and he eventually escaped the country from Brighton.

Lower Sea Lane will take you towards the shore, but about 200m short of it you turn left over the River Char and climb the broad, grassy flanks of Stonebarrow Hill. Cain's Folly, a deep, rambling undercliff above which the path rises to 500ft (152m), is sufficiently stable to have become colonised by brushwood, and wildlife flourishes on its slopes, inaccessible to man. Views back to Lyme Regis and beyond are truly magnificent, but this is a walk of visual delights and the best is yet to come!

Walking along the crumbling edge of orange-hued cliffs past a National Trust signpost (a car park and information centre lie 500m inland) Golden Cap is still some 2 miles (3km) distant. The approach, a popular local walk, is mostly seaward of pasture and copses around Westhay Farm and is well waymarked. Once over the final stream above St Gabriel's Mouth, the going gets tougher, first up a dangerously eroding cliff edge then across a stile and up rough steps mounting the rugged summit of Golden Cap itself. You have climbed to the highest clifftop on the entire Channel coast. Indeed, at 627ft (191m) it is as fine a panoramic viewpoint as any in Britain's south-west peninsula and in clear weather presents you with a situation to savour. The corollary is that wind and rain will rob much of the pleasure from you, except possibly a masochistic satisfaction at having tussled with the elements and won, so try to choose a promising day for this ascent.

The name Golden Cap is thought to derive from patches of yellow gorse and from the effects of sunlight on expanses of the yellowish Jurassic limestone near the summit. Leaving the coast path monolith and OS pillar behind you, descend steps to the left and fork right at a path junction. (The left fork leads to the little, ruined thirteenth-century church of St Gabriel's and a farmhouse of Tudor origin). Steep grass leads down towards the pub and seasonal café at Seatown, a favourite haunt of sea-anglers who cast for bass and mackerel.

A stiff climb lies ahead up Ridge Cliff to Doghouse Hill summit above East Ebb Cove and by the time you have reached Thorncombe Beacon with its World War II pillbox, you will have notched up another 509ft (155m) of ascent! However, this degree of exertion, as well as the proximity of subsiding cliffs, while not disappearing altogether, will moderate from now on.

Down at Eype's Mouth, stepping stones cross the little stream and a straightforward climb ensues over West Cliff, ending past holiday homes and sea defences on West Bay's promenade. Bridport Harbour, as West Bay was known before the railway came in 1884, was constructed in 1740 here at the mouth of the River Brit and was busy with net and rope exports from nearby Bridport, as well as with general cargoes and ship-building, until the end of the nineteenth century. Exposed and always prone to silting up, harbour sluice gates were installed in 1823 to scour sand and shingle from the entrance channel. West Bay's harbour is used today by pleasure craft, a fishing fleet and ships carrying away pea-gravel which has been extracted from the beach for years and is used mainly in filter beds. Underscoring the town's vulnerability to the sea, even in our resourceful times, considerable sums have been spent re-strengthening sea defences following an inundation by high-tide storm waves in 1974 which caused much damage.

You have to walk round the harbour basin and back past the Bridport Arms to regain the shore. Bathing is dangerous from the steeply shelving shingle, a characteristic of the coast from here to Weymouth. A short, sharp pull from the east end of the beach takes you up onto East Cliff and level walking outside golf links, with extensive views ahead of the Chesil Bank. Beyond a small valley, the path drops to beach level and proceeds inland atop a grassy embankment through Burton Freshwater's vast camping and caravan site. This deviation is necessary to cross the River Bride, a hazardous undertaking at its mouth, and is achieved by heading over a camping field to a finger post in a bank, crossing the river footbridge and veering right towards the sea.

Pleasant, easy walking leads on to Burton Beach. Opinions differ as to the exact location of Chesil Bank's western extremity: there can be no definitive demarcation point since shingle extends right back to Charmouth. Vestiges of a true pebble ridge can be traced as far west as Eype's Mouth, but its identity is dissipated, in my view, beyond Burton Cliff.

The Chesil (Anglo-Saxon for 'stones') is best seen in its entirety from the war memorial above Fortuneswell at Portland. It is an extraordinary topographical feature, an evenly curved blade fringed with surf extending 18 miles (29km) from south-east to north-west from the butt of Portland Bill. Four thousand years ago the whole area was marshland and borings have established that higher ground was colonised by alder and pine, so the Chesil, in geographical terms, is quite young. Piled up to 40ft (12m) high in places on a foundation of blue clay, its pebbles are gradated in size by west-to-east currents and range from 3ins (76mm) at Portland to fine pea-gravel in the west. Local fishermen claim to know their whereabouts when landing in fog or darkness by examining the size of the stones.

Low cliffs and a rough road head on to Cogden Beach, lonely, open flats of shingle and reeds where the path dwindles to nothing. There is a car park here but no commercial exploitation. Once much larger, Burton Mere's marshy lakes and cultivated reed beds are being smothered by encroaching pebbles which make for less than comfortable going to the seafront at West Bexington. Vehicular access and the provision of a good café and toilets have probably encouraged the growth of sea-angling here, but catches too are generally good and it is the venue for numerous fishing competitions.

You now take to a rough track rising imperceptibly past chalets and fields behind the Chesil which, as yet, is little more than a low slope of medium shingle. Being National Trust property, this is a popular walking route, with plenty of interesting wild flowers and bird life. Passing old Coastguard cottages and a few tarred boats drawn up onto the beach, you enter the surfaced Smugglers Walk, a pretty lane flanking the shoreline.

Before the walk draws to a close, do scramble out onto the Chesil again. To seawards, only the occasional broken wartime blockhouse, upturned boat or sea fisherman interrupt the vastness of this great pebble ridge which stretches almost to a vanishing point in both directions. Theoretically it is feasible to walk the entire bank, but the going can be very arduous, normal walking pace halved by the energy absorption of displaced pebbles at each footfall. Devoid of shelter, it is no place to venture in a storm; records remind us that the sea has the capacity to breach the bank and even thrust ships over its crest, hard though this is to imagine on a benign summer's day.

Arriving at a car park, you continue ahead on a track through a handgate into a green lane. Where this swings inland there is a choice of two conclusions to the walk. Either go on inland, forking right through a gate and up past St Catherine's Chapel into Abbotsbury village; or cross the stile and climb round the base of Chapel Hill to the Swannery. South-east of Abbotsbury, Chesil Bank is separated from the mainland by a large, brackish lagoon known as the Fleet. Many hundreds of mute swans may be seen at the Swannery which occupies the Fleet's western end; their protection dates back to 1393 when Abbotsbury's Benedictine monks reared them for meat. Development of any kind is prohibited in the Fleet Sanctuary Nature Reserve and its shallows, rich in wildlife, are acknowledged as an internationally important wetland. In fact, the coast path diverts inland here and does not reach the Fleet's shore until south-west of Langton Herring.

Apart from its sub-tropical gardens, open

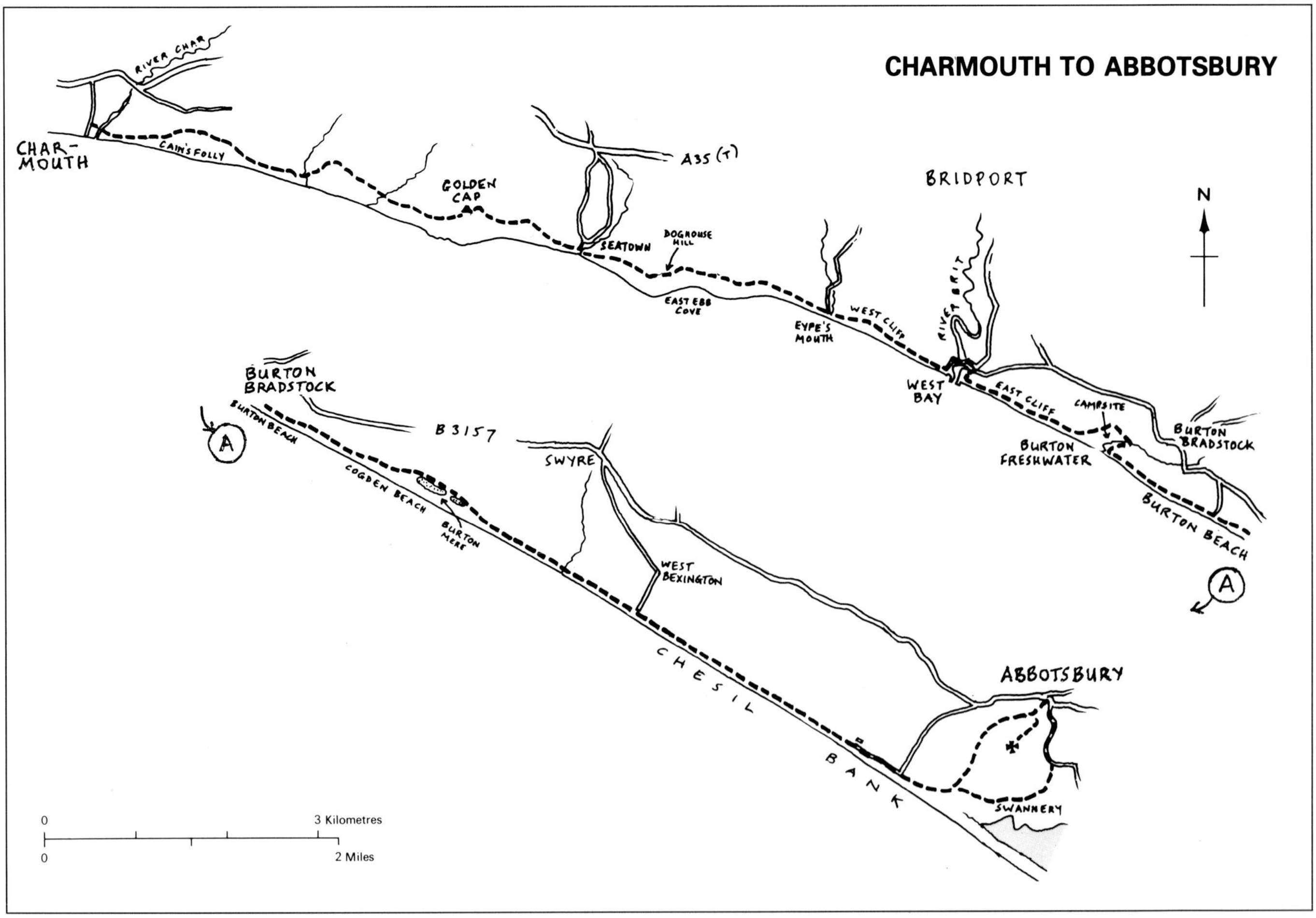

CHARMOUTH TO ABBOTSBURY

from mid-March to October, Abbotsbury is well worth looking round if you have time. It is one of those picture-postcard places, faintly reminiscent of the Cotswolds. The eleventh-century abbey ruin and thatched, fifteenth-century tithe barn—one of the largest in Britain—are the main 'sights', but there are many attractive perspectives over thatched cottages and the fourteenth-century hilltop St Catherine's Chapel commands unsurpassed views of this remarkable stretch of coast.

The harbour, West Bay.

Facing page: ***Looking back to Gad Cliff.***

WALK 19: *Dorset — Lulworth Cove to Kimmeridge Bay*

Maps: OS Landranger Sheet 194 (Dorchester, Weymouth and area) and 195 (Bournemouth, Purbeck and area). **Start:** Lulworth Cove slipway. **Finish:** Car park, Kimmeridge Bay. **Distance:** 7 miles (11km)—allow at least 5 hours. **Access:** Lulworth Cove lies at the end of the B3070/1 south of the A352 between Dorchester and Wareham. Kimmeridge Bay is reached by toll road from Kimmeridge village, west of Corfe Castle. Nearest railway stations—Wool and Wareham. **Type of Walking:** A strenuous switchback along precipitous chalk cliffs. The clearly marked paths are slippery in wet weather and contain some very steep gradients. No refreshment points along the way. **Features of Interest:** Lulworth Cove and nearby Stair Hole; Fossil Forest; Tyneham 'ghost village'; Kimmeridge oil well; chalk cliff scenery of unsurpassed drama and beauty. **Accommodation:** Plentiful at West Lulworth, otherwise non-existent. Youth hostel at West Lulworth.

A Spectacular Walk through the Lulworth Ranges

In 1974, following the Defence Lands Committee report chaired by Lord Nugent, the government agreed to increase public access to 7000 acres of land east of Lulworth which had been used since 1916 as a Royal Armoured Corps gunnery range. This decision gave birth to the famous Lulworth Range Walks of which the coast path is a major component. It is, however, not permanently open to the public, as the ranges are still used by the Army. Around 70,000 shells are fired here each year and inevitably some ricochet off target or fail to explode.

Every time the Range Walks are opened they are first thoroughly searched for unexploded shells, but this procedure cannot guarantee total freedom for walkers who stray from the marked paths. A common sense code of safety requests that walkers remain on waymarked paths, comply with instructions from wardens, avoid picking up ammunition or using metal detectors, keep away from buildings (except at Tyneham), refrain from lighting fires and collecting wildlife or fossil specimens without permission and take care near cliff edges. This may all sound excessively officious but in fact puts nothing whatever in the way of the sensible walker wishing to experience

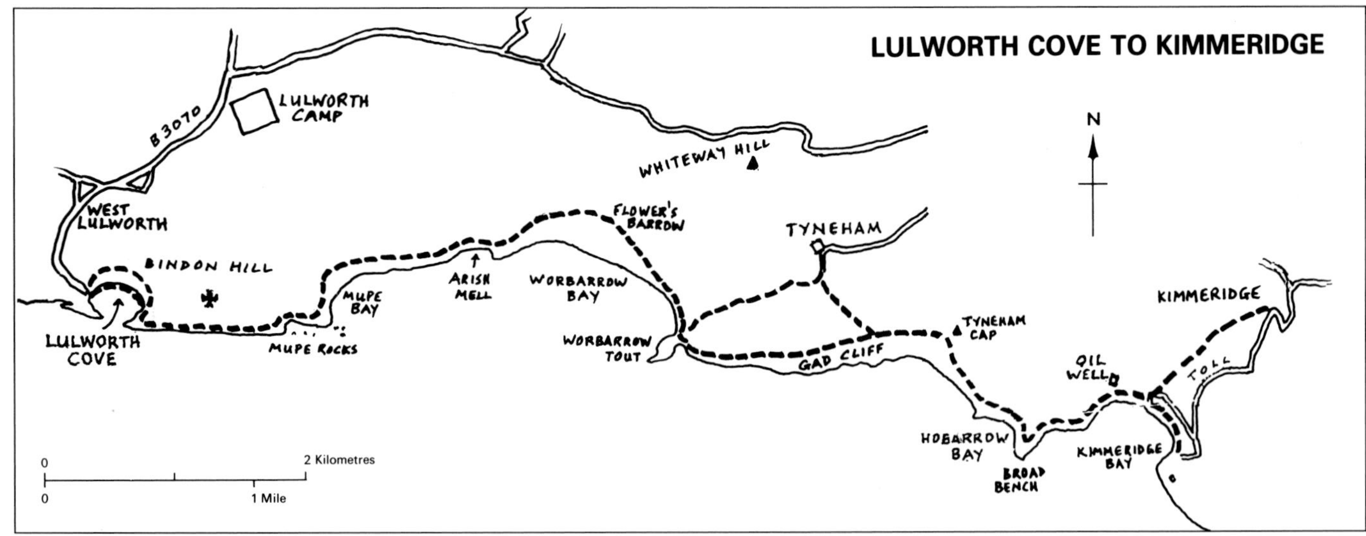

this stunningly beautiful coast.

The Range Walks are normally open to the public every weekend (except for about 6 per year) and during traditional holiday periods, ie. Easter, Spring Bank Holiday, Whitsun, from the end of July to the beginning of September and at Christmas. It is always prudent to check opening dates before planning a walk; information is available in the local press and the annual handbook published by the South West Way Association, as well as from the Range Officer, RAC Gunnery School, Lulworth, Dorset. Tel: Bindon Abbey (0929) 462721, ext. 819.

Whatever your views on the Armed Forces occupation of this and other pockets of Britain's countryside for the purposes of military training, their claim to have protected the Lulworth Ranges area from the negative aspects of exploitation by man does seem well founded. Much that would otherwise have disappeared beneath the plough has been preserved, including ancient earthworks, medieval field systems and features of pre-war land use that have reverted to natural development. Grasslands here are 'unimproved', herbicides and pollutants unknown, so that habitats support an exceptional variety of flora and fauna. Of course, the environment does incur damage, but it avoids the systematic manipulation of natural resources that characterises so many modern agricultural practices, not to mention the wholesale despoliation caused by new building development and the construction of roads.

And so to the walk itself. Try to choose a fine day, for the great pale cliffs reflect sunlight magnificently and colour flows into sea and clifftop turf. In wind and rain the 7 miles will seem like 14; in hot sunshine, remember to carry drinks!

West Lulworth, a smugglers' haunt in the early 1600s, has been extended seawards by tourist development and the cove, already heavily patronised by sub-aqua divers and boat owners, becomes overrun by trippers in the summer months. Nevertheless it is an interesting spot, the circular bay formed by the sea having breached a band of harder Portland limestone along the outer cliff line and worn back softer clays with remarkable symmetry. By walking a short distance from the car park's southern corner, signs lead you up to Stair Hole, a collapsed sea cave with arches and spectacular folding of the so-called 'Lulworth Crumple', rock strata contorted by the same movements in the earth's crust that formed the Alps.

Provided the tide is low enough, the walk begins along coarse shingle below high cliffs backing the cove. At the far end you climb steps and veer right across an overgrown stream bed onto Peppler Point. (If you are starting at high water, you must take a more elevated route which leaves the road above the cove and follows a path rising 300ft (91m) along the clifftops, dropping to the main route at Peppler Point.) Soon after swinging east along the shoreline, watch below for the well-known Fossil Forest, which can be reached down steps. What you see are the fossilised remains of algae which grew around the trunks of cycads—relatives of conifers—some 150 to 200 million years ago during the age of the dinosaurs.

At a white flagpole you pass through a gate in the Ranges fence and walk past a radar installation before coming round by a concrete bunker above Mupe Rocks. The long ridge of Bindon Hill rises inland parallel to the coast, while ahead in the distance lie the big earthworks on Flower's Barrow, Gad Cliff's jagged profile and the bulk of St Aldhelm's Head.

Unspoiled grassland dotted with gorse leads on above Mupe Bay and at a gravel track, loins must be girded up for the climb to Cockpit Head at the eastern end of Bindon Hill. A wire fence provides welcome hand holds on the first severe gradient, but soon the chalky path veers away right and zig-zags near the top to avoid dangerous ground above an impressive drop. Views are tremendous, taking in Weymouth and Portland Bill to the west, Poole Harbour and Bournemouth to the east, with the seventeenth-century Lulworth Castle inland beyond a foreground of battered hardware. The way now dips towards a narrowing ridge and descends very abruptly to Arish Mell; the beach here is out of bounds, being an outlet for Winfrith Nuclear Research Station $4\frac{1}{2}$ miles (7km) to the north-west.

Taking you temporarily away from the coastal edge, the ensuing long ascent reaches Flower's Barrow, an Iron Age hill fort of some significance on Ring Hill, 568ft (173m) above sea level. Its $15\frac{1}{2}$ acres of enclosures, ditches, banks, hut platforms and an entrance are all clearly discernible, but represent only two-thirds of the original site, the rest having slipped into the sea sometime back in the 1600s. Also on this lofty summit you join the old Dorset Coastal Ridgeway which heads inland to Lowford Sheard, Whitway and Kimmeridge village.

Worbarrow Bay is approached by negotiating a steep and potentially slippery descent of some 560ft (171m). The beach offers good bathing but is only accessible from this eastern end near Worbarrow Tout. This curious whaleback promontory ('tout' is Old English for 'lookout') is geologically an outlier of the South Purbeck Downs and can be walked out on for wonderful views of the coast in both directions. Just how the little complex of estate buildings here looked in pre-Army days (foundations and low walls are all that remain) is the subject of an artist's impression mounted on a tablet above the beach.

Instead of continuing up the shoulder of

Gad Cliff, I recommend a detour inland to Tyneham village, rejoining the coast path further on with no extra mileage involved. Simply cross the stile and walk on the track up Tyneham Gwyle ('gwyle' is a local word for a wooded ravine) for about 15 to 20 minutes.

Tyneham was a small rural community with roots as far back as the Domesday census. The valley was appropriated by the Army for use as a gunnery range in 1943 and its inhabitants were rehoused on the understanding they could return at the end of the war. In fact, this promise was never honoured and the 'ghost village' has remained unoccupied ever since. It is surrounded by evidence of Iron Age and medieval settlement, notably extensive ancient field systems, but the fact that so much has been preserved is due to a considerable irony, for the village itself is derelict.

To cater for increasing public interest, permanent exhibitions have been installed by the Heritage Coast team in the Church and the Schoolroom, explaining the history and development of the Ranges environment. Though there are no facilities here apart from toilets, the village is much visited by motorists who drive down from West Creech Hill when the Ranges are open. It makes an excellent picnic spot!

To regain the clifftops, walk back past the toilets onto a path signed 'Tyneham Cap' which mounts steep hillside onto the backwards-sloping flank of Gad Cliff above Brandy Bay. Cliff edge subsidence has opened up breathtaking views but great care should be exercised as any fall would certainly be fatal. From a signpost and stile, you fork right and angle down over grass, following the ubiquitous yellow-tipped posts. Zig-zags give way to easier slopes above Hobarrow Bay, bounded to the east by the extraordinary low-tide rock platforms of Broad Bench. On the descent, be sure to look back at the impressive multiple buttresses on Gad Cliff, unseen from the path above them.

The flowery track winds gently downhill, taking its leave of the Ranges at Kimmeridge Gate and presenting you with the astonishing sight of a working oil well! Dark brown bituminous shale found hereabouts and known as Kimmeridge Coal was once burned as fuel but attempts to market it were thwarted by its emission of unpleasant sulphurous fumes. Prospecting for oil began in 1936 yet 25 years were to elapse before production began. British Petroleum owns the green painted, electric powered 'nodding donkey' which extracts about 4.6 million gallons of oil per year: it is a great favourite with school field trips! Substantial oil reserves have been discovered in the region, particularly at Wytch Farm, and it is estimated that Dorset's total oil reserves would meet Britain's need for about 10 months.

One hundred and fifty metres along the tarmac road you fork right past old cottages, cross a stream, and reach the grassy car park at Gaulter Gap, part of the private Smedmore Estate. Other than toilets and ice cream vans, there are no amenities here, but the post office/stores at Kimmeridge village a mile inland serves meals, snacks and drinks. Kimmeridge's rock-bound shoreline produces a large expanse of shallow water extending a mile offshore and especially rich in marine life. Sub-aqua divers are often active, but surfers too are drawn here when a good swell pours into the bay.

Before leaving, you might care to climb steps through trees from the slipway road and visit the Clavel Tower on cliffs overlooking the east of the bay. Built in 1820 by the Rev. John Clavel of Smedmore, this odd mixture of Tuscan columns and classical motifs began life as a folly (or possibly as an observatory) and was later used as a Coastguard lookout. The walk could be extended an extra 5 miles (8km) along the Kimmeridge Ledges, over Hounstout Cliff and up to the pretty village of Worth Matravers where some accommodation is available.

Right: ***Gad Cliff (distant left) and Tyneham Cap (top right) across Kimmeridge Bay.***

Below ***Lulworth Cove, Stair Hole and Hambury Tout (top right) from Peppler Point (photo C.W. Footer).***

WALK 20: *Isle of Wight — Blackgang Chine to Alum Bay*

Map: OS Landranger Sheet 196—Solent and the Isle of Wight. **Start:** Blackgang Chine car park. **Finish:** Alum Bay car park. **Distance:** 15½ miles (25km)—allow a full day. **Access:** Blackgang Chine is on the A3055 west coast road about 2 miles (3km) north-west of Niton. Alum Bay and the Needles are the most westerly point on the Isle of Wight, not far from Totland, Freshwater and the vehicle ferry port of Yarmouth. Nearest railway station—Lymington on the mainland (for ferry to Yarmouth) and Shanklin (for Ryde and ferries to Portsmouth). **Type of Walking:** Mostly along low cliffs but becoming more elevated as the walk progresses, and interrupted by several deep ravines (chines). Good waymarked paths throughout, but little shelter from wind and weather. **Features of Interest:** Blackgang Chine Theme Park, old sawmill and ravine; spectacular, open coastal views; Tennyson Monument; The Needles; Alum Bay. **Accommodation:** Available at Niton, 3 holiday centres along the path, and at Totland/Freshwater/Yarmouth. Youth hostels at Whitwell (north-west of Niton) and at Totland.

Coastal Ravines, Wide Views and Spectacular Cliffs

For a surface area of only 73 square miles (117 square kms), the Isle of Wight is exceptionally well endowed with footpaths—some 500 miles (800km) of them in all. Scenery, too, is wonderfully varied, from high chalk downland to lonely saltmarsh, shady woods to steep cliffs and bustling towns to rolling farmland and quaint villages.

Breaking free from the mainland after the last Ice Age 10,000 years ago, Vectis—as it was once known—was heavily clothed with forest and even today the northern half, with its poorly drained soils, has greater tree cover than the south's farmland and pasture exposed to salt laden south-westerly winds. The island's history, from Stone Age man through to the Roman and Norman occupations, the building of Carisbrooke Castle, prosperity during the sixteenth and seventeenth centuries, the patronage of Queen Victoria and Alfred Lord Tennyson and the development of today's tourist industry upon which the island's economy depends, is a fascinating story but beyond the scope of this book. Even without such background knowledge, the visitor will register subtle differences from the mainland landscape—narrower roads, an 'old fashioned' chequerboard of fields and villages, all good

ISLE OF WIGHT – BLACKGANG CHINE TO ALUM BAY

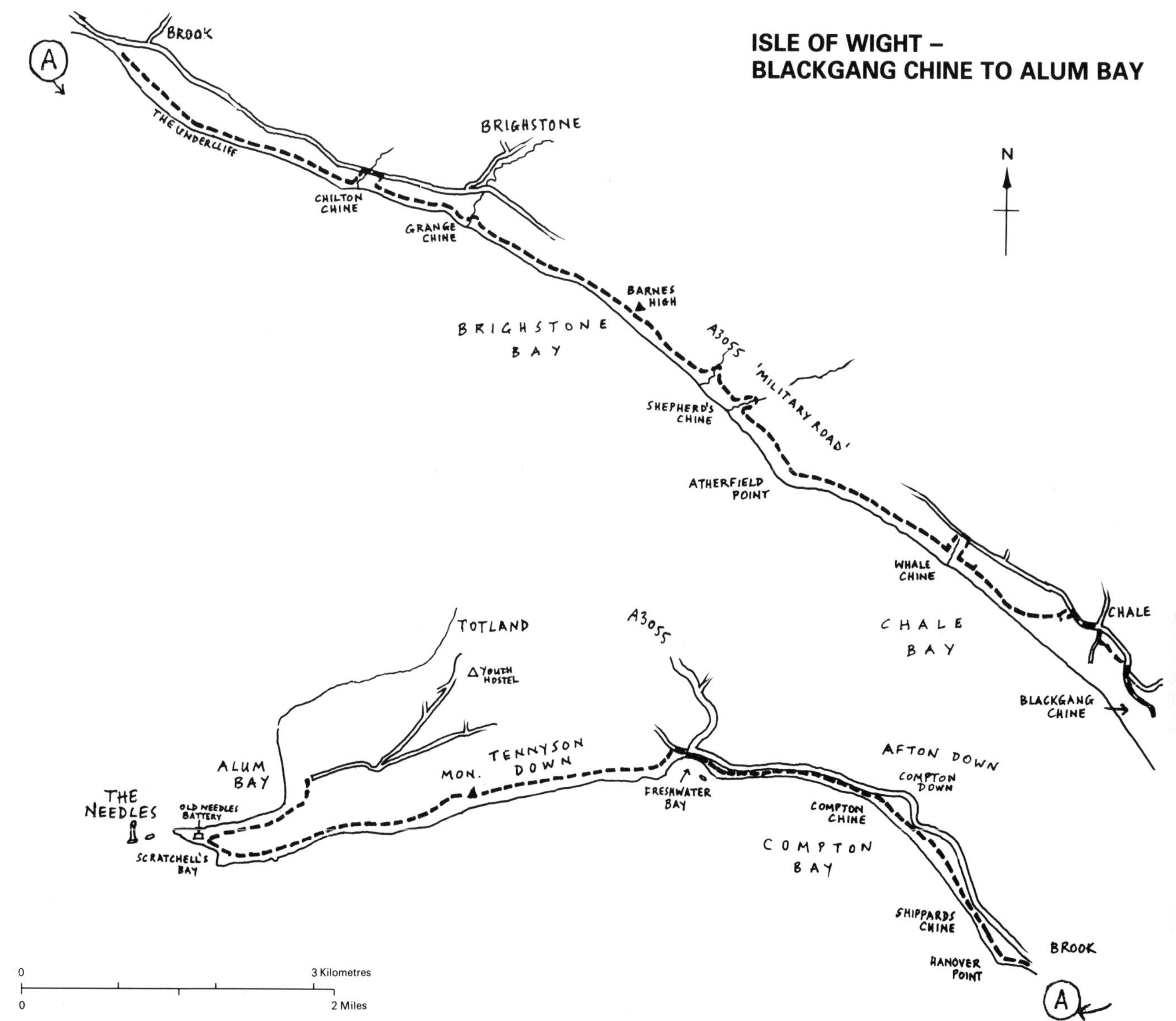

Facing page: ***Tennyson Down across Compton Bay.***

country, but a traverse of the south-west facing coast takes the honours for spectacular, wild surroundings and has been designated an Area of Outstanding Natural Beauty. Try to walk it in reasonable weather, for there is precious little shelter from a sou' westerly blow or driving rain, a fact I can personally vouch for having suffered just such conditions while prospecting the route for this book!

The size of Blackgang Chine's car and coach park will send trembles of apprehension down the spines of walkers to whom humanity *en masse* is anathema! Take heart, however, for the overwhelming majority of visitors will have come to see the Theme Park, not to walk the coast path. In common with other parts of the island, footpaths are generally well signed but are only thinly walked and you will have long stretches all to yourself.

Chines (from the Anglo-Saxon *cinan*, to crack) are steep sided, narrow gullies eroded into soft, sandy rock by streams and wave action and are characteristic of this coastline. Blackgang Chine is reputedly named after a local gang of smugglers; a monstrous, caricatured smuggler towers over the entrance to the Fantasy Theme Park opposite an old restored sawmill. It contains various impressive models and the skeleton of a 75ft (23m) whale washed up nearby in 1842. The chine itself may yet impress you more—a 400ft (122m) deep, landslipped fissure of blue-black Gault Clay which continues to gnaw away at the local shoreline, having already devoured the original coast road and several houses!

And so to the walk, which first aims for the main A3055 coast road, known as the Military Road from its construction in the nineteenth century to connect coastal fortifications. A public bridleway on the left by a road sign for Chale takes you over to The Terrace, a narrow lane leading to the cliff edge; here you turn right to rejoin the road through Chale village, passing St Andrew's church and continuing on a wide, grassy verge to a path signed 'Brook' opposite the entrance to the popular Mouse Inn. Soon on a true clifftop path, you pass Walpen and Ladder chines, once used by mackerel fishermen, and temporarily reach the road again before returning seaward—a manoeuvre necessary to cross Whale Chine. Timber steps have been installed in this miniature canyon for access to the unspoiled shingle beach beneath fossil-rich, striated cliffs.

Westward progress resumed, you are walking above rocks which claimed 60 ships between 1746 and 1808, earning Chale Bay the name Bay of Death. A neat row of Coastguard cottages stands above the reef at Atherfield Point, from where the entire south-west coast is visible, back to St Catherine's Point and ahead round the red cliffs of Brighstone Bay to Freshwater, Tennyson Down and the distant Needles.

Negotiating Shepherds Chine demands another inland detour to a small dam, then, passing a holiday camp, you cross a meadow and Cowleaze Chine before climbing past the OS pillar on the crumbling sands of Barnes High, 53ft (16m) above sea level. Grange Chine, over a mile of fine clifftop walking farther on, is steeper-sided, grassier and crossed by a beach level footbridge. Stiles to seaward of Brighstone holiday camp lead on above expansive sands and low-tide ledges of pale brown rock.

Yet another minor detour passes Chilton Chine and its holiday centre, crossing the road bridge and following the chine bank back to the shoreline. Yellow kidney vetch, sea carrot and sea-pink brighten the pathside in summer, while landslipped ledges on the Undercliff provide moist habitats for marsh orchids and other wildlife species of flora and fauna.

The path continues past Tomkins Plantation and along Roughland Cliff to Brook Green, the straggling, seaward end of Brook village where the writer J B Priestley took up residence. You cross a stile by the old Lifeboat Station and take to a gravel track to the Military Road where a left turn through the National Trust car park and a stile above the beach return you to the low, slumping, eroded cliff line at Hanover Point. Offshore, a small tower marks the 'Pine Raft': fossilised remains of a pine forest visible as rock flats at low water.

Beyond the headland lie Shippards Chine and a popular sandy bathing beach in Compton Bay. More significant to walkers, however, and anticipated from afar, are the sheer, 200ft (61m) chalk cliffs immediately ahead—a dramatic transition representing a time span of over 20 million years in geological history. As well as supporting a rich variety of lime loving plants, these downlands provide a venue for hang-gliding and give 1½ miles (2.5km) of gloriously unfettered coastal walking on springy turf.

From the climbing pole at the head of Compton Chine, the path veers away from the cliff edge to run along a bank just seaward of the Military Road beneath Afton Down. Having gained height, views are extensive and, once descending away from the road, include the miniature needles off Freshwater Bay—Arch Rock, Stag Rock and Mermaid Rock. Timber steps to Freshwater's sea wall conclude this exhilarating cliff section, but there is even better to come before the walk ends.

One hundred metres past the Albion Hotel, a tarmac lane leads off left, signed 'Tennyson Down', and a stile at the seaward end marks the foot of a hefty climb away from the cliff line onto the downland summit, the westernmost extremity of a chalk ridge extending the length of the island to Culver Down. Views of the island and adjacent mainland are magnificent and these breezy heights provide much to interest the ornithologist, archaeologist, geologist and botanist.

Here, 480ft (146m) above the sea stands a granite cross memorial to the poet Alfred Lord Tennyson who lived and worked at Farringford House, Freshwater for almost 40 years. In later times, his wife Emily suffered poor health and he would push her in her chair up to the old beacon. 'I do not think', she wrote, 'that on any spot on earth the air can be sweeter or more delicate', Tennyson himself declaring the air worth '6d a pint'!

Narrowing all the time to a green, west-pointing finger, the headland gives fine ridge walking between the Solent and unseen chalk cliffs to the south, against which seas pound and roar. The coast path proper bears right at a row of Coastguard cottages now owned by the National Trust, but it is worthwhile continuing out above Scratchell's Bay where the land falls and tapers towards the famous Needles; this was once a rocket testing site out of bounds to the public, but has been opened up by the National Trust. Comprehensive, photogenic views of The Needles are hard to come by—tourist posters often feature aerial pictures—but by scrambling around near old bunkers at the fenced cliff edge, one or two promising spots can be found. To approach significantly closer you must enter the Old Needles Battery, a restored fort open in summer, inside which a tunnel through the chalk brings you out onto a ledge above The Needles.

Short-cutting the initial dog-leg if necessary, you walk down the narrow tarmac lane on the northern flank of the headland overlooking Alum Bay. Originally the location for alum mining, its extraordinary riven cliffs of red, orange and ochre-hued sand have become a tourist attraction, spawning a leisure park complex and a chair-lift to the beach.

Storm at Freshwater Bay.

Layers of coloured sand—white quartz, yellow limonite, red iron oxide and other minerals—appear in a variety of souvenirs, the unmistakable trade mark of a visit to Alum Bay, set on mantlepieces and sideboards throughout the land.

Less well known is the bay's association with that pioneer of wireless telegraphy, Guglielmo Marconi. His telegraph station here exchanged radio messages with a tug offshore, then with Bournemouth 14 miles (23km) distant and next with Poole, 18 miles (29km) away, the range eventually extending to ships 40 miles (64km) out to sea. Between 1898 and 1900, Marconi's experiments attracted scientists from many countries and represented vital early pioneering work in the development of wireless communication.

Alum Bay.

WALK 21: *Sussex — Eastbourne to the Cuckmere Valley*

Maps: OS Landranger Sheet 199—Eastbourne, Hastings and area. **Start:** The south-western end of Eastbourne seafront. **Finish:**Seven Sisters Country Park Centre, Exceat. **Distance:** 7½ miles (12km)—allow 4 to 5 hours. **Access:** Eastbourne is a major south coast resort between Brighton and Hastings. Exceat lies approximately 6 miles (10km) west of Eastbourne on the A259. Nearest railway station—Eastbourne. **Type of Walking:** Well-walked paths on high, undulating chalk downland above sheer cliffs subject to erosion. Level walking in the Cuckmere valley. **Features of Interest:** Eastbourne itself; Beachy Head; Belle Tout old lighthouse; Birling Gap beach access; The Seven Sisters; Cuckmere river valley and Country Park exhibitions at Exceat Farm. **Accommodation:** Prolific at Eastbourne; hotel at Birling Gap; youth hostels at Eastbourne (west of the town by the A259) and near Alfriston (approx. 2½ miles/4km north of Exceat).

Beachy Head and the Famous Seven Sisters

Eastbourne enjoys many advantages—a mild climate, a history of well-planned development and the level of amenity which residents and cosmopolitan visitors alike demand from this relatively affluent corner of south-east England. Protected by rows of groynes, a shingly seafront runs from the Lifeboat Station, Butterfly Centre and Redoubt Aquarium eastwards past the classic Victorian pier, bandstand and 3-tiered promenade, on past floral gardens, museum and Wish Tower and west to the rising flanks of Beachy Head. It is here, where the road swings sharply up inland, that we begin this classic walk, in effect the initial, coastal section of the 80 mile (129km) South Downs Way from Eastbourne to Winchester.

From a signboard by the road, a stepped, chalky path climbs straight ahead over a low ridge with wide views back over Eastbourne,

Facing page: ***Cliff End and distant Belle Tout lighthouse from the beach at Cuckmere Haven.***

Below right: ***Beachy Head. Viewpoints from above are scarce and near the cliff edge.***

levelling off and waymarked through low, scrubby woodland. It emerges onto open downland overlooking playing fields before continuing across Heathy Brow. Views out to sea widen as we follow a narrow chalk trod—once used by Coastguards—through scrub some 50ft (15m) below the hilltop; the path becomes metalled towards Beachy Head, crossing the newly made Peace Path, to eventually attain the downland's crest near the old radar station.

During the main holiday periods and on fine weekends throughout the year, Beachy Head receives a steady stream of visitors, for a coast road approaches the cliff line here and farther on at Belle Tout and Birling Gap. The Beachy Head pub and coffee shop, car park and ice cream vendors do a roaring trade at such times! Just down the road stands a Visitor Centre worth taking in if time allows.

With every justification, the name Beachy Head derives from the French *beau chef*, or beautiful headland. Its precipitous limestone cliffs soar 534ft (163m) above the famous red and white lighthouse, clear views down to which are elusive. Except at very dangerous points, the cliffs are unfenced and it is patently unwise to risk life and limb by stepping onto an insecure edge; however, one good viewpoint is at map ref: 588 955! In clear visibility, the wide panorama from this lofty summit embraces the Isle of Wight to the west and Dungeness to the east. Passing a little walled enclosure commemorating World War II defences and equipped with a telescope, the way drops gently, parallel to the cliff line towards the old lighthouse at Belle Tout visible a mile ahead.

Eaten back by aeons of marine erosion, the South Downs end abruptly at the English Channel in vertical walls of chalk, dipping to ancient river valleys and topped by broad acres of grassland. 'But the glory of these glorious downs', wrote Richard Jefferies, 'is the breeze. It is air without admixture. If it comes from the south, the waves refine it, if inland the wheat and flowers distil it . . . ' From spring to summer, the short cropped turf will be studded with cowslips, sea lavender, orchids, harebells, bellflowers, samphire and vipers bugloss, and in fine conditions there is a rare fragrance in the wind. Gulls, jackdaws and rock pipits nest on ledges below.

At the bottom of the slope, quite near roadside car parking, the path takes to an old surfaced track, or the adjacent grassy clifftop which will inevitably diminish in size before the steady march of erosion. Belle Tout lighthouse, now a private residence, was built in 1834 and suffered the ignominy of becoming an artillery practice target during World War II, its subsequent reinstatement requiring major reconstruction work. Diverting inland round the perimeter wall, our onward route enters National Trust property, a welcome measure of protection for much of this Heritage Coast, and continues through sparse brambles and gorse. Ancient Iron and Bronze Age settlements were grouped hereabouts on Lookout Hill, as in numerous other locations on the South Downs, their remaining low banks and mounds still discernible here and there.

From open grass near the Coastguard lookout, a descent is made to a gravelly car park at Birling Gap, the final vehicular access point on this walk and once the haunt of smugglers and wreckers. A recent acquisition by the National Trust, the rather dilapidated row of grey cottages, ice cream booth, café and hotel are undergoing improvements, though investment cannot be easy to procure on a site so vulnerable to sea erosion. Nevertheless, refreshments—even accommodation—are on offer.

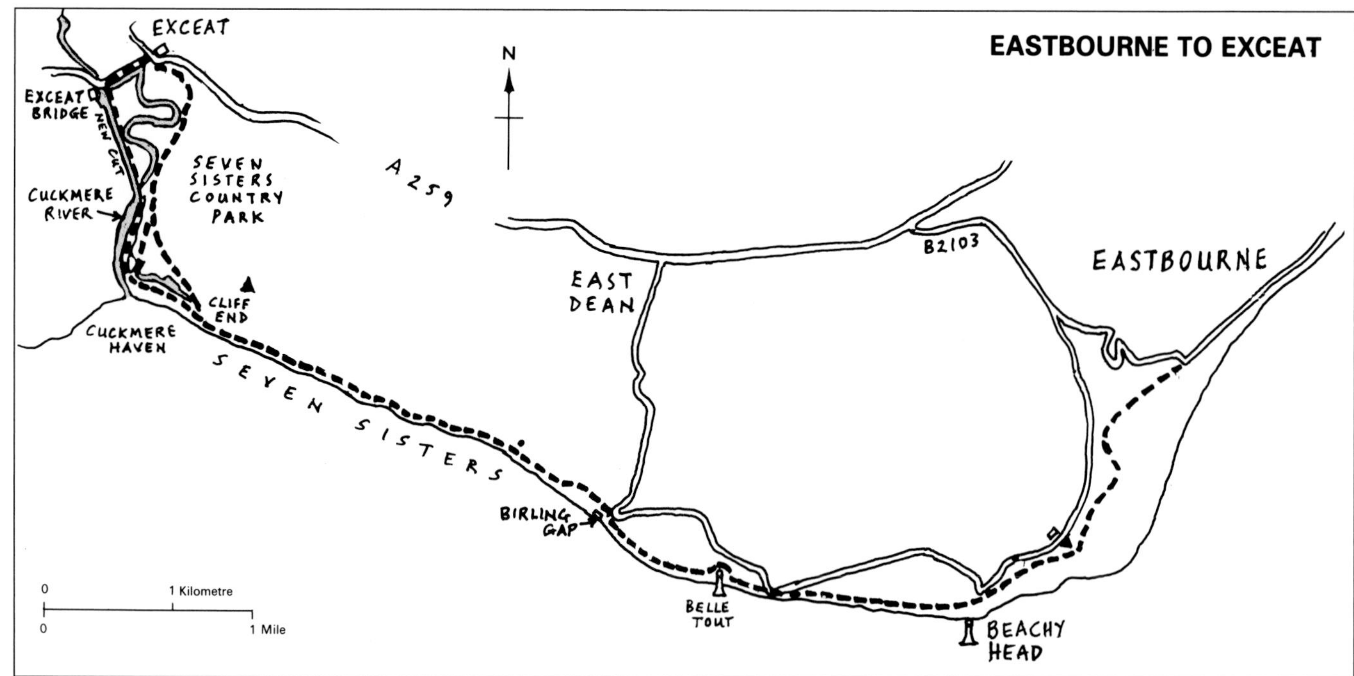

More likely to interest walkers who have now reached the half-way mark on this itinerary is a metal stairway leading down to beach level. Thanks to these entirely artificial means, we can enjoy the rare privilege of exploring low-tide chalk platforms or crunching along the flint-pebble beach between plunging surf and perpendicular walls of dazzling limestone. At high water there is a powerful, almost claustrophobic, sense of trespassing on land alien and hostile to man: *in extremis* there is no escape from heavy seas and incipient rock fall, so great care should be exercised to avoid getting trapped by an incoming tide. Back at cliff level, the presence of Coastguard rescue equipment and a safety boat confirms one's suspicions of potential danger, though in calm conditions nothing could be further from most people's minds! Birling Gap provides the only beach access between Eastbourne and Cuckmere Haven, as well as splendid views along the shallow curve of the Seven Sisters.

Where the coast road swings inland to East Dean village, a flint track beside the hotel is followed to the final building, beyond which a bridle gate returns us to the cliff edge. Ahead lie the Seven Sisters themselves, culmination of this elemental traverse along an interface between land and sea that could not be drawn more distinctly or more strikingly. Went Hill, Bailey's Hill, Flagstaff Point, Brass (or Bran) Point, Rough Brow, Short Brow and Haven Brow (or Cliff End) comprise the progression of tops, each separated by dips known on Normandy's equivalent Côte d'Albarte as *valeuses*, or hanging valleys truncated by erosion. The path is subject to minor changes due to occasional cliff falls, but stays exhilaratingly close to the open edge most of the way. En route a couple of memorial stones are passed, the second, at Flagstaff Point, commemorating the area's preservation from development and erected in 1926 by the Society of Sussex Downsmen.

From Cliff End, 253ft (77m) above sea level, a path dives down the grassy hillside to the broad mouth of Cuckmere Haven. Already having left National Trust property for the Seven Sisters Country Park, there are 3 options to conclude this walk:- 1) Follow the South Downs Way behind the pebble beach and inland along an embankment beside New Cut to Exceat Bridge, thence by roadside pavement to Exceat Farm. 2) Instead of the embankment tow path, take a track east of the Cuckmere river's meanders. 3) From the foot of Cliff End, follow a concrete road along the valley's east side. All three routes lead to the Seven Sisters Country Park Centre at Exceat Park, but before leaving the coast, it is worth pausing for a final reflection.

Although definitive views of the Seven Sisters are gained from Seaford Nature Reserve, an exciting beach-level perspective back to Belle Tout lighthouse is obtained from Cuckmere Haven, especially at low tide. During the eighteenth century when smuggling was rife, this coastal gap acted as a major landing point for brandy, lace and other contraband on its way to Alfriston. Today its great attraction is its inaccessibility to motor traffic, the A259 being a full mile distant.

Seven Sisters Country Park, inaugurated in 1971 thanks to the vision of East Sussex County Council and a grant from the Countryside Commission, covers almost 700 acres of beach, salt-marsh, water meadow, downland and scrub: one's impressions are of many stretches of water and reed beds, of sheep, birds and a haze of brightness back above the unseen sea. Canoes and small dinghies are allowed on the Cuckmere and several walking trails have been laid out in the mostly flat terrain. Refreshingly, the whole area is open to the public and there is a large, free car park by the handsome eighteenth-century Sussex barns converted to house an Interpretive Centre and 'Living World' exhibition at the foot of Exceat hill.

Facing page: ***The Meare, Thorpeness – 'House in the Clouds' centre right.***

WALK 22: *Suffolk — Aldeburgh to Dunwich*

Map: OS Landranger Sheet 156—Saxmundham, Aldeburgh and area. **Start:** Albeburgh seafront. **Finish:** Dunwich village. **Distance:** 9 miles (15km)—allow about 5 hours. **Access:** Aldeburgh is at the end of the A1094, north of Ipswich. Dunwich lies east of the B1125 between Leiston and Southwold. Nearest railway stations—Darsham and Saxmundham. **Type of Walking:** Tracks, pathways and compacted backshore; flat, except for low cliffs in one or two places. **Features of Interest:** Aldeburgh town and seafront; architectural fantasy at Thorpeness village; Sizewell nuclear power station(!); Minsmere Bird Reserve; Dunwich Heath and village; bird and seashore life. **Accommodation:** Available at Aldeburgh and Leiston (inland), also a little at Thorpeness and Dunwich. Several camp sites on or near the coast. Nearest youth hostel at Blaxhall, 6 miles (10km) west of Aldeburgh.

Man's Struggle against an Encroaching Sea

In his eighteenth-century historical account of Dunwich, Thomas Gardner described the Suffolk coast as 'destitute of rocks or some artificial means of preservation, exposed to the constant assaults of the raging waves of the sea'. Low, crumbling cliffs and shifting banks of shingle, mud and sand ensure that maps never remain accurate for long. There is a history of erosion and deposition here unequalled anywhere else in Britain: entire villages have been devoured by the sea and sizeable towns decimated, while elsewhere thriving little ports became silted up beyond hope.

The fact that Suffolk coastal settlements are more than usually vulnerable to wind and tide is of particular interest to walkers. Even on calm days, evidence of the sea's menacing power is not hard to find. Groynes and sea walls protect the more exposed communities but on long reaches of open coast it is impossible to influence the forces of nature engaged in that timeless conflict between land and water.

Aldeburgh's long main street of colour-washed houses and shops stretches towards the yacht club and Martello Tower where the River Alde, thwarted in its attempt to enter the bay, swings south for a further 10 miles (16km). From being a major Suffolk port in the sixteenth century, Aldeburgh was brought to its knees by plague and smallpox epidemics, marine erosion which swept away seafront properties and a relentless loss of trade to the then expanding Port of London. Fortunes change, however, and during the last century the town became a fashionable watering hole for the well-to-do. Elegant houses, new access roads and a promenade were constructed and Aldeburgh entered the twentieth century with optimism. In 1948, Benjamin Britten, Peter Pears and Eric Crozier founded the Aldeburgh Music Festival, now a world famous annual event held just inland at Snape Maltings.

The walk starts from the lifeboat at the northern end of the seafront. A small shanty town of black fishermen's shacks, each surrounded by a muddle of floats and boxes, backs the shingle foreshore. Ropes lead out to fishing boats atop the shingle's seaward slope—locally built craft are launched as they have been for centuries from the open beach. Beyond the promenade, a surfaced pathway shadows the coast road, making a beeline for Thorpeness. This eventually gives way to 'backshore'—firm, thinly vegetated levels between the shingle bank and the first beach houses.

Unless your momentum carries you irresistibly past the village, Thorpeness is well worth looking round. In the early 1900s, the author and dramatist Glencairn Stuart Ogilvie established a self-catering holiday village round The Meare, originally a marshy lake extending south to Aldeburgh but drained in the nineteenth century and landscaped by Ogilvie with islands and trees. Large, mock-Tudor and traditional East Anglian weatherboarded houses predominate (many built of heavily disguised concrete!) designed to accommodate affluent families and their servants. Architectural fantasy reaches a climax in Uplands Road with the House in the Clouds, a residence and water tower; opposite stands a windmill housing the Heritage Coast Centre. Duck ponds, pleasure boating, golf course, craft shops, tea rooms, pub and restaurant—you'll find them all here!

Thorpe Ness, by the sixteenth century already reduced from its considerable former size during Roman times, marks a subtle swing of direction to due north. Strong tidal currents scour large holes in the shingle hereabouts and bathing is not advised. Depending on sea conditions, the coast path route continues either below or along the edge of low, landslipped cliffs. Views ahead are dominated by the sinister, faceless bulk and gargantuan pylons of Sizewell's nuclear power station complex, at the time of writing undergoing extension. Neither are offshore waters any more welcoming, the notorious Sizewell Bank having claimed countless vessels throughout centuries of coastal trading.

Sparse clifftop trees and a few cottages lead to Sizewell Gap, a tiny fishing community once the venue for highly organised smuggling operations. There are public toilets here and the 'Sizewell T' café or Vulcan Arms will take care of the inner man if energy is flagging, while at the same time giving shelter from a keen easterly blow.

Without doubt the power station is something of a thorn in the walk's side—offensive to those who favour less potentially hazardous technology, anachronistic perhaps even to supporters of nuclear power considering its location close to holiday resorts and nature reserves on Heritage Coast. Outfall and inlet towers, for all the world like miniature oil rigs, stand close inshore, circulating 27 million gallons of seawater per hour to cool the reactors; enough energy is generated to satisfy the needs of a medium sized city.

Progress is resumed along the duney backshore (more stable here than to the north and south) alongside prolific shingle flora. For the uninitiated, like myself, to whom nuclear energy is a dark and inaccessible mystery, it is difficult not to dwell on an image of glowing reactor cores as you hurry through the site on sandy walkways between chain link fencing!

Ahead lie 1500 acres of tawny reedbeds, artificial lagoons and bushy islets backed by heath and woodland. Minsmere Nature Reserve and Bird Sanctuary, administered by the RSPB, shelters over a hundred breeding species, including marsh harriers, bitterns, nightjars, woodcocks, avocets and nightingales. Entry to the reserve itself is by permit only (tel: Westleton 281), but as you walk along this wild and beautiful coastline, you pass a large public hide for viewing shore birds. Tussocks of Marram grass have stabilised the low sand dunes which separate you from the shingle beach; with Sizewell now receding behind you, distant views to Southwold's lighthouse can be fully appreciated.

Fishing boats on the beach at Aldeburgh.

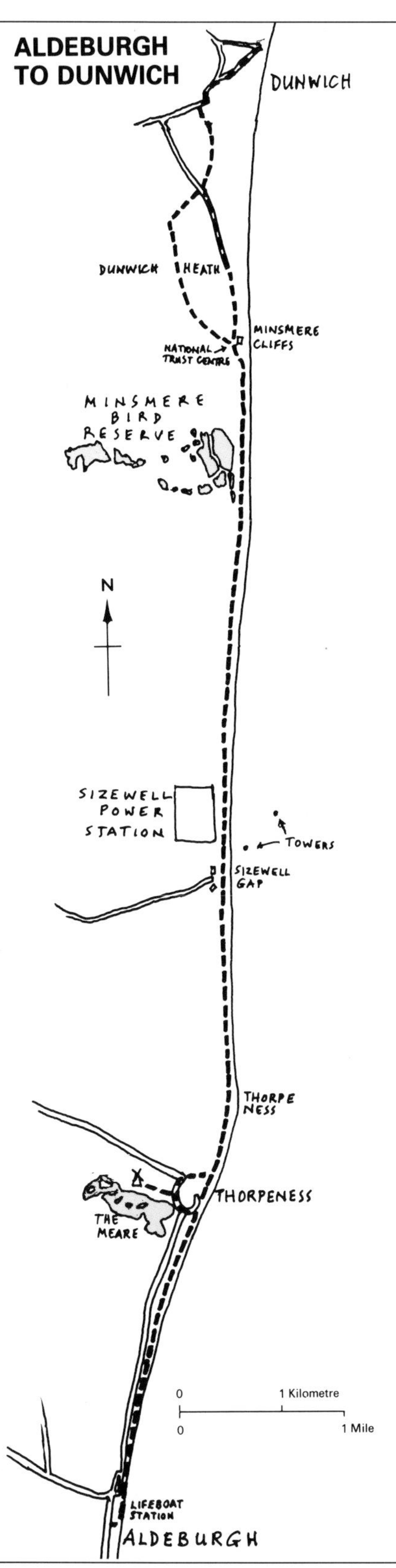

From the National Trust car park on crumbling Minsmere Cliffs, a fine retrospective panorama opens up over the Minsmere wetlands. An inscribed pillar, unveiled in August 1988 by the Admiral of the Fleet Lord Lewin of Greenwich, commemorates the lighting of beacons here to warn of the Spanish Armada's approach 400 years ago.

The most direct onward route follows the clifftops then the ramped road past a camping and caravan site, 500m beyond which a woodland footpath strikes off right, towards the centre of Dunwich. However, there is much to recommend following a waymarked trail north-west from the National Trust Information Centre by a row of renovated cottages (vacated by the Coastguard Service in 1909 and now owned by the NT). It crosses Dunwich Heath, veering right (north-east) at a junction near trees and reaches the same woodland path to Dunwich mentioned above. During World War I the heath was used as an army training area and as the site for a radar station in World War II. Clothed with bracken, heather, gorse and silver birch, it provides habitats for a wide variety of flora and fauna.

Lanes lead through Dunwich village to the seafront. Here, gazing eastwards from the little fishing shacks on the wave-washed shore beneath unstable brown and orange cliffs, it is sobering to reflect that in Roman times the sea would have been over a mile distant. Throughout recent centuries, erosion has been occurring at a rate of 1m per year so it will come as no surprise to learn that there is more of Dunwich on the seabed than above!

It is an extraordinary story of man's helplessness against the forces of nature. At the Domesday Survey in 1086, Dunwich possessed 3 churches and some 5000 inhabitants. Brushwood anchored to the shingle foreshore with heavy rocks each autumn protected this developing river-mouth port from serious erosion and by the mid-thirteenth century the town, as capital of Suffolk, prospered. A harbinger of its ultimate fate came in 1286 when a severe storm washed away land and properties; sand and mud were deposited in the river channel, hampering shipping. In January 1326, another raging storm completely blocked the river-mouth, diverting it north. Faced with the crippling loss of dwellings, churches, windmills and trade, people began moving away so that by 1602, Dunwich was less than a quarter its original size.

Periodic devastation continued, sea walls being breached and marshland inundated. Roads became undermined and the depopulated town lost its MP in 1832; by 1920 the last remaining church—All Saints—slipped to destruction. Only the ruins of Greyfriars Priory and those of the leper chapel beside the Victorian St James Church recall Dunwich's lost past. For a evocative glimpse of the town's history, visit the excellent little museum in St James Street.

A final retrospective view along the beach at Dunwich.

WALK 23: *North Norfolk — Sheringham to Burnham Overy Staithe*

Maps: OS Landranger Sheets 133 (North East Norfolk) and 132 (North West Norfolk). **Start:** Sheringham seafront. **Finish:** Burnham Overy Staithe. **Distance:** 23 miles (38km)—2 days suggested. **Access:** Both Sheringham and Burnham Overy Staithe lie on the A149 coast road west of Cromer. Nearest railway station—Cromer. (Sheringham is on the steam-hauled North Norfolk Railway). **Type of Walking:** Undulating cliffs to begin with, then pebbles (can be tiring) and well-defined paths beside saltmarsh and creeks on sea defence embankments. Very few gradients. **Features of Interest:** Beach angling; Bird Sanctuary at Cley Eye/Blakeney; Blakeney Point (boat trips); extensive tidal saltmarsh; the working port of Wells-next-the-Sea; Holkham Gap (and nearby Holkham Hall); vast, open coastal views throughout, specially interesting to lovers of boats, birdlife and angling. The entire walk is through an Area of Outstanding Natural Beauty. **Accommodation:** Available at Sheringham, Wells-next-the-Sea and to a lesser extent at intervening villages along the coast. Youth hostel at Sheringham and Hunstanton.

Pebbles, Dunes, Saltmarsh and Creekside Harbours

No map of the Norfolk coast will prepare you for its intoxicating qualities of space and distance. Walkers experience these extended horizons, these vanishing points of linear perspective, these visual infinities, in ways which are unique to them: journeying on foot frees the mind and senses through its deliberate, slow rhythms and unhurried progress.

It may be necessary for hill walkers to make a mental adjustment, to set the senses for more subtle, intimate changes in their surroundings, unfolding in their own time. Superficially, one saltmarsh, tidal creek or pebble ridge may

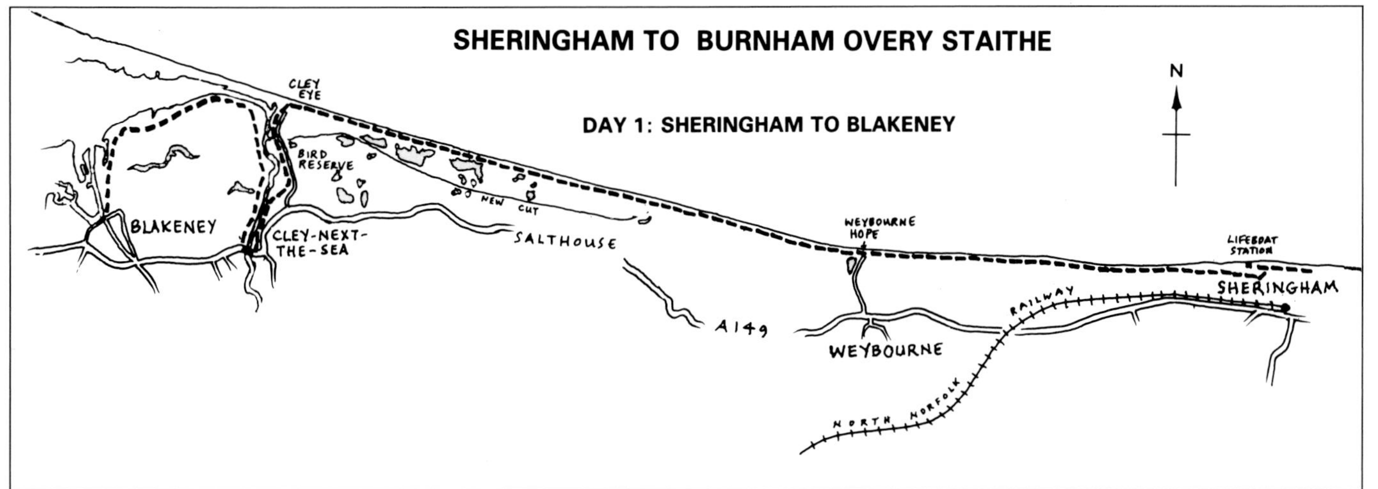

Facing page: ***The prospect ahead from Sheringham's lifeboat station.***

resemble the next (much as books or paintings are not differentiated primarily by their outward shape), but for the observant traveller the North Norfolk coast reveals a wealth of detail.

Impressions of a walk will vary according to season and weather but cannot fail to include the wild plants of sand dune, shingle and saltmarsh, glimpses of windmills and pantiled roofs, clattering footfalls on pebble beaches and the repetitive motif of small boats moored to quaysides or plying the tidal channels. In stormy conditions, the East Coast's inherent vulnerability to the sea is keenly felt.

Day 1: Sheringham to Blakeney ($10\frac{1}{2}$ miles/17km)

Sheringham, a bustling little resort with a clock-towered High street, grew from humble fishing village origins when the railway arrived in 1887. There is good sea bathing off its groyned beach during the summer, but the coast is a treacherous one and periodically threatens the heavily concreted seafront. Sheringham's lifeboat is housed at the western end of the pedestrian promenade—a good place from which to take your bearings and gaze past eroding ochre cliffs towards the low, pale line of Blakeney Point

The walk starts on clifftops above, heading west past the Coastguard lookout and along the perimeter of golf links. Gently undulating, gorse-fringed fields ensue, never far from the North Norfolk Railway whose steam engines will doubtless bring a tear of nostalgia to the eyes of enthusiasts during summer weekends! Inland lie copses and woodland surrounding Sheringham Hall, renowned for its exotic plants and rhododendrons and before long you will sight the windmill at Weybourne.

Cliffs, as such, finally fizzle out at Weybourne Hope's pebble beach and a conspicuous daymark beacon. There is deep water immediately offshore here and back in 1588 the location was garrisoned against the Spanish fleet, so seriously was the threat of landing taken. As the old rhyme goes:

He who would old England win
Must at Waborne Hoop begin.

Today, sea anglers huddle behind green umbrellas and cast for flounder, bass, whiting and cod.

Beyond a reedy 'mere', the path continues along the crumbling edge of land—hardly cliffs. At one point east of Gramborough Hill the right of way has slipped down onto the beach. Behind the pebble bank stretches a broad corridor of flat marshland grazed by sheep, cattle and horses. Punctuated by lagoons and drained by numerous ditches, it separates coastal roads and villages from the shoreline, providing a haven for bird species. As the pebble bank approaches Cley Eye (always try to walk on the seaward slope to avoid erosion of this vital sea defence), you are skirting above a Norfolk Naturalists' Trust Bird Reserve. Bought in 1926, it was their first acquisition and is complemented by the thatched Visitor Centre just east of Cley-next-the-Sea on the A149. Without interruption, the sloping pebble bank runs on westwards to Blakeney Point, ruler straight.

From the car park and Coastguard lookout (the café sells fresh crab salads!), you veer inland past old tractors and boats along the river embankment to Cley village, in the Middle Ages a thriving fishing port. Keeping seaward of the eighteenth-century windmill (a guesthouse), you reach the High Street, cross the River Glaven on the roadside sluice and turn shorewards along the bank. Opposite Cley Eye, the way swings in a big 180-degree loop to the popular sailing village of Blakeney, passing mud flats and saltings and the distant dune-backed spur of Blakeney Point.

Blakeney harbour, though much silted up since its heyday as a great seaport serving the Crusaders' sailing ships, is served by a navigable channel lined with colourful small craft. Passenger ferries offer trips out to view seabirds, seals and shoreline flora on Blakeney Point during the holiday season. There is a good choice of accommodation, including the harbour-front Blakeney Hotel and a nearby camp site, making this an admirable place at which to overnight.

Day 2: Blakeney to Burnham Overy Staithe (13 miles/21.5km)

From the quay's western end, the coast path stays close to creeks parallel to the A149 past Morston Salt Marshes (National Trust); local boatmen will take you by arrangement out to Blakeney Point from the sandy foreshore here. Crossing the River Stiffkey's mouth, you reach Stiffkey Greens, the path itself threading a sequence of delightful, flowery and sometimes tree-shaded embankments inland of one of Britain's largest surviving natural saltmarshes. Walking through these quiet, elemental spaces, you are treated to some of our country's most unspoiled rural heritage—a quietly exhilarating experience which, on fine sunny days, is little short of idyllic.

Covered diurnally by tides, some plants have developed a tolerance to submersion in sea water. One of the first plants to colonise the mud flats is samphire (or glasswort), gathered locally as a summer vegetable. Other species include eelgrass and enteramorpha, a narrow-fronded green seaweed devoured with relish by overwintering Brent Geese! On higher ground, sea aster and sea lavender thrive, the latter forming a delicate purple carpet in summer. Cockle fishing is virtually finished these days, but some folk still take rake and bucket out on the marshes to collect 'Stewkey Blues', a famous local delicacy. The uninitiated

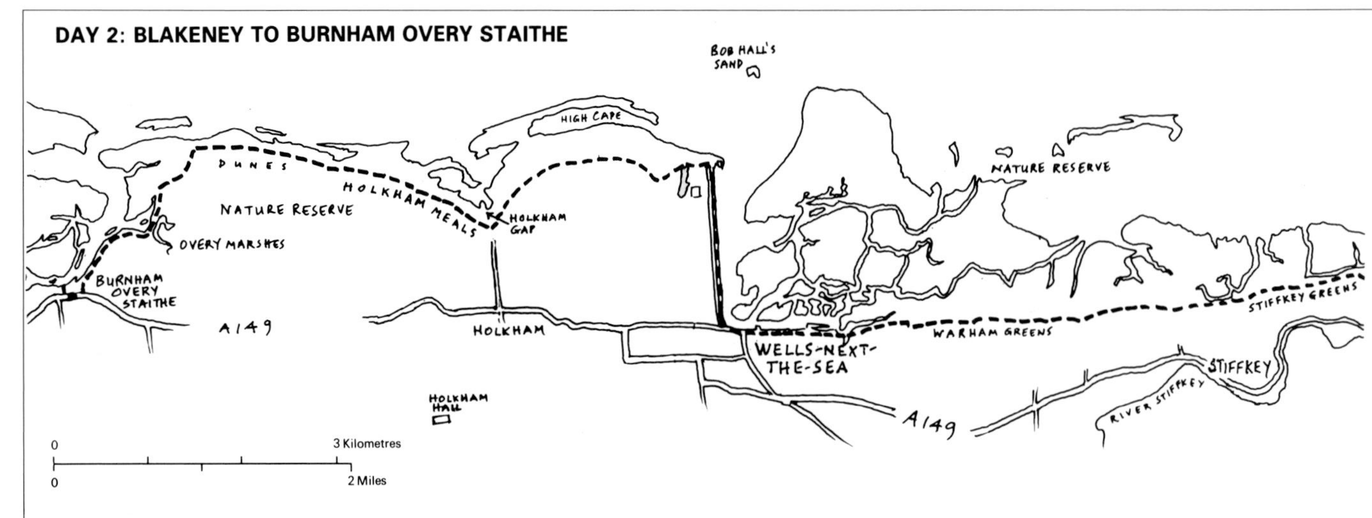

Blakeney harbour.

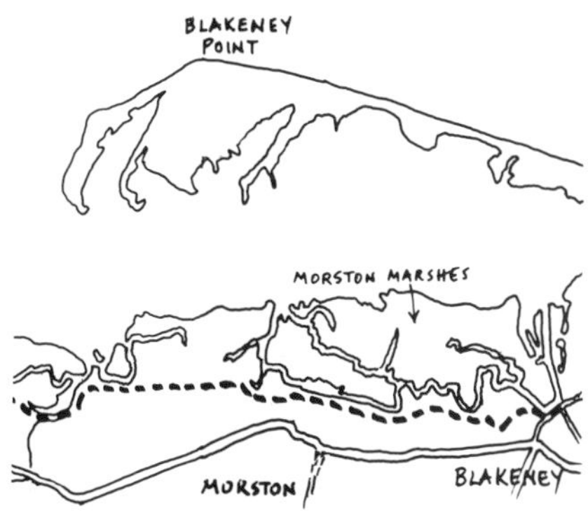

are advised not to stray from paths across this half-land, half-sea, as tidal creeks fill rapidly and can cut off a retreat.

The way heads on due west, skirting Stiffkey village, crossing Warham Greens and approaching Wells-next-the-Sea. Like Cley to the east, Wells now finds itself more than a mile from open water, thanks largely to land reclamation work by the Coke family of Norfolk during the eighteenth and nineteenth centuries. Wells, however, retains a viable harbour—the only one on the North Norfolk coast—used by coasters carrying mainly grain and fertiliser. The port is a modest enclave of industrial activity on a notably unindustrial coast, carrying with it a complement of seafood stalls, amusement arcades, shops, cafés and ships' chandlers. There are old streets too, behind the quayside, but coastal walkers will be pondering the next step: Wells' 'seafront' is a half-hour away on foot along the surfaced riverside embankment (or, for non-purists, by miniature railway in the holiday season!). At the end are a boating lake and refreshment kiosk, car park and camp site.

If a swim is contemplated, take good note of the warning notices—currents out on these wide expanses of sand and mudflats are deceptively strong as an impetuous sea rises and sinks, never resting to catch its breath, its tidal cycles spent sliding from horizon to foreshore and back again. A klaxon is sounded when it is time for those who have ventured out onto Bob Hall's Sand and adjacent dune-edged marshland to return to the mainland and safety.

Although there might be a beachcombing route from the huts and groynes out round High Cape, the coast path turns left along the landward side of Holkham Meals conifer plantation. The scent of pine resin and absence of traffic is reminiscent of parts of France's western seaboard—its *Côtes Sauvages*; here, as there, hardy conifers prevent the sand dunes extending inland.

At Holkham Gap—a 'V' shaped indentation with motor access from the coast road near eighteenth-century Holkham Hall (open to the public)—you swing seaward on a timber walkway. You then keep left, either through the shady plantation itself or along the back of an immense duney foreshore on any of several paths. In fact, firm sands extend almost as far as the eye can see at low water, allowing, with the necessary vigilance, a gloriously unfrequented onward walk.

By keeping to existing tracks through the dunes of Holkham Nature Reserve, or staying on the beach (below high tide line to avoid disturbing nesting terns during May, June and July), you will pick up the sea bank beside the mouth of the River Burn. It takes you straightforwardly in a mile or so the pretty sailing village of Burnham Overy Staithe—reliant on a frequently absentee sea but busy, nonetheless, with small craft.

Positioned on a river whose creeks, tentacle-like, probe the saltings out to Scolt Head Island, yet still connected to the ebb and flow of the open sea, Burnham Overy Staithe encapsulates the very essence of this unique coastline. A plaque on a harbourside house reads: 'Richard Woodget, master of the *Cutty Sark*, lived here 1899-1926', while Nelson's birthplace can be found 2 miles (3km) inland at Burnham Thorpe. Rigging slaps lazily against the masts of dinghies waiting for the tide and, although you can walk west as far as Hunstanton, there is surely no better place to call a halt than here.

The woodland path at Holkham Meals.

WALK 24: *Humberside — Flamborough Head*

Map: OS Landranger Sheet 101—Scarborough, Bridlington and area. **Start and Finish:** Danes Dyke car park (being circular, the walk can be started from any convenient point). **Distance:** 9 miles (14.5km)—allow 4 hours. **Access:** Danes Dyke car park is signposted south of the B1255 between Bridlington and Flamborough village. Nearest railway station—Bridlington. **Type of Walking:** Good level going on open clifftops with a few sharp gradients through stream valleys, mostly provided with steps. Field paths and a little road walking complete the circuit. **Features of Interest:** Danes Dyke; Flamborough Head lighthouses, old and new; a Heritage Centre; marvellous chalk cliffs, stacks and caves. **Accommodation:** Widely available at Bridlington, also some around Flamborough village. Nearest youth hostel—Scarborough.

Round a Major East Coast Limestone Headland

Flamborough Head juts defiantly into the North Sea, interrupting a largely unbroken sweep of coastline between the Tees and Humber rivers. The prominence of this flat-topped peninsula is all the more surprising when one finds it composed of chalk, usually a soft crumbling rock easily eroded by the sea. However, as so often is the case, limestone provides good walking terrain and the Flamborough Head plateau is no exception.

Gently rolling farmland bisected by lanes and punctuated by copses narrows towards the blunt headland with its conspicuous lighthouse. Some way back, a deep ravine known as Danes Dyke cuts north to south across the promontory—an extraordinary feature marked by a thin line of woodland. Constructed long before the Danes' occupation in the ninth century and even pre-dating the Iron Age (flint arrowheads have been found on the site), this mostly man-made ditch once served as a fortification to defend Flamborough Head against territorial threats from the 'mainland'. A circular nature trail has been established around the southern end, taking walkers through dense woodland and into the dyke itself. It is from the car park here that the walk begins.

By following the beach path, climbing steps on the left and forking seawards, we find ourselves out on low chalk cliffs with magnificent views back along the great arc of Bridlington Bay. The first of several stream valleys ('wykes') on this walk is soon encountered—unexpected little down-and-ups equipped with steps and

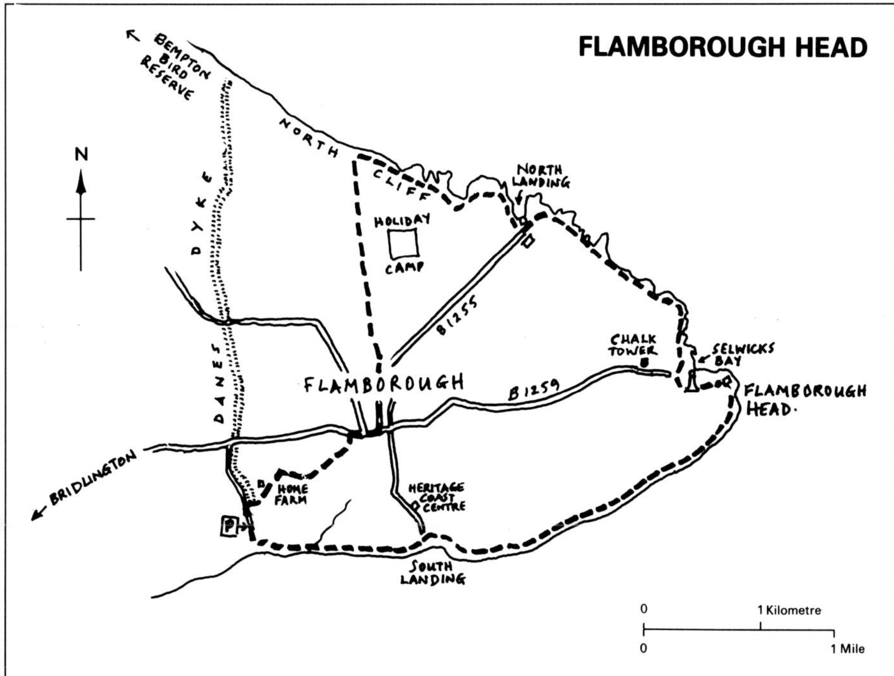

Facing page: ***The bold thrust of cliffs at Selwicks Bay.***

virtually invisible until you are upon them. Beyond an old wartime pillbox the ground rises to Beacon Hill and passes a path to nearby Flamborough village; the lighthouse on Flamborough Head, already visible, is still a good hour's hike away. Before long the path reaches South Landing—a few fishing boats, an emergency lifebelt and a beach of brilliant white pebbles held in a shallow cove.

When fishing was still profitable, canny Flamborough fishermen would station their 'cobles' (boats of the east coast with high, sharp prows and built wide amidships on the old Viking pattern to deal with heavy seas) at both South Landing and North Landing across the peninsula, enabling them to put to sea whichever direction wind and weather were coming from. A little way up the lane inland stands a new Heritage Centre and car park—well worth a short detour during the holiday season when it is open.

Erosion has closed the old cliff edge path out of South Landing and new steps have been provided a short distance back from the beach. At the top we fork right and resume glorious open walking between undulating fields and a sheer drop to the sea. Two more stream gullies are crossed and within a mile, just after a path to Lighthouse Road, there is a 'Dangerous Cliffs' sign. This is not, however, a harbinger of risk to life and limb but rather a reminder that the interface between land and sea is a shifting, unstable one, subject to constant erosion or deposition. In fact, with normal care the path leads safely on and one's sense of anticipation at reaching the headland tip is heightened. Fields end and a grassy track makes a beeline for the lighthouse building, though paths continue round above High Stacks to the Fog Signal Station road.

Flamborough Head's original octagonal lighthouse—England's oldest surviving example—dates from 1674 and can be seen rising above rooftops 400m or so inland to the north-east. This so-called Chalk Tower was built for Sir John Clayton, who leased the site for £70 a year, and was coal fired. It was superseded in 1806 by the present structure, designed and built without recourse to scaffolding in five months by John Matson of Bridlington and now controlled by Trinity House. Fog is a serious hazard to shipping, nowhere more so than on this coast which experiences the notorious 'roak' or sea mist. A cannon shot Fog Signal was established in 1859, replaced in 1877 by the firing of rockets and in 1913 by a 'bull horn' siren. Since 1985, piercing electronic 'bleeps' penetrate the gloom and assail the eardrums of passing walkers!

A large café behind the lighthouse will yield welcome refreshment before continuing along the coast path above Selwicks (pronounced 'Silex') Bay. This dramatic indentation, backed by grassy slopes and a low-tide beach, reveals for the first time on this walk the majestic rock architecture that characterises Flamborough Head. If the tide is right, (and this is no place to get cut off!) an entertaining hour can be spent descending the footpath and exploring foreshore chalk stacks, blowholes, boulders, rock pools and caves beneath beetling cliffs.

Our onward way skirts the edge of golf links above chalk promontories with names like Stottle Bank Nook and Cradle Head and heads straight for North Landing. Set back in a deep, cliff-girt cove, altogether more picturesque than South Landing, it is, alas, also more commercialised. A vast café/restaurant and car park serve the needs of summer trippers, but a more serious note is struck by the presence of Flamborough lifeboat station. Once again, the scene is enlivened by brightly painted fishing cobles and there are caves to enter at low water, the best being Robin Lythes cave on the east side of the beach.

By keeping to the waymarked path seaward of the car park, a deep stream valley is soon negotiated and signs warn of dangerously eroding cliffs. There are, indeed, some evil looking sections where the path hugs an unstable edge above precipitous drops, but it is always possible to keep well back where necessary. Coming round to a bungalow, there are magnificent views ahead of North and Bempton cliffs, a forbidding vertical wall 2 miles (3km) long and over 300ft (100m) high.

We soon meet a motorable track leading from the B1255 and find ourselves just up from the little beach at Thornwick Bay. This is yet another location where access to the foreshore is possible in favourable conditions. Walking round the back of the bay, we descend into the last of the stream valleys, climb out and continue up the boundary of two fields on North Cliff to a stile.

Whilst it is possible to extend the walk along Bempton Cliffs, site of an important RSPB reserve, and thence into Filey Bay, a return to our starting point becomes increasingly problematic. Unfortunately there is no public right of way along Danes Dyke—surely the most elegant of lines for a circuit of Flamborough Head—so we must turn left at our stile on North Cliff and follow three field edges past a holiday camp to Flamborough village. The church stands due south and here we turn right on a pavement alongside the B1255 Bridlington road. A left turn into Water Lane leads to a kissing gate and a field path south-west towards Maidlands Plantation. A short way along the exit drive beyond Home Farm lies the car park and the conclusion of this circular walk.

WALK 25: *Yorkshire — Saltburn-by-the-Sea to Whitby*

Map: OS Landranger Sheet 94. **Start:** Ship Inn, Saltburn-by-the-Sea. **Finish:** Whitby harbour. **Distance:** 19 miles (31km)—a long day's hike which could be split by staying overnight at Staithes or Runswick Bay. **Access:** Saltburn lies on the A174 east of Middlesbrough. Whitby is reached off the A171 between Guisborough and Scarborough. Nearest railway stations—Saltburn and Whitby. **Type of Walking:** A clear path along rugged, eroding cliffs with some substantial ascents. Some beach walking and a little road work at high tides. **Features of Interest:** Sites of Roman Signal Stations; derelict nineteenth-century ironstone harbours; numerous old jet, alum and ironstone workings; picturesque fishing villages; dramatic marine erosion and eastern England's highest cliff; Whitby town and harbour; Captain Cook associations at Staithes and Whitby. **Accommodation:** Readily available along the coast. Youth hostels at Saltburn and Whitby.

Captain Cook Country

It has always struck me that what the Yorkshire coast may lack by comparison with the balmier south and west of Britain is more than compensated for by a different, more forceful order of beauty. In places, the alum, jet and ironstone industries have left their mark and what remains is not always pretty to look at. Yet for the visitor, particularly the walker, such relics underscore the essential paradox between current attitudes towards the environment and the needs of those who lived in less affluent times to wrest a living from mineral deposits. Though diminished, this industrial tradition lives on in the Skinningrove steel works and the potash mine at Boulby, but the most profound influence on settlements here has been exerted by the bullying North Sea. Bitter east

Facing page: ***Skinningrove beach, looking south to Boulby Cliff.***

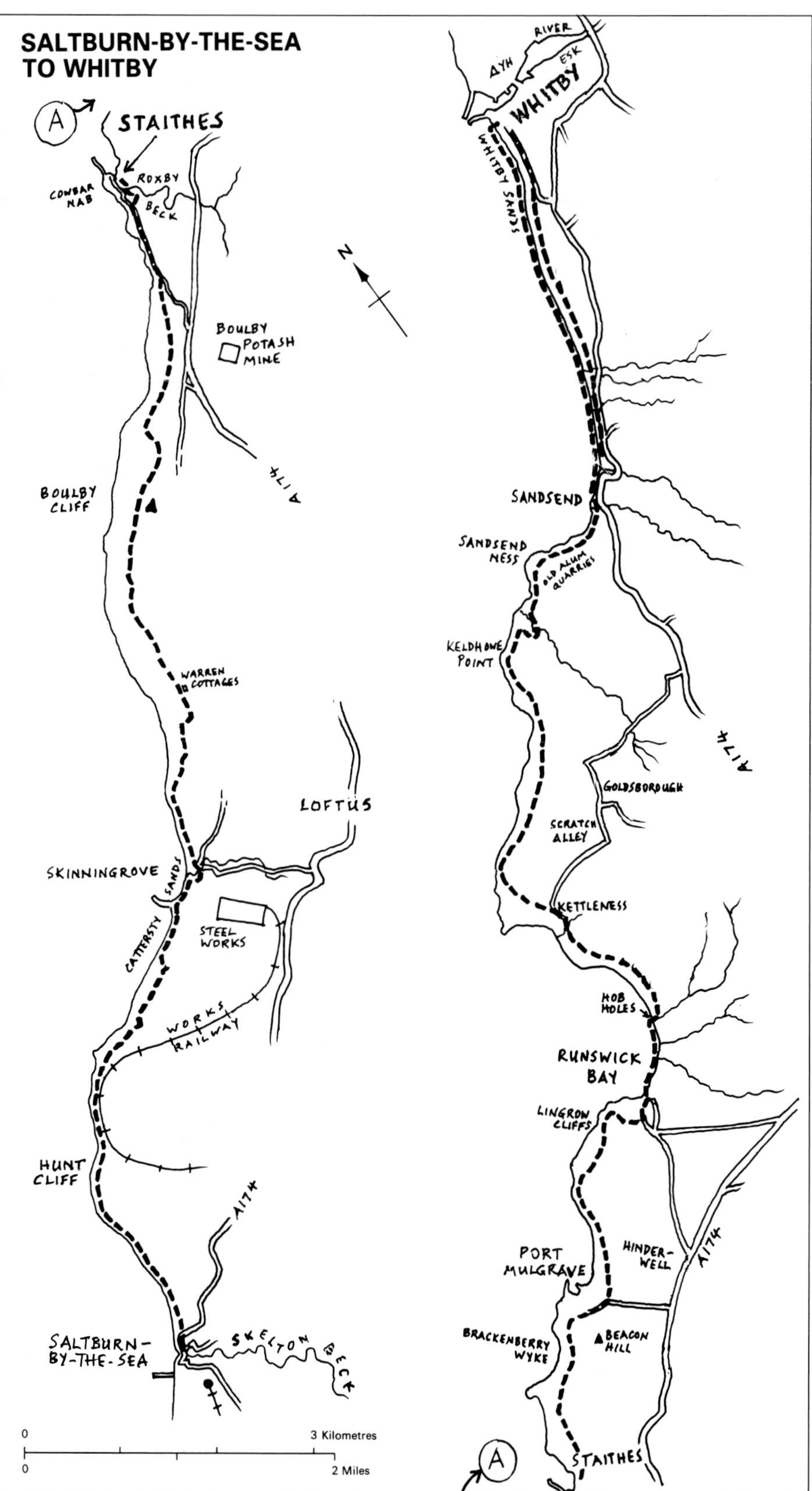

winds, atrocious sea conditions and the notorious 'roak' sea fog make this a treacherous coastline for shipping. The proud, sad records of lifeboats from Redcar south to Bridlington and the stoic resilience shown by fishing communities who have suffered the loss of their menfolk down the centuries bear witness to the sea's dominating presence.

Despite boasting some of England's highest cliffs, much of this coast is composed of soft shales and boulder clay and marine erosion is occurring at an alarming rate. Indeed, the sea's incessant onslaught and its capacity to strip the land to its geological underclothes, so to speak, are a perfect foil for the sanctuaries of town and hamlet visited on this walk. It may be perverse of me to suggest that calm, sunny weather will mask the coast's true character, but there is a real sense in which lowering skies and an angry sea heighten one's appreciation of these great sombre cliffs and rock scarred foreshores. One April I walked from Saltburn to Whitby amid violent squalls. Keeping a steady course was practically impossible, but the wind was mercifully at my back. Streamers of snow swept inland above a maelstrom of spuming surf, the entire landscape animated with Turneresque curtains of vapour. However agreeable, no fine day can compare with such elemental drama or leave so enduring a memory.

Saltburn-by-the-Sea, it must be said, has seen better days. Until 1850 when the railway came, it was no more than a fishing hamlet clustered around the Ship Inn beside Skelton Beck. Railway transport brought prosperity to Redcar, Marske and Saltburn and their firm, flat sands were used for motor racing in the early days of the sport. Saltburn's grand houses ranged above terraced paths in the steep little Skelton valley reflect its Victorian heyday as a select resort, but fashions change and the town's proximity to an industrially expanding Teesside contributed to its decline. Today it has a faded, rather down-at-heel charm and its stub of a pier, once thronged with paddle-steamer trippers, is popular with anglers.

The walk begins from behind the Ship Inn at Old Saltburn (the seaward path has disappeared) where colourful fishing cobles are drawn up on the shingle bank before it gives way to rock scars beneath Hunt Cliff. Steps take you up to clifftop level at over 360ft (110m) and past the site of a Roman Signal Station, one of a series down this coast. Excavations in 1923 unearthed the incomplete skeletons of 14 people thought to have been murdered by raiding Picts or Saxons during the Roman withdrawal from Britain. For a short distance the path follows the cinder bed of a railway track then skirts pasture and fields before dropping through boot-clogging slag and boulder clay to Cattersty Sands.

Fishing cobles moored in Roxby Beck, Staithes.

Skinningrove's old jetty has been disembowelled by waves. It still protects the little bay, but inconsequentially, for Skinningrove, despite some modern housing, is an industrial ghost. Caught between gaunt cliffs, it exudes impoverishment and an aftertaste of soiled shabbiness from its labouring origins. Skinningrove's ironstone seam was one of the first to be mined during the mid-1800s boom which was centred inland at Rosedale. Terraced dwellings in which miners were housed and the steel works at the valley head where the old mines were located seem blatantly misplaced on this Heritage Coast, but it must be remembered that the iron industry offered relative wealth to people whose only source of income would otherwise have been agriculture or fishing. Skinningrove developed because ore, coal and a moderately sheltered harbour allowed profitable production to take place—at least until the first decades of this century when higher quality imports and the effects of the General Strike sounded the industry's death knell.

You cross the stream outlet, permanently stained from iron-ore waste, and pass fishing cobles and jumbled rows of pigeon lofts before climbing to the cliff edge path outside field fences round Warsett Hill. Below, the cliffs behind Hummersea Scar saw much activity between the seventeenth and nineteenth centuries as the mining and purification of alum reached its zenith. Alum was employed as a fixing agent for textile dyes and to cure animal hides and size paper; it was later produced more economically from coal shales treated with sulphuric acid.

At Snilah Ponds, the way ducks inland to a field road through Warren Cottages farmstead. You will already be feeling the pull of gravity and a steady ascent ensues to Boulby Cliff, at 666ft (203m) the highest on England's eastern seaboard. These are not cliffs in the mould of a Beachy Head or a Land's End whose steep rock faces plummet to the sea. Boulby's summit is less determinate, set back above sprawling undercliffs riddled with alum, jet and ironstone mining levels. Dropping in stages reminiscent of moorland, the path is exhilarating and (excepting the potash mine to the right of the coast road) provides wonderful views ahead of indented cliffs and a tableland of green fields.

Staithes is approached by a short road walk along Cowbar Lane and a descent into the gorge of Roxby Beck, from where you can enjoy a classic panorama over the intimate huddle of tall houses. The old village, protected by Cowbar Nab headland, has retained much of its original character as an important fishing harbour. Three hundred local men and women were once employed in the industry and after 1885 fish was distributed to cities by train. Steam trawlers from larger ports eventually monopolised catches and the 120 cobles based at Staithes dwindled to the handful we see today, though crab and lobster fishing continues the seafaring tradition.

If there is time to spare (you may even consider overnighting here), be sure to explore the cobbled streets and alleyways and to cross the beck footbridge where the cobles are moored. Round on the seafront itself, houses were periodically damaged or washed away by storm waves until the two breakwaters were constructed: there are plans to extend the height of the northern one, as it only partially breaks heavy seas. The Cod and Lobster Inn forms a focal point above the small sandy beach and one can imagine that little has changed since 1744 when, as a lad, James Cook served his apprenticeship to William Sanderson, a haberdasher here. Eighteen months later he would answer the call of the sea to begin an illustrious career as a Royal Navy navigator and explorer of new lands.

Immediately past the Cod and Lobster, you turn right up a cul-de-sac, past Captain Cook's cottage, climb steps and turn left in a gully onto the cliff path (waymarked Cleveland Way, of which this walk is a part). Beyond modern farm buildings, the way is seen clearly ahead, crossing stiles through fields some distance from the cliff edge and rising steeply over pasture onto Beacon Hill. At over 325ft (99m) above sea level, the next stretch offers magnificent views of the vast Lias Limestone 'scars' of Brackenberry Wyke, uncovered at low tide on the shore below.

In no time at all the path leads out to houses and the road end at Port Mulgrave. The little harbour is hopelessly choked with mud and stones, its jetty half derelict, yet until the ironstone mine at nearby Dalehouse closed in the 1920s, ore was carried from the workings by rope-hauled railway wagons through a mile-long tunnel and shipped to the furnaces of Jarrow.

From the Ship Inn you resume clifftop walking along the edges of arable fields, negotiating a slippery little gully at Rosedale Wyke. Old fencing below Lingrow Cliffs provides a graphic reminder of this coast's propensity for slipping into the sea! Indeed, the entire original village of Runswick disappeared one fateful night in 1664. Being careful to turn right inland at a stile, you soon reach the Runswick Bay Hotel and drop down the lane to Runswick Bay village.

Like most similar communities, the village's fortunes hung on fishing, its decline mirroring that of nearby Staithes. Smuggling and salvage from shipwrecks yielded another source of income, along with the Kettleness alum quarries and Grinkle ironstone mines, but it was the railway that heralded real change. New houses were built above the bay, locals moved away, shops closed and by the 1950s Runswick Bay had become the holiday settlement it is today. Although renovated and modernised, many original buildings remain and are worth looking at.

At high tide, especially in rough weather, the

Whitby harbour from the Old Town.

onward route becomes distinctly problematic and there is really no alternative but to wait for a clearance at the top of the sands. I once set out determined to force a way through the dense scrub and thorn bushes and soon found myself among derelict holiday chalets. Their foundations lay akimbo, little garden plots choked with brambles, a lawn mower abandoned and kitchen implements strewn around, for all the world like some terrestrial *Marie Celeste*. Twenty years ago, the chalets were occupied, cared for, supplied with water and connected by neat pathways, but subsidence has put an end to all that. Scrambling along the shoreline bank in the face of huge waves, I managed to locate an overgrown track up into fields and emerged thankfully onto the dismantled trackbed of the old Yorkshire coast railway. None of this was on public rights of way and underlines the difficulties of the landslipped terrain behind the bay.

From the rows of brightly coloured cobles hauled up by tractor onto hard standing by the car park, you walk along the sands past the Sailing Club to the foot of cliffs. Though rather silted up, Hob Holes can still be seen to the right. 'Hobs', or goblins, that haunted the Yorkshire moors and dales feature in many legends. Runswick's hob was reputed to cure whooping cough, so ailing children were taken to the cave and their mothers would call out

Hob—hole Hob!
My bairn's getten't kink-cough:
Tak't off! Tak't off!

Beyond Hob Holes you climb a distinctive stream valley, crossing its bed by footbridge and mounting steps on a stiff ascent to Kettleness. This cluster of redbrick houses is associated with the disused coastal railway, while 800m to the south-east rises a grassy mound, the site of Scratch Alley Roman Signal Station. Views from here are commanding enough, but during its operational period in the fourth century warning of possible invasion from the North Sea, the station comprised a high timber or stone lookout tower. It is one of a chain stretching from Hunt Cliff near Saltburn, already encountered on this walk, to Filey Brigg south of Scarborough.

Shadowing the old railway track until it plunges into a tunnel, the coast path undulates above rugged cliffs and swings south-east round Keldhowe Point, a far more extensive promontory before being seriously undermined by jet workings in the nineteenth century when Whitby jet ornaments and jewellery were in great demand. Once past the railway tunnel portal, you are walking the trackbed again through the remains of large alum quarries at Deep Grove and Ness End. Wildlife has recolonised the quarries and railway cutting; among birds seen here are woodcocks, snipes, sparrowhawks and green woodpeckers, while ponds, marshy areas and adjacent woodland provide diverse habitats for a wide range of plants and insects. (For more information about this fascinating location and the old alum industry, see the North York Moors National Park booklet—*Sandsend Trail*). From Sandsend itself, the stark ochre headland of Sandsend Ness, hewn into by 300 years of man's labouring, reveals something of its geological structure—a complex series of shales overlying jet rock and capped by boulder clay from the last Ice Age.

I hope you arrive here at a low or falling tide, since the final 2 miles (3km) to Whitby are far more pleasantly accomplished by walking along the sands than near the A174! The former route also reveals more signs of the sea's relentless power in the form of numerous landslips and broken retaining walls. The roar of surf will ring in your ears and boots will be encrusted with salt, but there is no finer way to enter Whitby, a vigorous Yorkshire town and historic port at the mouth of the River Esk. Amusement arcades, ice creams, candy floss and fish and chips there may be in abundance, but one is never left in any doubt as to the town's auspicious heritage and seafaring heart. It is a place I never tire of visiting, but doing it full justice lies outside the scope of this book. Make a point of seeing the harbour and fish quay, the great breakwater piers and lifeboat station, the east bank old town beneath the abbey ruins, the Pannet Park Museum and the little gallery of Frank Meadow Sutcliffe's century-old photographs of the Whitby area and its people.

WALK 26: *Northumbria — Bamburgh to Craster*

Maps: OS Landranger Sheets 75 (Berwick-upon-Tweed) and 81 (Alnwick, Morpeth and area). **Start:** Bamburgh. **Finish:** Craster. **Distance:** 14 miles (22.5km). **Access:** Bamburgh is reached on the B1341/2 east of the A1. Nearest railway station—Chathill. Craster lies north-east of Alnwick on the B1340 then country lanes. Nearest railway station—Alnmouth. **Type of Walking:** Dunes and sandy beaches, low clifftops and a little road walking. Few gradients of any consequence. **Features of Interest:** Bamburgh Castle and Grace Darling Museum; boat trips to the Farne Islands from Seahouses; Beadnell harbour and old lime kilns; Football Hole; Embleton Bay; Dunstanburgh Castle; Craster harbour; beautiful, unspoiled sandy bays and rocky foreshore throughout. **Accommodation:** Available in varying degrees at Bamburgh, Seahouses, Beadnell and Craster. Several camping/caravan sites on or near the coast.

Castles and Harbours on a Wild, Open Shore

To the first-time visitor, Northumbria seems a vast county. Within its rolling, agricultural horizons, its empty switchback roads, its castles and woodlands, it is easy to find echoes of Normandy. The Northumbria coast, too, spreads its dunes, pale sandy beaches and stony foreshore over apparently limitless miles.

In many places, offshore rocks are revealed by low tide—earth's bare floor running out beneath the waves and underpinning the land. Reefs help dissipate the destructive power of North Sea storms but in rough weather surf and salt spray roll intimidatingly against this low shoreline whose harbour villages have been hardened by centuries of exposure to the elements.

Hadrian's Wall and Northumbria's many castles bear witness to the area's embroilment in historical conflicts between England and Scotland, north and south. Perched dramatically on outcrops of the Great Whin Sill, one of several basalt intrusions running across northern England, coastal castles here are conspicuous features in a horizontal landscape. Tyneside's industry may lie a mere 30 miles (48km) to the south, but Northumbria's wide bays and clear sea bear no obvious signs of its proximity. Indeed, there is a greater sense of spaciousness and unsullied natural beauty here than the rest of England prepares you for: somehow the scale of the coast is grander, more expansive.

Appropriately for a region so steeped in history, this walk begins and ends near great

Facing page: **Looking back to Football Hole from Newton Point.**

Top left: **Beadnell harbour.**

Top right: **Many visitors take a boat trip out to the Farne Islands, visible clearly from Seahouses.**

Bottom left: **Dunstanburgh Castle's Lilburn Tower stands high on an outcrop of the Whin Sill.**

Bottom right: **Craster enjoys a wide reputation for its delicious seafood.**

castles. Between them unfolds a sequence of dune-backed sands, rocky promontories, harbours and low, grassy cliffs. It is perfect golfing country and links occupy several sections of the immediate hinterland.

Bamburgh village, a delightful cluster of eighteenth-century cottages, tasteful shops, a few hotels and refreshment places, is utterly dominated by its castle which stands to seaward on an outcrop of the Whin Sill. Romantic and imposing, the castle monopolises your attention on arrival, but Bamburgh itself is worthy of a little exploration before setting off. Of particular interest is the Grace Darling Museum and, opposite, her memorial in thirteenth-century St Aidan churchyard.

The name Grace Darling became synonymous with bravery at sea after she and her father William Longstone, lighthousekeeper on Farne Island, rowed a coble out to the foundering steamship *Forfarshire* during a violent storm in September 1838. Nine survivors were rescued and the Darlings became national heroes, the Royal National Lifeboat Institute awarding them its silver medal.

The walk begins down towards the castle, where you turn left and cross a recreation field to its far right corner near a pavilion. Here, close under the sheer 130ft (40m) rocky base of Bamburgh Castle, overhung with foliage and soaring to pink sandstone walls, the path dives round left and leads through dunes to the beach.

Such vast sands, where sea and dunes meet in distant, glittering perspective, are more characteristic of the French coast than Britain's. You might encounter galloping horses and a scattering of fellow humans, but walk south for a while and you will probably be alone. From this angle Bamburgh Castle resembles a small fortified city. Its position is virtually impregnable and occupation is thought to date back to Roman times.

The complex took its name from Bebba ('Bebban burgh'), wife of Ethelfrith whose grandfather—Ida, King of Northumbria—constructed the original timber fortress in AD 547. Twice stormed and pillaged by the Danes in the tenth century, the castle went into decline until eventually rebuilt by Henry I who added the massive stone keep. In royal hands it played an active part in the border wars, though of less strategic importance than nearby Alnwick Castle, and in the seventeenth century passed from James I to the Forster family. Through reckless extravagance they ultimately faced bankruptcy and were forced to sell their assets, Bamburgh Castle being purchased in 1704 by Lord Crewe, Bishop of Durham; restoration began and he established a trust so that work could continue after his death.

By the late 1800s, objections were being voiced at the castle's use as a girls' school: drainpipes, smoke-cowls and artificial battlements detracted from the building's historical dignity. Soon it was acquired by Lord Armstrong and restored at great expense, though much of its architectural authenticity was lost during rebuilding under the personal whims of this Tyneside inventor. Today divided into apartments, the castle is nevertheless open to visitors and contains much of interest, including an old 150ft (46m) well and the massive original keep wall up to 11ft (3.5m) thick. Views are tremendous.

If the tide is high, paths meander through dunes to the south. The normal beach route passes Islestone, frequented by shags and cormorants, and crosses Greenhill Rocks. Out to sea lie the Farne Islands, of which more when we reach Seahouses. Brock Burn is usually shallow enough, but if full you can dodge in to the coast road at Monks House. Otherwise the walking continues seaward of St Aidan's Dunes until, approaching the first buildings of Seahouses and before the foreshore becomes

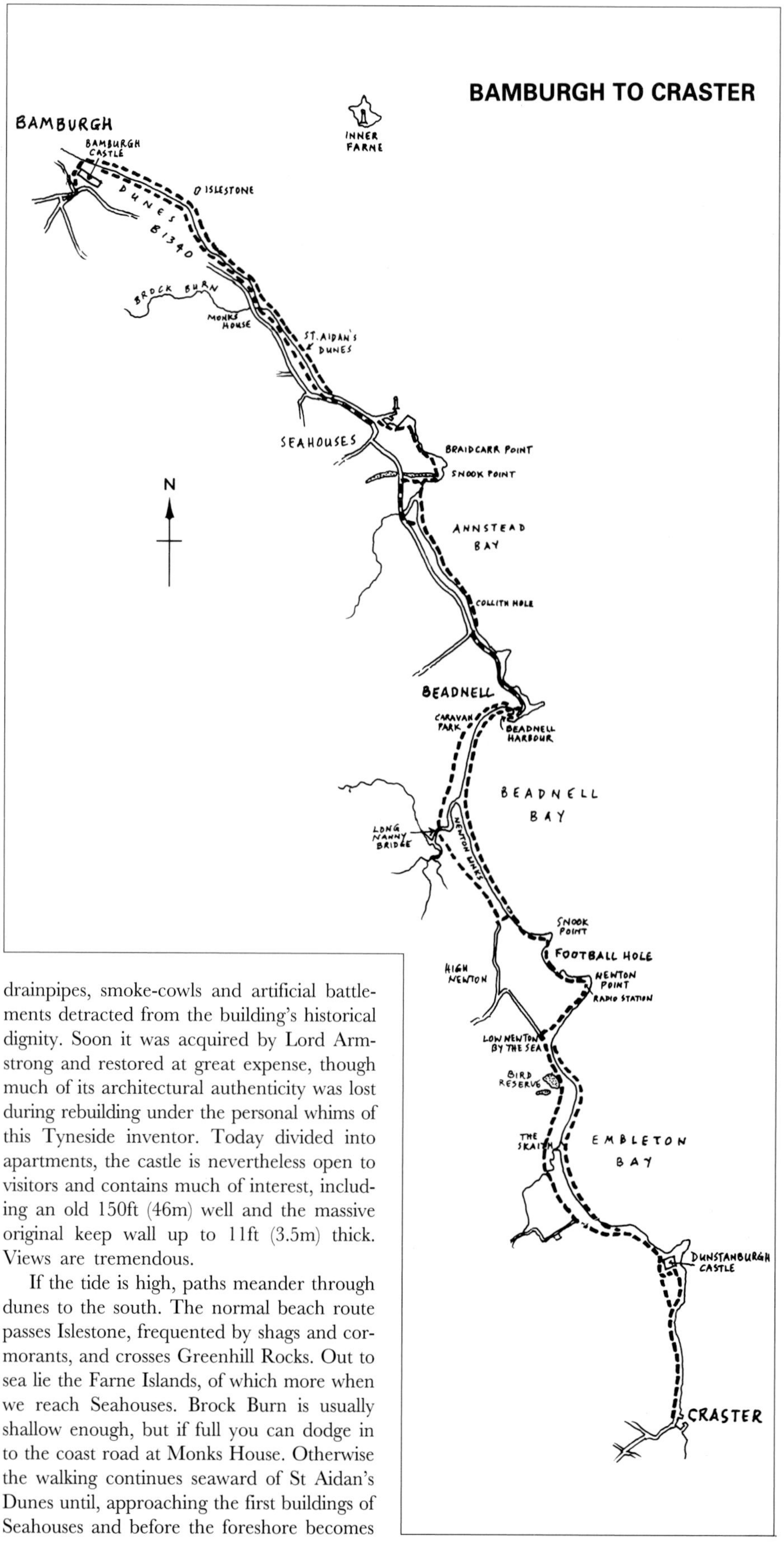

BAMBURGH TO CRASTER

rocky, you turn right beside the road to enter the village.

Rather unfairly decried by some as vulgar, Seahouses does, at least, have a living heart. Fish and chips, ice cream and amusement arcades there may be, not to mention coach loads of trippers, but this is where you jump on a boat for the Farne Islands and no-one will deny the memorable experiences such trips provide for everyone who takes them.

Resistant to marine erosion, the Great Whin Sill asserts itself to the east as this group of low islands covering some $7\frac{1}{2}$ square miles (12 square km) offshore. A National Trust Nature Reserve, they are a paradise for sea birds who breed there in vast numbers, and for grey seals too. Landing is allowed on Farne Island (or Inner Farne), largest in the group and associated with St Cuthbert who lived alone here and to whom the fourteenth-century chapel is dedicated.

In all but the worst weather, Seahouses harbour acts as a magnet for visitors. As well as superlative views back to Bamburgh Castle and across to the Farne Islands, there is all the paraphernalia of a working port—fish boxes, crab pots, floats and ropes along the quaysides, nets being mended, boats coming and going and colourful ticket stalls for Farne Island trips.

Onward from the harbour, you skirt the cliff edge at Braidcarr Point, cut across Snook Point and walk along a rib of higher ground between the sea and an old quarry lake. Swinehoe Burn is only safely fordable at low tide; at other times you are advised to detour inland by the lake and over the road bridge. Foreshore rock beds in Annstead Bay are mostly limestone with some coal layers and a dyke of dolomite, the way keeping to the top of this rugged beach past Collith Hole before retreating to the road at Beadnell near a camp site. The village centre lies a little way inland.

The coast road eventually ends at Beadnell Harbour, a tiny anchorage for cobles held between massive masonry piers and protected by rock reefs. Warm-coloured sandstone boulders form fascinating rock pools and Beadnell Bay is a popular location for canoeing, windsurfing, dinghy sailing and sub-aqua diving. Quite unexpectedly, the harbour is backed by a towered and arched fortress-like building of honey-hued stone—in fact, eighteenth-century limekilns matchlessly preserved by the National Trust.

In common with much of this route, best walking is along the beach, here an open, flat seascape punctuated only by dinghy masts and a dark blue farm silo. It seems to me that planning regulations condoning the erection of such obtrusive structures in visually sensitive areas fail to represent the interests of society at large who wish to maintain the integrity of our coastal heritage: the silo, large as a lighthouse but not half as elegant, is visible for miles.

Parallel to the beach should conditions there be unsuitable, a continuation of the roadway through Beadnell Bay Caravan Park will take you over Long Nanny Bridge and on through Newton Links to a National Trust car park at Newton Links House. Here you walk seawards and turn right towards grey-brown rocks which end the magnificent sweep of Beadnell Bay. There is a duney path round Snook Headland with unimpeachable views back to Beadnell Harbour almost 2 miles (3km) away.

Except on the busiest holiday weekends, the delectable sands of Football Hole bear the imprint of sea birds' feet rather than those of humans! Despite its proximity to High and Low Newton, the bay offers a real sense of seclusion and I can only assume that half a mile of walking from the nearest road access is enough to deter the majority of visitors. At low tide, beds of weed-covered rock—pungent to the nostrils—stretch far out to a line of crashing surf.

As you round Newton Point, an extraordinary conjunction of buildings occurs: in the foreground a modern radio station, long and low beneath its aerial tower, and behind it, two miles distant across Embleton bay and six centuries older, the brooding, ragged silhouette of Dunstanburgh Castle.

Friendly cows and columnar cliffs lead on as you swing south-west past rolling hayfields and acres of richly textured, pool dappled rock platforms. Just above these tilted planes of dark limestone, the field path ends at a roadside stile in Low Newton-by-the-Sea. Its pretty grass square is flanked by a pub, small café and low-built fishermen's cottages, while a mixed foreshore of rock and sand offers the best of both worlds to beachgoers.

Already sights will be set on Dunstanburgh Castle, excitingly poised on Whin Sill cliffs at the far end of Embleton Bay. To reach it, you continue south, either on the sands or on a public footpath through dunes past Newton Pool Bird Reserve, summer breeding ground for black-headed gulls. Beyond the last chalets, Embleton Burn has to be negotiated and at high water or after heavy rain you may need to use The Skaith footbridge. Another of the coastline's golf courses extends along to Dunstan Steads and from here the scenery increases in drama by the minute!

To seaward, above a jumble of pale, mottled boulders, rise the cliffs of the Whin Sill. Sheer and fluted, they support a raucous population of sea birds which has turned the rocks white with guano. Standing sentinel high on the grassy outcrop, Lilburn Tower alone betrays the presence of Dunstanburgh Castle from this low angle. Skirting the promontory below John o'Groats Gateway, the path slants up left to enter the main castle ruins; if you are satisfied with distant perspectives, however, keep down over a boggy stretch and ahead past little rocky bluffs towards a gate and fence where the path from Craster comes in.

'Surpassing all other Northumbrian castles in the grandeur of its site, it alone abides as a castle should abide in all the majesty of a shattered ruin' (Freeman). Dunstanburgh Castle covers 10 acres and is administered by English Heritage. Its history begins in 1313 when Thomas, Earl of Lancaster, ordered a castle to be built on this prominent rocky knoll, naturally defended to the north by unassailably steep ground. After the Battle of Boroughbridge seven years later, he was executed for treason and custody of the castle changed several times, John de Lilburn and John o'Gaunt adding a tower and gatehouse respectively. At that time, a small harbour existed just to the south, now a marshy depression.

During the Wars of the Roses the castle changed hands twice but subsequently fell into disuse and in 1550 was described by Sir Robert Bowes as 'in wonderful great decaye'. J M W Turner was to immortalise the great ruin in watercolours some three hundred years later. Being remote from centres of population and a mile from the nearest road, Dunstanburgh Castle remains unspoiled by modern development. It receives a steady flow of pedestrian visitors, however, and its thorough exploration is well worth an hour of anyone's time.

There are no complications in the final leg of this walk. A well-trod path over turf close-cropped by sheep and docile cattle leads for just over a mile above the rocky shoreline to Craster. Inland there is a National Trust Information Centre and a Nature Reserve at the old whinstone quarry, also a car park and tea rooms.

Eyemouth harbour.

WALK 27: *Borders Region — Eyemouth to St Abb's Head*

Maps: OS Landranger Sheet 67—Duns, Dunbar and Eyemouth area. **Start:** Eyemouth harbour. **Finish:** St Abbs, or St Abb's Head. **Distance:** 8 miles (13km). **Access:** Eyemouth lies near the A1107, off the A1 8 miles (13km) north of Berwick-upon-Tweed. St Abbs is at the end of the B6438 a little further north-east. Nearest railway station—Berwick. **Type of Walking:** Undulating cliff tops with moderate gradients; path near the sheer edge in places. A little road walking and some field paths during the circuit of St Abb's Head. **Features of Interest:** Eyemouth Museum, harbour and old town; Coldingham Bay; St Abb's harbour; St Abb's Head National Nature Reserve with seabird colonies, Mire Loch and sensational cliff scenery (binoculars advised for maximum appreciation). **Accommodation:** Available at Eyemouth, Coldingham Bay and St Abbs. Youth hostel at Coldingham.

Fishing Harbours, Spectacular Cliffs and Seabirds Galore!

This is not a route to be hurried, for there is much to see as each new point is reached. Few coastal walks hold such variety and contrasts—from a busy fishing port to holiday beaches and a major east coast headland noted for its seabird populations. Fine weather can be maddeningly elusive in these Scottish reaches of the North Sea, but it will increase your enjoyment, especially of St Abb's Head which is at its best during the seabird breeding season between April and July. On the other hand, there is something to be said for a rough weather encounter with a coast renowned for its savage indifference to man.

Whatever conditions prevail, I suggest starting at Eyemouth Museum and Tourist Information Centre housed in the Auld Kirk, previously Eyemouth's parish church. Not only does it sketch in the life and times of this border region, but there is a moving exhibition based around the Eyemouth Tapestry, a memorial to those lost in the Great East Coast Fishing Disaster of 1881.

No visitor to Eyemouth worth his salt will ignore the hazards faced by fishermen in these often inhospitable waters. For onlookers in fine weather there is a colourful picturesqueness about the quaysides here—a picturesqueness which belies the hard realities of putting to sea, even in these days of radar, sonar and radio. Eyemouth and neighbouring fishing communities will not forget October 14th, 1881. Following an unseasonably poor summer, Britain was hit by a storm of such ferocity that widespread damage was sustained to property as far apart as the Orkneys and the English Channel. Scotland's eastern counties fared worst, but conditions offshore were unimaginable. The great storm and its consequences are indelibly stamped upon the town's history.

Despite an exceptionally low barometer, Eyemouth's fishing fleet had put to sea in calm sunshine that fateful morning. Eight or nine miles (13 to 15km) out they were laying nets when an eerie silence descended, followed by wind which rapidly increased to hurricane strength. Sails were ripped apart, masts demolished and boats overturned but, miraculously, a few craft managed to make harbour. Many sank without trace in the maelstrom while others foundered close to safety in sight of helpless friends and relatives on shore. One hundred and twenty nine Eye

Top: ***The nesting season in full swing at St. Abb's Head.***

Bottom: ***West from Pettico Wick.***

mouth fishermen and 60 more from nearby ports lost their lives in a tragedy which must rank as one of the greatest national disasters of its kind in recent centuries.

If you have time to follow it, Eyemouth's Town Trail will take you past fish smoking sheds (still used daily), the quayside fish market, boatyard, eighteenth-century harbour buildings, narrow streets once used by smugglers, and much besides. Eye Water snakes inland to form the harbour, its entrance modified more than once to improve access for the fishing fleet.

Although pleasure craft come and go during the summer, large ocean-going trawlers and seine-netters dominate the port, festooning quaysides with a purposeful miscellany of nets, ropes, floats and fish boxes. Above the town's grey hilltop houses, not far from the A1 trunk road, fish freezing and canning plants process much of the catch. When the fleet is in, one could spend hours absorbed by sights, sounds and smells against a backdrop of harbour architecture vaguely Flemish in character—the Ship Hotel, the 'Contented Sole', the Mission for Deep Sea Fishermen. Moored in readiness at the port's seaward end, the RNLI's *Eric Seal* provides a constant reminder of the sea's menacing presence.

From rocky promontories east of the harbour entrance, there are views right along the coast to the squat white lighthouse on St Abb's Head, but the walk itself begins from Eyemouth's sea front. Beyond the swimming pool, a path ascends forbidding red cliffs and swings right past a large caravan park to Fort Point. Humps and hollows in the ground are all that remain of the fort itself, built in 1547 at the instigation of the Duke of Somerset, protector to young King Edward of England, but it was demolished 13 years later after seeing various actions between the French, Scots and English. Two cannon and a Coastguard lookout mark the Point, overlooking Eyemouth and the Hurkur Rocks offshore.

Continuing on the coastal path towards the industrial estate, you veer down right then cut across Callercove Point and on along field edges. An inland detour is necessary to negotiate the large, overgrown stream valley at Linkim Shore and in less than a mile you turn west from Yellow Craig headland, dropping down steps to the rock and pebble cove of Buskin Burn. (If sea conditions are unsuitable here, simply continue at clifftop level inland through a small wooded nature reserve to the bridge, here turning right on a lane past the youth hostel to the car park above Coldingham Beach.)

Having crossed Buskin Burn on stone slabs, you take the clear path zig-zagging up to a stile between small hills. A marvellous prospect across Coldingham Bay to St Abbs awaits you and a sandy path leads ahead past timber chalets of dubious vintage to the Beach Café and toilets. Should a high tide prevent you walking along this popular bathing beach—apart from Eyemouth's the only one for miles—go up the access pathway and turn right past houses onto the cliff path. A more pleasant alternative climbs the broad path up vegetated slopes from the far end of the beach.

St Abbs' southernmost buildings have already been in view and in no time at all you are rounding the little headland and arriving at the harbour. Named after a seventh-century monastic settlement established by St Aebbe, daughter of King Edilfred of Northumbria, St Abbs is sheltered by extensive concrete sea walls. They were built during the mid-1800s onto natural foreshore rock formations and enclose two large basins with a slipway and lifeboat station. Fishing operations are modest—mostly inshore for crab and lobster—and the village appealingly sleepy, though in July, during the week-long Herring Queen Festival, fishing vessels bedecked with bunting escort the newly elected Queen from here to Eyemouth.

Guano-smeared cliffs to the north across Starney Bay provide a foretaste of what is to come, for if Eyemouth and Coldingham Bay reflect aspects of man's engagement with the sea, St Abb's Head belongs in no uncertain terms to its extraordinary concentration of wildlife. This 192-acre National Nature Reserve is owned by the National Trust for Scotland who co-manage it with the Scottish Wildlife Trust. Public access, supplemented by a Ranger Service, is year-round and a hilly, single-track lane threads out to the headland where there is parking space for only about 15 cars.

Several options exist for the last leg of this walk, depending mainly on transport arrangements. If at all possible, I recommend making a loop round the headland as described below, finishing at St Abbs village. Indeed, such an excursion would provide an admirable half-day stroll in itself, especially if transient bad weather spoils things on your first visit.

Walking inland on the B6438 towards Coldingham, you will find a signposted path by a wall on the right just past the church. However, a short distance farther on at Northfield Farm—worth detouring to—are the Head Start coffee house and a National Nature Reserve Interpretative Centre. A leaflet issued by the Gordon family who farm St Abb's Head details crops, stock and working methods.

Back at the coastline, you soon enter the Reserve and pass the sheer seabird cliff of White Heugh. Beyond Wuddy Rocks you drop virtually to sea level at Horsecastle Bay where a stile leads behind the steep slopes of Kirk Hill and the Reserve perimeter turns sharp left. Meandering uphill temporarily back from the sea's edge, the coast path brings you up to the lighthouse/fog signal complex; commissioned in February 1962, it acts as a main marker for shipping approaching the Firth of Forth. Keepers here maintain radio contact with several remote lighthouses and are generally too busy to receive casual visitors, though special arrangements can be made in advance through the Principal Keeper.

There could be no finer culmination to a coastal walk than this lofty headland with views extending south-east to Eyemouth and north-west to Bass Rock from the viewing table on Harelaw Hill. Between April and the end of July, eclipsing all else with their mewing, screaming calls and wheeling flight, some 50,000 seabirds adopt these spectacular cliffs as their own. With nests occupying every ledge and crevice, pale guano transforms natural rock colours and sends its pungent smell wafting up on the wind. Here you will see guillemots, kittiwakes, razorbills, shags, puffins, gulls and fulmars—a pair of binoculars will be worth their weight in gold!

We may marvel at the dizzy drops to the sea from rock face and pinnacle, but inaccessible sites such as these are chosen by breeding seabirds for protection against predators and for their close proximity to seawater. Indeed, razorbills and guillemots, which may number over 40,000 individuals, require an uninterrupted fall to the water for their chicks who tumble from nest ledges several weeks before they are capable of flight. Unlike gulls who often feed inland, true seabirds are totally reliant upon the sea for their survival. Techniques for obtaining food vary from species to species, but adult birds often fly many miles to procure sustenance for their young.

It will come as no surprise to find birdwatchers here. Strategically installed with telescopes and notebooks, theirs is perhaps the definitive experience of a moving and immensely vigorous natural process. Even without specialist knowledge and equipment, however, our human senses are awakened by the magnitude and drama of this annual regeneration.

If you follow the access road down for about half a mile, you will reach a pull-in for divers above Pettico Wick. (The sea off St Abb's Head is uniquely rich in marine flora and fauna, thanks to an eddy of the North Atlantic Drift which mixes Atlantic and Arctic species.) Here, on the St Abb's Head Fault, you are standing at the conjunction of two kinds of rock: resistant lavas form the headland just traversed, while ahead lie sedimentary rocks laid down 50 million years earlier on an ancient sea bed and contorted by immense geological pressures over subsequent millenia. From the cliff edges, views are stunning, especially west to dark, stratified bastions of rock leading along to Fast Castle Head.

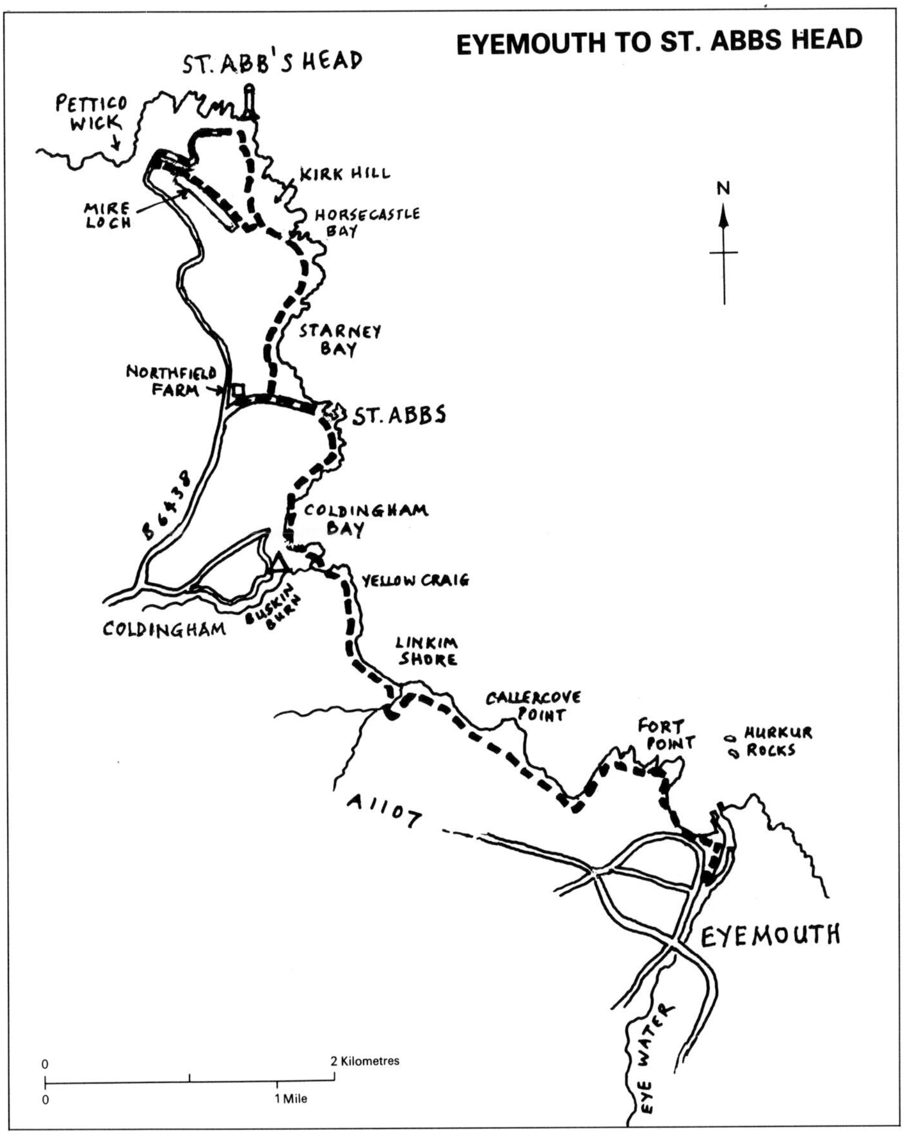

EYEMOUTH TO ST. ABBS HEAD

ST. ABB'S HEAD
PETTICO WICK
KIRK HILL
MIRE LOCH
HORSECASTLE BAY
N
STARNEY BAY
NORTHFIELD FARM
ST. ABBS
B6438
COLDINGHAM BAY
YELLOW CRAIG
COLDINGHAM
BUSKIN BURN
LINKIM SHORE
CALLERCOVE POINT
FORT POINT
HURKUR ROCKS
A1107
EYEMOUTH
EYE WATER
0 2 Kilometres
0 1 Mile

At a cattle grid below, you turn back inland across sheep pasture and beyond a fence walk along the crag-topped valley of Mire Loch, excavated by glacial meltwater during the last Ice Age. A dam erected around 1900 formed the loch itself—it is not a natural feature despite appearances. Several kinds of water bird nest here and adjacent reed beds provide habitats for wetland plants.

Half a mile or so after leaving the road, you turn sharp left to meet the Reserve boundary at Kirk Hill and retrace your outward steps to St Abbs. Alternatively you could simply follow the access road all the way back to Northfield Farm: traffic is light and, of necessity, slow!

Below left: ***St Abb's harbour.***

Below right: ***Approaching Coldingham Bay.***

WALK 28: *Fife — Earlsferry to Lower Largo (by Catherine Mowat)*

Map: OS Landranger Sheet 59—St Andrews and Kirkcaldy Area. **Start/Finish:** Start at the car park at the west end of Earlsferry village High Street. Finish at the small car park in Lower Largo village. **Distance:** 5½ miles (9km). Allow 3–4 hours. **Access:** By road—A917 links Elie/Earlsferry to Lower Largo. Bus Services: Direct services from Elie/Earlsferry/Lower Largo to Leven and Dundee via coast. Timetables in bus shelters, tel: 996 74238. **Type of Walking:** The Chain Walk at the west side of Earlsferry is a tough, exciting, low-tide rock scramble, not suitable for the unfit, but fun for the more adventurous walker. Check tide times with Coastguard, tel: Crail 50666. An easier route follows the cliff path to the sandy beaches of Shell Bay and Lower Largo. Cocklemill Burn can be forded at low tide otherwise a detour of half a mile upstream is necessary to the nearest bridge. **Features of Interest:** The Royal Burgh of Earlsferry; Chapel Ness with its ancient eleventh-century ruin; the challenging Chain Walk; wildflowers and bird life; picturesque Lower Largo; 'Robinson Crusoe' country. **Accommodation:** All year round accommodation in hotels, guest houses and B&B at Elie/Earlsferry and Lower Largo. Caravan and camping at Shell Bay Caravan Park. Nearest youth hostel at Falkland, near Cupar. Tel: Falkland 0337 57710.

From Shakespeare to Robinson Crusoe

The East Neuk of Fife is a picture-book land with its colourful, highly individualistic villages and seaside towns overlooking the Firth of Forth.

The character of the houses has survived from the sixteenth century, still with red pantiled roofs, crow-stepped gables and colourwashed walls. The visitor to the East Neuk resorts is forcefully struck by the colour and variety of the neat rows of cottages, no two quite the same, with windows of differing sizes and ornately moulded doorpieces, some revealing a plaque above the door inscribed with the initials of the owner and his wife and the date the house was built. In the past, an anchor or sailing ship sometimes appeared on the plaque, the ships changing in design over the years.

The sea formerly gave these coastal towns their main livelihood but now only a few harbours support fishing vessels. Local boats still operate from Elie, fishing for lobster and crab,

Facing page: ***The Crusoe Hotel, Lower Largo (photo Stan Mowat).***

and some harbours, including Elie, are used successfully in the summer months for water sports.

Neighbouring Elie and Earlsferry are nearly always mentioned in the same breath, like Siamese twins. It is difficult to separate the two. The adjoining royal burghs were officially amalgamated in 1929, the 'royal' status denoting their importance to the Crown as prosperous marketing towns, well sited geographically to conduct foreign trade.

Earlsferry, the smaller of the two burghs, is also the oldest. According to legend it was made a royal burgh by Malcolm Canmore (a name derived from the Gaelic for 'Great Head' or 'Chief'), King of Scotland from 1057 to 1093, at the request of Macduff, Earl of Fife, who was given sanctuary there while escaping from Macbeth. (Shakespeare's portrayal of Macbeth is not, in fact, historically accurate as Macbeth was a great king, renowned for his strong leadership and desire for law and order.)

The car park at the west end of Earlsferry High Street is close to the golf course and a short walk down one of the side streets leads to the beach and the ruined hospice or 'rest house' at Chapel Ness. The remains of the ruined chapel perch precariously on the rocky headland overlooking the wide sweep of Elie's south beach and the old granary building at the end of the harbour causeway.

In its day, the chapel was used as a hospital or guest house for weary travellers crossing the stormy Forth from East Lothian. The Cistercian nuns of North Berwick ran the sanctuary which was one of a series of similar 'rest houses' founded in the reign of King David I by Duncan, Earl of Fife, a much needed place of refuge in troubled times.

Skirting the golf course, the footpath follows an easy route close to the stony beach with plenty for the botanist to enjoy. Rocky inlets are thickly carpeted with sea pinks and the celery-like Scots lovage and sea wormwood can be found along the shoreline.

At the end of West Bay, the path dips beneath Kincraig Point at the start of the Chain Walk and forks upwards towards the easier cliff top route.

The shore walk can only be tackled $2\frac{1}{2}$ hours either side of low tide. People have been stranded so it's wise to check the tides before starting out. Don't attempt this route if you have a dog with you or if you're unfit and don't have a head for heights. Take the cliff path instead and enjoy the panoramic views.

The pebbled beach now gives way to something entirely different, a dramatic change from open skies and sandy bays to dark volcanic rock. These basalt cliffs date back 325 to 280 million years—standing beneath their shadow is like taking a step back in time. Weirdly-shaped rocky outcrops pounded by the sea rear up in all directions, some in almost vertical formations resembling organ pipes. Deep, narrow gullies carved out of the soft rock form caves and crevices beneath the cliffs and the first of these is the historic Macduff's Cave.

It was here that Macduff, Thane of Fife, the minor lord responsible to the King for collecting rents from the Fife villagers, is reputed to have hidden while trying to escape from Macbeth.

Macbeth's contest with his arch rival, Duncan I, made famous by Shakespeare, cast him forever in the villain's role but his claim to the Scottish throne was fully justified through his mother's family links with Kenneth II. He also appears to have been a strong king, ruling well with his queen (Gruoch), for 17 years.

When you stand in the cave's dark entrance listening to the sea constantly breaking on the rocks and hissing through the narrow channels it's not difficult to imagine Macduff's relief when he was eventually ferried away by a local fisherman to the safety of East Lothian. From that day on, this part of the village has been known as Earlsferry.

Tradition has it that when Malcolm Canmore became Scotland's king, he repaid Macduff's loyalty by decreeing that fugitives could not be pursued from Earlsferry until they were halfway across the Forth.

The name Chain Walk quickly becomes obvious. To get from one secluded cove to the next you have to make use of a series of chains and steps which have been set into the rocks. The chains are reassuringly large and heavy and well stapled; nonetheless, there are places where you can find yourself dangling with a drop of 10–13ft (3–4m). This is not for the faint-hearted.

There is no easy way round; the tide sees to that. It's either up and over or admit defeat and take the cliff walk. It may not be easy, but it's fun and well worth the challenge. Each cove has its share of strange rock formations and hidden caves; the Doo's or pigeon's cave and the Deil's cave, whose former occupants are more likely to have been smugglers, come at the end of the Chain Walk. Perched high on grassy ledges nesting fulmars keep a wary eye on the human intruders scrambling awkwardly below them.

A low, flat, ledge of rock, another steep scramble and the shoreline is left behind as the cut-out steps on the cliff path lead to the top of Kincraig Point. On a clear, sunny day, the view rivals anything on the Mediterranean.

Facing west lies the beautiful sweep of Shell Bay and, beyond, Largo Bay. In early summer the brilliant yellow rape fields, a crop used to make cattle feed, contrast with the ever changing blue-green seas and pale sandy beaches. Looking back towards Earlsferry, the path winds along the cliff top where the remains of Second World War concrete gunnery bunkers scatter themselves at regular intervals, some intact, some in ruins. Far across the Firth of Forth, the solid outline of the Bass Rock rears 350ft (105m) out of the sea, its steep cliffs white with nesting sea birds, a favourite breeding ground for around 7500 gannets. Further south the Isle of May can also be seen. It's the largest island on the Forth, measuring one mile by a quarter of a mile, and a national nature reserve.

Below the cliffs the stacks and rocky outcrops of the Chain Walk guard the string of sheltered coves pummelled by the tide. Shags and cormorants collect in large numbers on the rocky islets and as many as 40 will stand preening and drying their wings, hustling for positions, while others dive in the rough surf awaiting their turn for a quick spin dry.

The cliff-top's lime-rich grassland, strewn with cowslips in the spring, attracts many butterflies in the summer months and the Common Blue, Small Heath and Small Copper can all be found here.

After admiring the view and getting your breath back, it's time to return down the cliff path which drops quickly to the rocky shore before curving gently towards Shell Bay and its caravan park.

Walking either through the caravan park or over the dunes brings you to the western peninsula of the bay known as Ruddon's Point or Shooting Ho Point where there used to be a rifle range. The identity of the mysterious Ruddon has been lost in the mists of time. Shell Bay, as the name suggests, is home to a number of shells including cockles, mussels, razors and periwinkles.

If a high tide prevents fording at Cocklemill Burn follow the track over the sand dunes. Some of these are as high as 30–50ft (9–15m), making ideal nesting sites for sand martins, and on the quieter stretches of the deep, flowing burns, shelducks go peacefully about their business.

Cross the bridge and enter Largo Bay. If the tide is out the walk can continue along the shore or, alternatively, along the old railway embankment which takes you into the village of Lower Largo. Choose the shore walk if you want a long, invigorating stroll along unspoilt beaches. You may well be following in the footsteps of the real Robinson Crusoe—Alexander Selkirk—born in Largo in 1676, one of the town's most famous seafaring sons. His adventures on the high seas and survival on a desert island inspired Daniel Defoe's *Robinson Crusoe.*

Always a headstrong lad, Alexander Selkirk

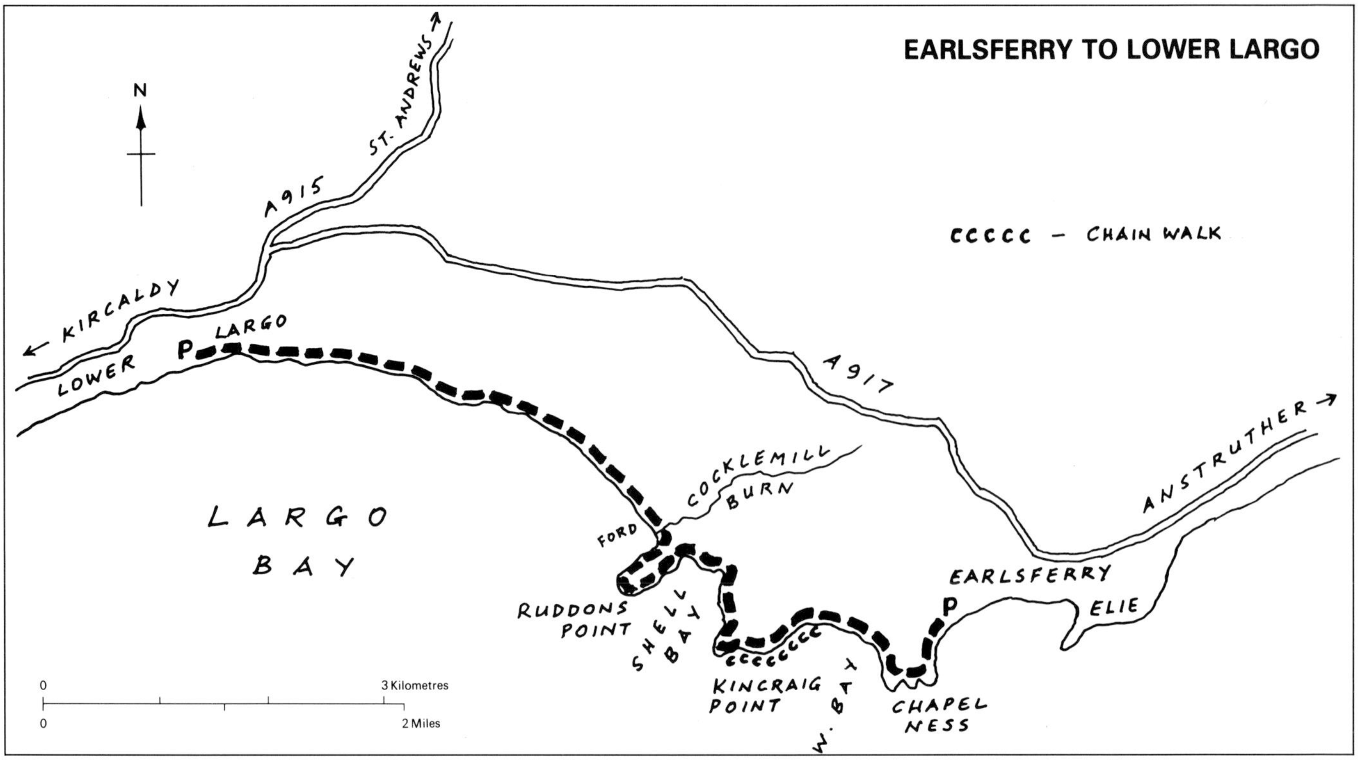

EARLSFERRY TO LOWER LARGO

N

ST. ANDREWS →
A915
CCCCC – CHAIN WALK
← KIRCALDY
LOWER P LARGO
A917
ANSTRUTHER →
COCKLEMILL BURN
LARGO BAY
FORD
RUDDONS POINT
SHELL BAY
EARLSFERRY
P
ELIE
KINCRAIG POINT
W. BAY
CHAPEL NESS
0 3 Kilometres
0 2 Miles

reputedly left home after a violent quarrel with his family and joined a privateering expedition to the French and Spanish colonies. His flair for navigation earned him early promotion. In 1704 he set sail for the South Seas on the ill-fated vessel *Cinque Ports*. The voyage was doomed to failure and no trace was found of the two Spanish galleons the crew had hoped to capture. Their captain died and his successor was highly unpopular. After quarrelling with his skipper, Selkirk demanded to be put ashore on the island of Juan Fernandez, 400 miles off the Coast of Chile, uninhabited except for some wild goats.

He could not have foreseen that instead of waiting a few weeks for the next friendly ship to hove into sight, he would be forced to survive for 4 years and 4 months on very basic provisions. After he was rescued, Selkirk again spent some time at sea risking more adventures with the privateers before returning to Britain a wealthy man. He stayed for some time with his family in Lower Largo, but the years of solitude had left their mark and by 1720 he was again back at sea as a lieutenant on HMS *Weymouth*. One year later the captain's logbook recorded that Alexander Selkirk had died and been buried at sea.

Largo Bay is a haven for wildlife. Sandpipers scurry ahead in anxious groups, oystercatchers and ringed plovers add their cries to the sea breeze. Nature lovers of a different kind also use the privacy of the dunes and quiet beaches for a spot of all over tanning on sunny days. It is not one of Scotland's official naturist beaches, but the area is a popular choice because of its easy access and secluded bay.

A few miles further west, at the golfing village of Lundin Links, the mysterious Standing Stones of Lundin Links can be found on the ladies golf course. The stones are uncut, standing in a rough triangle, and are thought by some historians to be the remains of a temple erected by mathematically sophisticated sun worshippers who used the stones as 'markers'. Local people believe they were erected to mark a battle with the Danes.

Leaving the beach as the houses of Lower Largo come into view, walk along Main Street where you'll pass Selkirk's birthplace and a small museum.

The car park is alongside the tiny harbour, close to the comfortable Crusoe Hotel—a fitting place for any seasoned traveller to while away a few hours.

The 'Deil's Cave', Earlsferry. (photo Stan Mowat).

Hackley Bay, Sands of Forvie (photo Fred Gordon).

WALK 29: *Grampian — The Sands of Forvie (by Fred Gordon)*

Map: OS Landranger Sheet 39—Aberdeen. **Start/Finish:** The car park just over the bridge across the River Ythan, one mile north of the village of Newburgh. **Distance:** 7 miles (11km)—allow 3½–4 hours. **Access:** This is a circular walk but it can be cut in half if you arrange to be picked up at the village of Collieston. Easy access at both ends with ample car parking facilities just off good public roads. **Type of Walking:** Easy walking over grass and sand with few ups and downs. **Features of Interest:** Sand dunes, cliffs, heathland; an old ruined church; interesting birds and plants; small lochans. **Accommodation:** B&B and hotels locally and in Aberdeen, 12 miles (20km) south. Camping locally and in Aberdeen. Youth hostel in Aberdeen.

A Walk through one of Britain's Largest Sand Dune Systems

The Sands of Forvie lie on the east coast of Scotland, some 12 miles (19km) north of Aberdeen. The area is the fifth largest sand dune system in Britain and has been described as the least disturbed by man. It is easily reached by taking the A92 Aberdeen to Ellon road out of Aberdeen and turning right on the A975 road for Newburgh some 8 miles (13km) north of Aberdeen. About three-quarters of a mile north of the village the road crosses the River Ythan and the car park, just over the bridge on the right, is where this walk begins.

Leave the car here and follow the unsurfaced road past the signs for the Ythan Estuary and Forvie Centre. If at this point you look across the river you will see the ruins of Knockhall Castle. This was once the stronghold of a branch of the Sinclair family who were the lairds of Knockhall. The castle was built in 1565 and was occupied until 1734 when it burned down accidentally. It was never rebuilt and remains a ruin.

Follow the track for about 200m and turn left at the sign marked 'Footpath to Beach'. After about a quarter of a mile there is a gate and an old railway carriage. The closely mown field on the left is an airfield for a local radio-controlled model aircraft club and you might be lucky enough to see several of these in the air around you. Pass through the gate into the Forvie National Nature Reserve where there is a large sign indicating what may be seen in the Reserve and the Bylaws affecting visitors.

The Reserve was established in 1956 as one of the first in Scotland and covers some 1018 hectares. The area before you has been largely unaffected by reclamation for agriculture and its rolling sand dunes and heathland contrast with the farmland round about. However, man has lived here in the past and much evidence of prehistoric man lies preserved under the sand. This has led to the area being described as 'an archaeological landscape with few equals in lowland Eastern Britain'.

Follow the track across the sandy heathland into the dunes. The sand is composed of quartz grains much finer than those found on the beach. Being lighter it is easily transported by the wind and over the centuries these dunes have gradually moved northwards. The dunes around you are still on the move but those to the north have now stabilised.

After about half a mile you get your first glimpse of the sea and the salmon fishing station. Here the nets are taken from the shore to dry. They are used to catch the salmon in the shallow waters as they head for the northern rivers of Scotland. Turn left here at the sign for Forvie Kirk. In medieval times there was a settlement here and Forvie Kirk was the parish church for over 700 years. The ruin dates from the twelfth century but it is likely that a chapel has stood on the site since AD704.

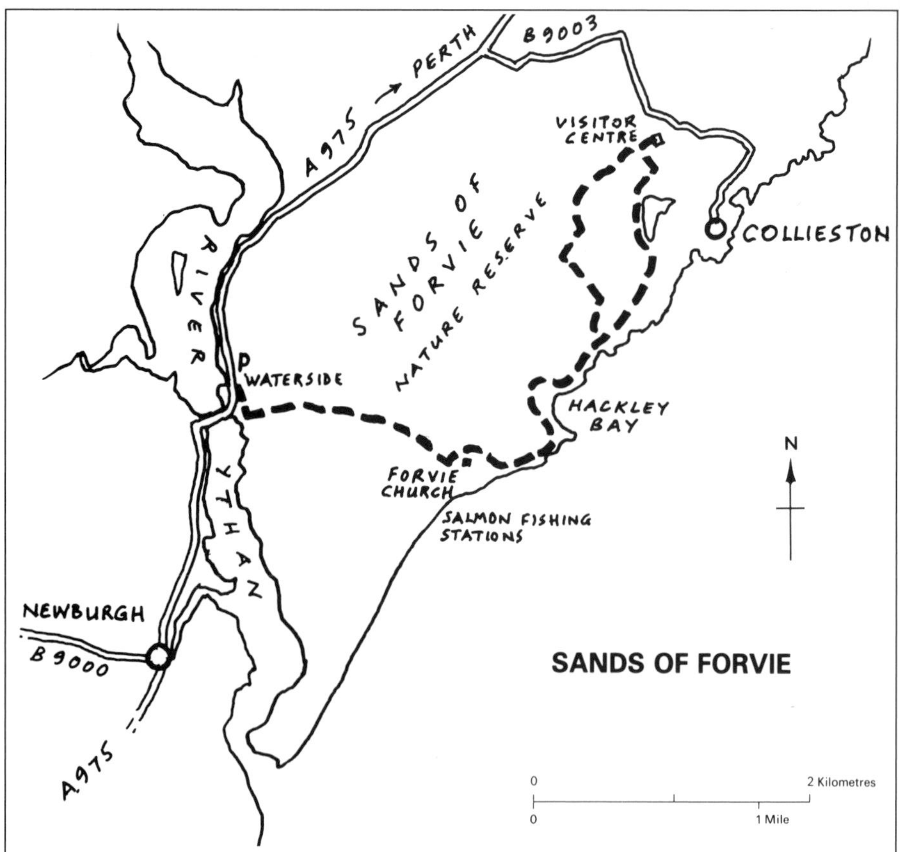

The plant community on Forvie sands is very interesting with over 350 species so far recorded. Colourful plants such as sea campion, bird's-foot trefoil, wild pansies and beautiful violets are all worth looking out for here. On the steeper slopes to the right are thrift, common scurvy grass and kidney vetch.

Out at sea giant North Sea oil rigs can often be seen lying just off Aberdeen. The low-sterned oil rig supply boats are also to be seen carrying essential items such as cables, pipes and food out to the rigs up to 100 miles (166km) away. Overhead fly helicopters ferrying men to and fro from the rigs in a seemingly endless cycle. There is a close association, locally, between the oil companies and wildlife. Companies have given large sums towards creating wildlife sanctuaries in the north-east and several of the oilfields are named after birds, for example, Fulmar, Tern and Cormorant.

Continue along the path near the cliff edge. There are several points here where you can look down steep gullies to the sea below, and there are small sandy beaches but many of these are difficult to get to safely.

Just over half a mile beyond Hackley Bay there is a gate and another sign indicating the boundary of the Reserve. Bear left here along the fence down to Sand Loch. This is a lovely haven used by many sea birds as a drinking station as it is a freshwater loch. Study the reeds surrounding the loch for coots, mallard and other ducks often found here—several may well have chicks with them. A few minutes spent quietly sitting here can be very rewarding.

The track comes to a stile over a fence. Pass this and go on for a further few hundred metres to a large gate. Turn right through this gate and make for the Forvie Visitor Centre. The Centre is open to the public and is well worth looking round. Displays illustrate the work of the Nature Conservancy Council on the Reserve and indicate the plants, animals and birds which can be seen throughout the year. There are badges and an excellent wildlife game for small children, and outside are several exciting displays. A very informative booklet on the reserve is also available, free of charge.

Just outside the Centre is a wildlife garden containing many local species of flowers and behind the Centre there is a Tree Nursery. Here native species are grown and it is possible to purchase trees for replanting in your own garden. The Warden, or his assistants, will be glad to advise you on these.

Perhaps the most exciting display is the wildlife pond. This was established a few years ago with the assistance of children from a local school and won a Kodak Conservation Award in 1985.

Return to the gate into the Reserve and walk straight ahead. This marked path meanders through the centre of the heath and enables the walker to appreciate the unspoilt heathland once very common in this part of Scotland. There are several small lochs here but in dry weather many of them are empty. Look out for tormentil, lousewort and heath milkwort amongst the bell heather and cross-leaved heath. There are several scrub trees in places such as birch, willow and pine.

In just over a mile the main path is rejoined near the cliffs. Turn right here and retrace your steps past Hackley Bay and Forvie Kirk. On the way back the views are quite different with the large sweep of beach visible past Newburgh and on to Aberdeen. On a clear day the higher buildings of the city can be seen.

Return through the heath and sand dunes to your car.

Facing page: ***Lochan near Scourie (photo Fred Gordon).***

WALK 30: *Highland — Scourie to Tarbet (by Fred Gordon)*

Map: OS Landranger Sheet 9—Cape Wrath. **Start/Finish:** Walk starts near the pier in the small village of Scourie. It ends at the hamlet of Tarbet further north. **Distance:** 6 miles (9km) return. Allow 4½ hours. **Access:** Parking at the start of this walk is quite easy as there is an adequate car park next to the toilets in the centre of the village of Scourie. At the Tarbet end of the walk there is also a car park next to a small tearoom where the ferry departs for the Island of Handa. **Type of Walking:** The path is fairly good and well marked with cairns. Stout shoes or walking boots are to be favoured as the path can be very wet after prolonged rain. **Features of Interest:** Crofting village of Scourie; lochans and rocks along the coast; the bird sanctuary of Handa and the fishing hamlet of Tarbet. **Accommodation:** Hotel and B&B in Scourie. Good camp site near the beach. The nearest large village is Ullapool some 35 miles (58km) to the south. Here there is ample hotel and guest house accommodation plus a youth hostel and camp site.

Coastal Moor with Lochans and Superb Views

This coastal walk begins at the crofting village of Scourie set at the head of a wide sandy bay. The name Scourie is said to be a corruption of Norse and Gaelic: 'Skoga' meaning a copse, and 'Airigh' a shieling or summer pasture. The area of Sutherland was once a stronghold of the Vikings and many names locally are either Norse or Gaelic in origin, or as in this case, mixtures of the two.

Scourie was the birthplace of General Hugh Mackay, a famous soldier of the seventeenth century. He rose to fame when he wrote a manual on infantry tactics which became a classic work in the history of the army. Despite this, his forces were defeated at the Battle of Killiecrankie in 1689.

The walk begins in the centre of the village, by the public toilets (parking available here). Follow a route to the camp site about a quarter of a mile to the west. Turn down the track to the right of the camp site towards the large, white house with the walled garden. The mildness of the climate in this area, largely due to the influence of the Gulf Stream, has enabled the owner of this house to grow palm trees in the garden—quite possibly the most northerly palms in the British Isles.

Turn right along the garden wall and follow the path to where it joins the road. At this point turn left along the road with a small stream on your left. After about 500m the road ends but the footpath climbs up the hill and is well marked with small cairns all the way to Tarbet. If tempted to walk to the sea at any point, care should be exercised as the cliff along this part of the coast can be very greasy due to algae and lichen. The lichen are well worth looking at more closely. They are not, in fact, plants but are formed by the symbiotic association of a fungus and an alga, the various combinations producing different growths. They were—and in some areas still are—collected and used in the dyeing of wool giving a variety of colours.

Several other plants found on this path were also collected for dyeing. Tormentil, a small yellow flower very common here, gives a yellow dye. Common Sundew, a small; red-leaved plant found in boggy areas, gives a purple dye. Silverweed, common in grassy places especially near shores, gives a red colour. Dyeing is experiencing something of a revival and is often described as an art, like cooking.

After about half a mile the land opens out onto a gently undulating plain of Lewisian gneiss, a wilderness of lumpy crags and small lochans. Here bare rock surfaces abound since heather does not flourish very well on this type of rock. Over 1000 million years old, Lewisian gneiss is one of the oldest rocks in the world. Many geologists come from all over the world to study the rocks here and the walker may well meet one chipping off a sample along the way.

After a further half mile the path passes close to two small lochans, Lochain Bealach an Eilein. It is worth approaching these lochs quietly as they often contain some of Scotland's rarer and more interesting birds, namely the red and black throated divers. These birds are about the size of cormorants and lie very low in the water, diving frequently to chase small fish which form their staple diet. They are very well adapted for their way of life with legs set well towards the back of the body. They always nest close to the edge of their chosen loch so that they will not have to walk far to the water. Care should be taken not to disturb them as they are very shy and easily scared off.

The path now drops down and crosses two small streams both of which are outflows from a number of lochans to the east. They should not present any difficulty.

Out to the west over the Sound of Handa can be seen Handa Island which is an important nature reserve in the care of the RSPB. Handa, the Sandy Isle, is wild and beautiful and composed of Torridonian sandstone laid down some 600 million years ago. It is low lying with some excellent beaches in the east but rises in the north and west to huge cliffs over 400ft (120m) high. Along these cliffs lie crevices and ledges which form part of an extremely important nesting area for over 100,000 seabirds such as puffins, razorbills, guillemots, fulmars and shags.

The interior of the island is largely peat bog with six small lochans. Around the edge of the island are several areas of richer grassland and machir. In the interior great skua and arctic skua breed. During the breeding season the skuas are likely to 'dive-bomb' visitors to protect their nests. As a mark of respect to the wealth of wildlife living here, the whole island is designated a Site of Special Scientific Interest.

At one time, over 60 people in 12 families lived on the island and the remains of their crofts can still be seen. They cultivated the land by a system known as lazy beds, a form of strip farming. Oats and potatoes were grown and this staple diet was supplemented by fish and seabirds. However, the potato famine of 1845 and the landowner's wish to turn the whole island over to sheep in 1848, resulted in the island being evacuated. Many left for Canada and others settled on the nearby mainland.

The way is easily followed here and after about three-quarters of a mile the path drops sharply to a burn flowing into Lochan a Mhuinean about a quarter of a mile to the left. After another half a mile it rounds a small crag and turns east into a small gully. Offshore are several small islands and it is worth scanning these with binoculars for seals as they often haul out onto these to sun themselves between fishing trips. The path then climbs for a short distance before dropping the last quarter of a mile to the fishing hamlet of Tarbet.

To the east of the village is Loch Dubh, the dark loch, which is full of water lilies and in common with many lochs in the area, full of lively brown trout. Permits to fish these lochs can be obtained in Scourie. In many cases the trout are small but they fight very hard and provide good sport for the fly fisherman with light tackle.

Tarbet is a small fishing community. The local fishermen fish for crab and lobster but, during the tourist season, ferry visitors out to Handa. There is an excellent tea room down by the pier and car park and a pleasant half hour or so can be spent here before embarking on your return journey. If time allows, it is well worth taking the ferry out to Handa and spending a few hours walking round the island. During the breeding season the birds are truly magnificent.

The return walk is the reverse of the outward journey.

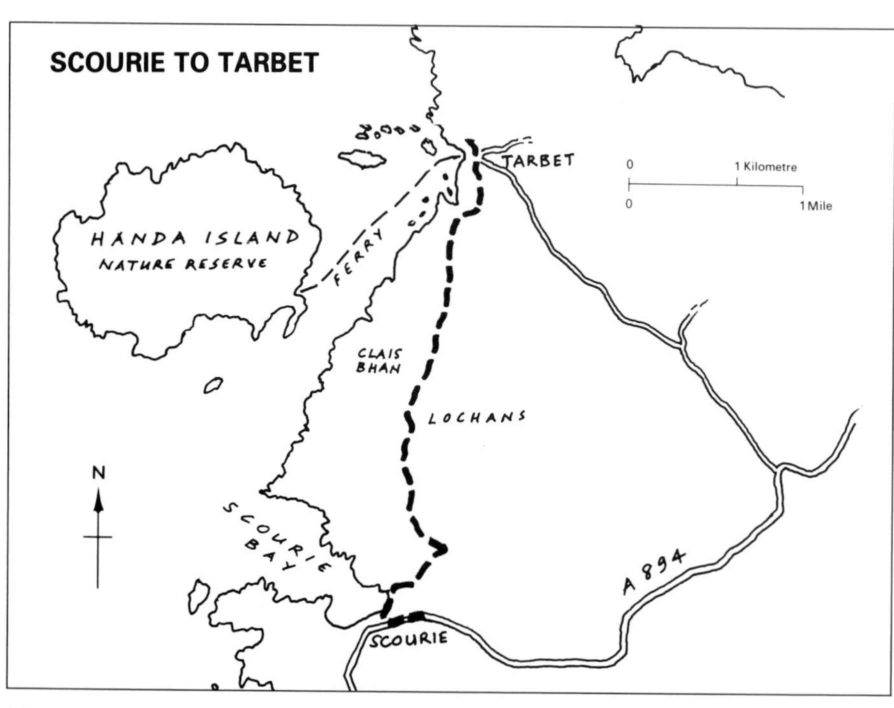

Facing page: ***Looking west on the cliff path (photo Fred Gordon).***

WALK 31: *Highland — Ben Mor Coigach Cliff Path (by Fred Gordon)*

Map: OS Landranger Sheet 15—Loch Assynt. **Start/Finish:** Blughasary to Culnacraig, car parks at both ends. **Distance:** 5½ miles (8.8km). Allow 6½ hours plus time for stops. **Access:** Take the A835 north from Ullapool through Ardmair and over the hill to Strathcanaird. Turn left at the sign for Blughasary and follow to the end of the road, about 1 mile, where there is a small car park. To reach Culnacraig continue north on the A835 for another 5 miles (8km) and turn left at the road for Achiltibuie. Follow it through part of the Inverpolly National Nature Reserve to the village of Achiltibuie. Continue to the end of the public road at Culnacraig. **Type of Walking:** Quite rough and wet especially after rain. Boots should be considered essential and care taken to keep to the path. Not recommended as a walk in misty conditions. The views on a clear day, however, are very rewarding. **Features of Interest:** Views over Loch Broom to Isle Martin and the Summer Isles; glimpses of the saw-toothed ridge of An Teallach to the south and Ben Mor Coigach immediately to the north; small fishing boats and Soviet trawlers out on the loch. **Accommodation:** Wide selection available in Ullapool. Youth hostel on Shore Street and a camp site on the shore of Loch Broom on the outskirts of the village. Hotel, B&B and youth hostel accommodation at the end of the walk.

Torridonian Sandstone and Island Views

This is a fairly challenging but rewarding walk over Torridonian sandstone along sea cliffs on the lower slopes of Ben Mor Coigach. In bygone days the path was in regular use by the postman delivering mail to the remote Reiff peninsula. The post is now delivered by an easier route but it is still possible to experience the thrill of walking high above Loch Broom with superb views out over Isle Martin and the Summer Isles.

The walk starts at the small car park at Blughasary. Proceed through the small gate at the end of the car park and cross the bridge over the River Runie. It is worth pausing here for a few minutes to look at the falls below where jumping salmon can often be seen. Turn left and walk to the gate across the Land Rover track and turn right onto the path marked by white posts. Down to the left is the River Kanaird which is well known for its salmon and sea trout fishing and they can sometimes be seen jumping in the various pools trying to rid themselves of sea lice.

Follow the path for about 1¼ miles (2km) to the small gate through the deer fence (not to be confused with the large gate passed about a quarter of a mile earlier). Turn right up the steep slope. From here on the way is mainly well marked by either posts or cairns and due to the nature of the terrain, care should be taken to follow the path carefully. After climbing about 750ft (250m) the path veers inland. Directly below can be seen the Pictish fort of Dun Canna. This was built centuries ago on the small promontory to be defended in times of local trouble.

After about a quarter of a mile the path descends into a gully. Cross this gully and turn west parallel with the fine cliff of Torridonian sandstone on your left. Torridonian sandstone was laid down as a sediment in shallow seas or lochs about 400 – 600 million years ago. It has a distinctive reddish colour and in many places is built up to 1800ft (600m) in depth. In some places it contains fossils of Trilobites which were small, crab-like animals which preyed on other sea creatures. Close inspection of the rock shows that it contains pebbles which were rounded as they were carried down by ancient streams.

From here the path bears right to cross a fair-sized stream flowing from Loch Slac a Bhuilg Mor about half a mile to the north-east. Across the stream are the ruins of a drystone dyke and what looks like a small ruined house. This is most probably the site of a shieling or upland pasture. In past centuries it was common in many parts of Scotland for crofters to move with both family and animals away from their homes in the glens to allow their animals to feed on the rich pastures to be found higher in the hills. The men would travel up first to repair any damage done to the shieling during the previous winter and then the rest of the family would bring up the animals. The time spent at the shielings would depend on the area, and the weather, and could include any time from May to September.

At the shieling the animals would feed on the rich pasture and their milk would be used to make cheese and butter for the family. Once made, it was buried in the peat bogs where it was safe from summer heat and bacteria. The children were sent out to gather plants and herbs which were used either to dye wool or for medicinal or culinary purposes. From here the path continues west and care must be taken on the next section as you pass along the cliff top with iron fence posts on your left. Notice the single Scots pine tree growing on the cliff face—it is the only tree of any size here and has escaped being eaten by sheep and deer due to its inaccessible position.

The path then bears away from the cliff

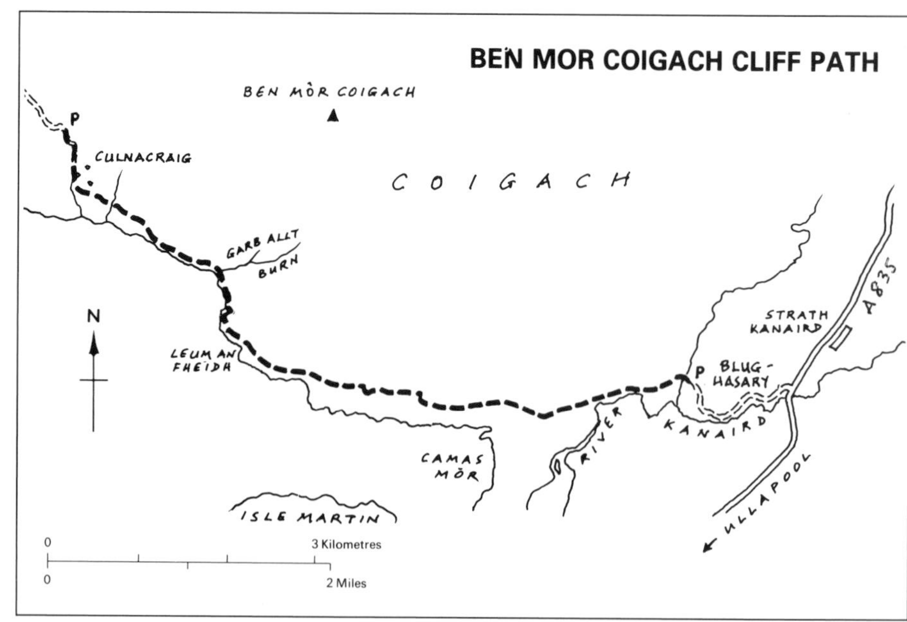

edge and over the next half mile crosses two small streams, the second barely visible on the 1:50,000 OS map. From this point there are very good views of the long ridge of Ben Mor Coigach stretching away to the right. Coigach means 'Place of the Fifths', derived from the old Celtic custom of dividing land into five parts. Rising to 2415ft (743m) this mountain is very popular with hill walkers and from the path it is often possible to see people high on the ridge above.

The onward route descends down to the Garbh Allt, or Rough Burn, half a mile ahead. Just before the final descent to the bay at the burn's mouth the path comes near to the cliff again. Take care as it is not always possible to see the next post or cairn, but the path is fairly clear.

At the Garbh Allt cross the fence and the burn. This presents little difficulty in dry weather but if the burn is high, cross on the shingle down on the seashore. Once across, the path climbs steeply up the hillside and along the clifftop through some scrub birch trees. Once round the headland the first house at Culnacraig, Seaview, comes into view. From here there is also an excellent view of the Summer Isles.

The Summer Isles guard the mouth of Loch Broom. The largest island, Tanera Mor, lies just 1½ miles (2.5km) off the coast near the end of the walk. Its total area is only 800 acres but it had a population of over 70 up until 1900. The once thriving community lived by inshore herring fishing but as this declined people gradually left the island and by 1946 it was uninhabited. However, life has returned and there is now a fish farm in the main bay, reviving the importance of fish as a local product.

Tanera Mor is rich in birdlife. The naturalist Dr Fraser Darling lived on the island and listed over 40 species of birds including buzzards, sheld-ducks, red grouse and many others.

Another of the islands, Horse Island, may well conceal some of the treasure from the Spanish Armada. It is said that gold was hidden there in 1588 and a local shepherd did discover a gold coin some years ago.

Most of the islands in the Summer Isles group are rich in wildlife and it is worth taking a boat trip to visit some of them. Two companies run trips lasting a few hours, or a whole day, from the pier in Ullapool.

The next landmark is the Coisiche Burn about a mile further on. This burn runs in a deep gully and is best avoided after heavy rainfall. A short descent to the shore, however, enables an easy crossing on the beach. Once across the burn follow the path up to the first cottage where a Land Rover track is reached. This leads through several crofts, and passes a small fish farm on the left where young salmon are reared, before joining the public road, and the pick up point, by the Allt a Choire Reidh burn.

Facing page: ***The top of Dun Caan, Raasay, looking to the mainland (photo Rennie McOwan).***

WALK 32: *Highland — Dun Caan and the Rim of Raasay (by Rennie McOwan)*

Map: OS Second Series Sheet 24—Raasay and Loch Torridon. **Start/Finish:** Inverarish village, on the south-west corner of Raasay, just over a mile north of the ferry pier. **Distance:** 20 miles (32km) round journey if turning at Brochel Castle on the east coast, but shorter permutations possible. **Access:** Raasay is served by roll-on, roll-off car ferry from the village of Sconser, on Loch Sligachan on the Isle of Skye. The crossing takes 15 minutes. Take the A850 road from Portree or Broadford on Skye (11 and 12 miles) to Sconser. Ferry times change with the seasons and according to school holidays. In summer expect them to be 5 times daily (no ferries on Sunday). Contact Isle of Skye and S.W. Ross Tourist Board, Portree. **Type of Walking:** Strenuous walking over very rough moorland; can include small hills and a metalled road. Allowances must be made for much upping-and-downing but the expedition can be split into sections and spread over a number of days. **Features of Interest:** The hill of Dun Caan and the island of the MacLeods of Raasay. Nature Conservancy Council 'area of special interest': botany, geology, archaeological sites, wildlife, loch and sea angling. Magnificent views to Torridon and Applecross on the mainland and to the hills of Skye; spectacular cliffs. **Accommodation:** Borrowdale House, at the township of Clachan, 2 miles (3.3km) from the pier, is a hotel run by the Highlands and Islands Development Board. A Grade 3 youth hostel, Creachan Cottage (12 bed), now the Alan Evans Memorial Hostel, is 3 miles (4.5km) north of the pier (seasonal; booking advised July to mid-August). When closed, send bookings to the national office: 7 Glebe Crescent, Stirling.

Coast and Moorland on a Lovely Scottish Island

Skye is such a delightful island that it is hard to leave it and many visitors do not consider it worthwhile making the additional ferry crossing to Raasay, but theirs is the loss. It is not a big island, about 13 miles (21km) long if one takes into account offshore islets and about 3½ miles (5.5km) wide in the southern section, but it is a truly beautiful place and worth taking the time to savour. It has witnessed the mysterious people of pre-history with their standing stones, forts and mounds; the Celtic saints, the probing Norsemen and the later clansmen. It has received distinguished visitors like the fugitive Prince Charles Edward Stuart during the 1745 Jacobite Rising, the literary figure, Dr Samuel Johnson, who in 1773 produced interesting but ponderous and often inaccurate memoirs of his Highland visits, and his Scottish satellite and biographer, James Boswell.

It is an island of controversial land history, of 'cleared' people and a variety of lairds. For modern visitors it is also an island of marvellous views and superb wildlife, including its own species of vole, as well as eagles, otters and at least 60 different bird species. There are red deer on the moors and the name Raasay derives from the Norse for a roe deer, *raa*, and an island, *ey*.

It is also botanically varied including mixed woodland and Forestry Commission plantations, moorland and shore terrain. Bluebells and rhododendrons abound in season and field and alpine flora include lesser butterfly orchids, early purple and green winged orchids, the spotted orchid, field felwort, sea aster and bog asphodel, as well as saxifrages, mosses and ferns. It lends itself to coastal wandering and the prominent, flat-topped, highest hill, Dun Caan, is seen from many corners of Skye and the mainland and must be one of the best, small-height, viewpoints in Scotland.

To enjoy Raasay, it helps if you are an island-going enthusiast and fairly philosophical about the weather, but if the sun shines you will be as captivated as a former laird who visited the island, fell in love with it and named one of the hills 'Temptation Hill' as a tribute to its appeal.

The Raasay ferry departure point on Skye, the township of Sconser, is one of those tiny places whose name might have changed the course of Scottish and British history. It was here, in 1745, that the chiefs of the MacDonalds of Sleat on Skye and the MacLeods on Skye and in the Outer Isles met to decide whether they would support the Jacobite cause when Prince Charles Edward Stuart landed in Scotland from France. They decided to hold back, a decision of major importance because they could have added many men to the Prince's cause. Over 100 MacLeods of Raasay, under Malcolm, the ninth Chief, joined him and the island suffered severely from the brutal behaviour of the Hanoverian forces when the Rising of '45 failed. Houses were burned, people killed or molested and goods and cattle stolen, but Malcolm prudently made over his lands to his son who stayed at home and the lands were not forfeited.

Few feelings can often be dismissed as wild romanticism, but parts of the island have a sense of sadness about them, perhaps a relic from the times of bloodshed or from the nineteenth-century Clearances. The walker passes the remains of old homes and on higher ground, the stone foundations of shielings, the temporary summer homes of the Gaelic people who in past times took their cattle, goats and sheep up to the fresh grass for the spring and summer. Some of the most beautiful Gaelic songs were written at or about the shielings which were also places for courtship and enjoyment

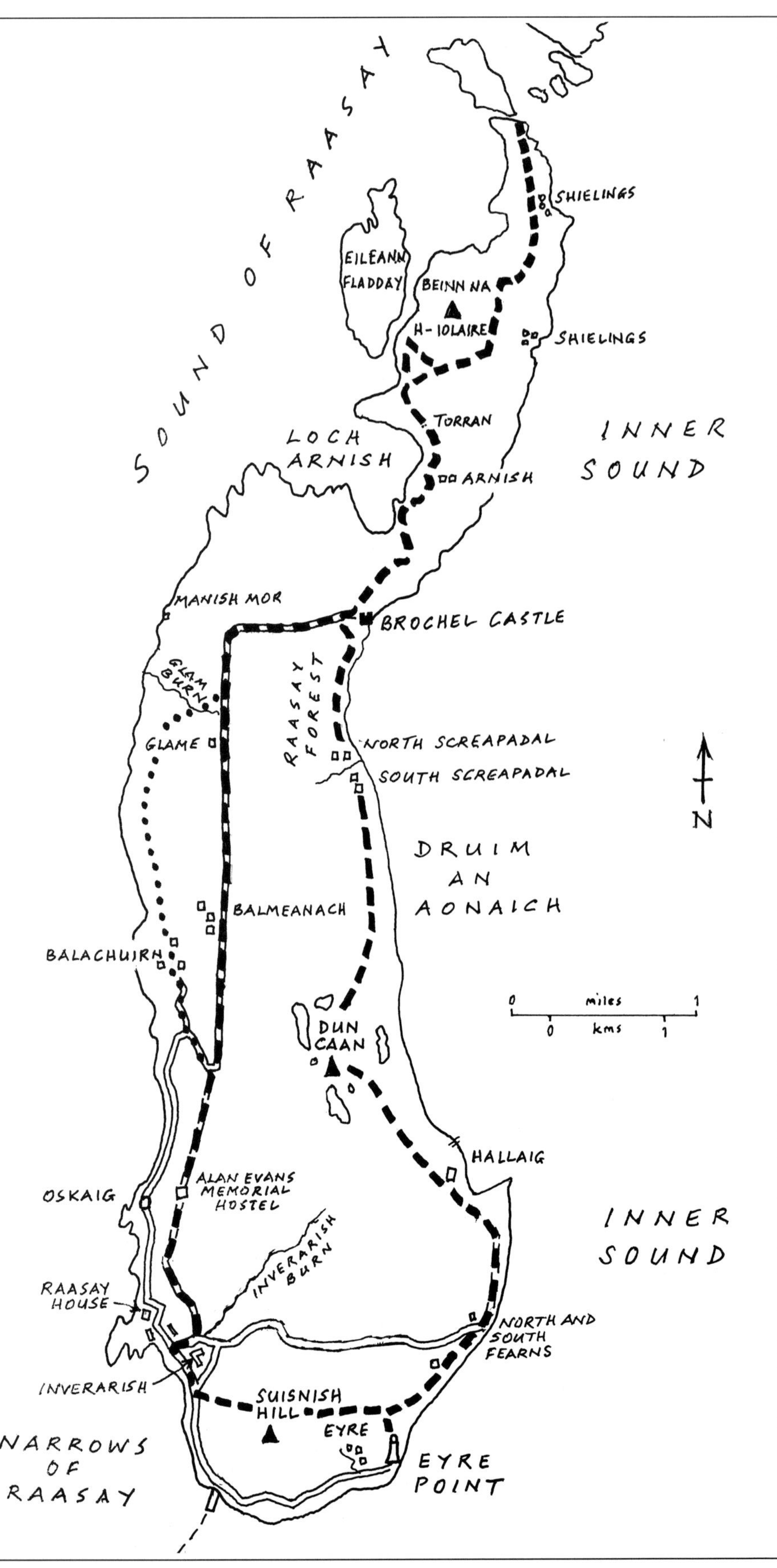

In Dr Johnson's time the population totalled over 900; it is now about 100. He recorded that they were happy and healthy people but by the nineteenth century the island was overcrowded and some people emigrated willingly. The importation of sheep and the creation of sporting estates resulted in many people being forcibly cleared off the land by lairds in conditions of great hardship. To this day it can make the blood boil to read the evidence of crofters to the Napier Commission which was examining this tragic period in British land history. One man said the scene at the pier as the people left for America, their homes burned or destroyed, was like watching lambs being separated from their mothers, such was their distress.

In ten years one-third of the people had emigrated and the cleared townships included the tether-peg area of Balnakeipan where small children were tethered for safety on the steep slopes. At one stage the island had three owners in four years. A crofter who was forbidden by the laird to marry but who secretly did so had his home destroyed. The couple built a makeshift shieling but that too was destroyed.

In more recent years men returning from the First World War were refused good land for crofts and seized their own plots. There was a public uproar when they received jail sentences and a settlement of a kind was later reached.

The island was bought by the Department of Agriculture in 1922, but parts were later sold. There was more public controversy in 1977 when the Highlands and Islands Development Board bought out landowner Dr John Green, of Cooden, Sussex, who was accused of blocking island development and who was called 'Dr No' by the Scottish media. His home, Borodale (Borrowdale) House, is now the hotel.

The walk starts in Inverarish village where there is a shop and post office but it can, of course, start from wherever you are staying. Begin at a high concrete pier on the right of Glen Road about 600ft (222m) from Henderson's Bridge. A small path rises immediately to the left of this pier (at the time of writing marked with a white triangle) and about 55m along the disused track of an old railway. Cross a forestry fence by a stile.

The double row of cottages and single row of larger houses which largely form Inverarish village are relics of an ironstone mine opened by William Baird & Co. of Coatbridge in 1913. German prisoners of war were once housed in the cottages and worked in the mine. It became uneconomic and closed in 1919. Some buildings near the ferry pier and the pier itself are relics of the mining days and so is a line of the railway which ran from the pier to the mine, north-east of the village. The firm was scandalously responsible for holding up land-grants to First World War Servicemen, awarded under the 1919 Land Settlement Act.

Pass through a forestry plantation for about a quarter of a mile and then walk onto the moor. There are good views to the island of Scalpay, off Skye, and to the mainland hills. Moorland cairns mark the descent to Eyre Point (itself a pleasant walk) where there is a shingle bay and a lighthouse, built in 1893, but contour instead over rough moorland for just over a mile in an easterly direction until you strike the minor road at North Fearns township and walk on clear of the trees which lie to the north-east of Eyre Point. Both Fearns and Eyre suffered greatly in the Clearances.

The made-up road ends and the walker continues on a wide grassy track for another $2\frac{1}{2}$ miles (4km) to Hallaig where there are birch groves, an attractive waterfall and a cairn to the Gaelic poet Sorley Maclean *(Somhairle MacGill-Eain)* who was born in 1911. Social justice, the Spanish Civil War, his experiences in the Western Desert during the Second World War, love-poetry, praise of the landscape, and a lament for his brother, the Celtic scholar Calum Maclean, all feature in his work. One poem, about the nineteenth-century Clearances, is called 'Hallaig' and he is widely regarded as one of the outstanding poets of the twentieth century.

From Hallaig pick your own route steeply uphill over high ground until you reach Loch na Mna, the loch-of-the-woman, to the south of the prominent hill of Dun Caan, one of a series of high level lochans which surround the peak. Legend has it that this loch held a kind of sea monster which devoured a local girl. Her father lit a great fire nearby and roasted a sow so the smell would attract the monster. He built a hiding place of stones and an avenue of boulders so that the monster would have to crawl through. All went according to plan; the father leapt on the monster, stabbing it to death with a red-hot spit.

The hill takes its name from its shape which is literally can-shaped. It is a Norse name and *dun* (which should be pronounced 'doon' but hardly ever is) means a 'fort' or 'stronghold'. Sailors call it Raasay's Cap because it also looks like a bonnet. The summit is surrounded by a rocky escarpment, but the walker only needs to wander around the foot of the rocks to find a clear way up.

When crossing moorland on Raasay, particularly to the south of Dun Caan, keep a look out for dangerous little fissures hidden in the heather. In cold weather water-vapour pours out of them and they can look like tiny volcanoes.

The view from the flat top of Dun Caan is magnificent: lobster boats and other fishing vessels in the Inner Sound look like toys. The mountains of Torridon, notably Ben Alligin, the peaks of Applecross, the Kintail hills and many other inland summits can all be picked out.

The views over the Narrows of Raasay and the Sound of Raasay to Skye are particularly striking. Glamaig's twin peaks are clearly evident, as are Blaven and Sgurr nan Gillean in the Cuillin, and the cliffs of the Storr and the Quiraing are also on view. Lewis, Harris, Eigg and Rum can all be made out. The sea east of Raasay is over 1000ft deep, deeper than anywhere else until the Atlantic shelf is left behind west of the St Kilda archipelago.

Johnson and Boswell were both happy on Raasay, well-entertained by the MacLeods. From the beginning, their impressions were favourable. Boswell wrote, 'We saw before us a beautiful bay . . . and beyond it hills and mountains in graduation of wildness. Our boatmen sang with great glee.' Dr Johnson remarked rather patronisingly 'the pleasing appearance of domestic society was not equalled in the most polished countries'. Boswell breakfasted on mutton, cheese, brandy and punch and then climbed Dun Caan. He was so taken by the flat top and the view that he danced a reel or jig on the summit where there is now a trig point.

If the walker has had enough at this point it is easy enough to angle down southwards and then south-west on a path which leaves from the foot of Loch na Meilich. Gaelic names are interesting and should be investigated because they often give a picture of the terrain or tell of past peoples and events. *Meilich* is an awkward one because it can variously mean 'a hollow', 'numbing cold' or 'bleating' (as in sheep). The tiny loch to the north-east of Loch na Meilich, Loch Meall Damh means the 'loch-of-the-stags-mound'. This path leads down to the road which connects Inverarish with the townships of South and North Fearns and which cuts across the southern section of the island.

Your next targets are the townships of North and South Screapadal, $3\frac{1}{2}$ miles (5.5km) from Dun Caan. Keep to the central moorland with the eastern Druim an Aonaich escarpment (possibly 'ridge-of-solitude') between you and the eastern shore. The walking is mainly easy on springy turf and there is a steepish descent at the end to the old settlements at Screapadal.

At North Screapadal you pick up a track through the woods which links with the road crossing the island from Inverarish and Clachan to Brochel Castle, an old Clan MacLeod stronghold, now ruinous with an eyrie-like site on a series of huge rocks. It was built by the MacLeods of Lewis and it speaks of times past when the sea was the highway, commanding

Top: ***Looking to Dun Caan.***

Bottom: ***Brochel Castle (photos Rennie McOwan).***

the Inner Sound and the seaways into Loch Kishhorn, Loch Carron, Lochalsh and the normal sailing routes to and from Lewis, in the Outer Hebrides. The Inner Sound has heard the swish of oars and the creak of sails from the vessels of raiding Norsemen and the galleys of the clan chiefs in their quests for power and land. The last MacLeod chief to live in the castle was Iain Garbh, a name often translated as Rough John, but the Gaelic can also mean 'haughty', 'harsh', 'boisterous', 'fierce' and 'terrible', and almost any one would be applicable.

Just offshore the MacLeods of Raasay sailed to meet the MacKenzies of Gairloch in an uncivil war in 1611; both chiefs were slain at sea. Earlier, in 1263, the giant fleet of King Haakon and his son, Magnus, anchored offshore in their bid to reinforce Norway's hold on the Outer Isles and western seaboard. They were outwitted and outfought by the youthful King Alexander III, one of Scotland's finest rulers.

Again, a number of permutations face the walker at Brochel. Those who wish to abandon the expedition can be picked up by car at the castle. Personally, I prefer to save the expedition further north for another day but if you feel fit to continue, take a broad track or road for 2 miles (3.5km) to the township of Arnish. Look carefully at this road: it was cut out single-handedly and heroically by a crofter, Calum MacLeod, who died in 1988. It was later surfaced by the local authority who no doubt blushed. Continue on for a while to Torran township and take a path following the west shore to the tidal island of Eilean Fladday. You can cross over and explore the island, but it is *essential* to check tide times. Return to Creag an Eoin, 'crag-of-the-birds', on the main island and walk on another linking track to the south and east of Beinn na h-Iolaire (pronounced 'ben na yooler', 'mountain-of-the-eagle') and on over rough ground past old shielings to Caol Rona (the 'narrows-of-the-seals'), which separates Raasay from its northerly outlier, Rona, and the offshore island, Eilean Tigh ('island-of-the-house', pronounced 'tie'). The word 'Kyle' on maps, as in Kyle of Lochalsh, is a corruption of *Caol.* When the people were forcibly cleared from much of their best land in the nineteeth century, many had to eke out a living on Rona, creating tiny potato plots in little hollows among the rocks and living on shellfish and other shore and sea fare.

The walk from Arnish and Torran to Eilean Fladday and then on to Caol Rona is wild and beautiful. There are views to the Outer Isles and to Staffin on Skye. In recent years some helpful white triangle markers have been erected by the Forestry Commission at key turnings, although I know many walkers do not like waymarking of any kind. The area north of Brochel is often called South Rona. Go equipped for rough wandering on this outing.

An alternative route from Brochel Castle that explores much of Raasay follows the tarmac road westwards and then southwards down the middle of the island to where, after $5\frac{1}{2}$ miles (9km) it doubles back north, west and then south. Either follow it for a further 2 miles (3.5km) down to the township of Oskaig or take a subsidiary track at the most southern point (before the road doubles back) and walk down past the Alan Evans Memorial Hostel and on to Clachan and Inverarish. The hostel is named after a Raasy enthusiast who ran

Looking to Skye from Raasay (photo Rennie McOwan).

a private hostel here and then gave the building to the Scottish Youth Hostels Association. The tarmac road is the direct line southwards but many walkers do not like walking on tarmac. Another alternative, which involves much upping-and-downing over rough moorland, is to follow the road westwards from Brochel Castle for $1\frac{1}{2}$ miles (2km) and then leave it and cross the moorland westwards to Manish Mor on the western coast where there are old shielings. Keep wandering southwards along the coast until you strike Lochan an Rathaid ('small-loch-of-the-paths') and the townships of Balmeanach and Balachuirn where you pick up the tarmac road again. Either keep on the road to Oskaig or take the track south of the pronounced north/south twist in the road, the track which leads past the hostel. Keep an eye out for wildlife, particularly deer and seals. If you choose the road have a look at the Glame or Glam burn, 3 miles from Brochel, where Bonnie Prince Charlie hid in a hut. The road then takes the walker down to Raasay House and Clachan village where it is certainly worth spending a few hours or an evening exploring the neighbourhood.

Raasay House, at Clachan, is one of the sights of the western seaboard. It is a listed building and was the home of the MacLeods of Raasay until 1834 when bankruptcy forced the twelfth laird to emigrate to Tasmania. It stands on the site of a house built in 1745 and burned by the Hanoverian soldiers and sailors a year later when searching the island for the fugitive prince. Dr Johnson and Boswell both stayed at Raasay House. Early in the nineteenth century the house was renovated and reshaped and in 1846 it was sold again and then proceeded to pass into the hands of several owners. In 1876 the industrialist Edward Herbert Wood from Burslem, Staffordshire, bought it and created a sporting and farming estate. He sold up in 1912 and the house then became a hotel until 1960. It lay derelict for a time and suffered attacks from pillagers and violent weather conditions. It is now occupied by the Scottish Adventure School, run by a trust which helps young people enjoy life in the outdoors.

On the shore in front of Raasay House is a circular fortification known as The Battery; two stone mermaids and a small cannon. The Battery may have been built at the time of invasion scares during the Napoleonic wars, but it is more likely that, along with the cannon and mermaids, it simply formed part of the decor of the house and estate.

When standing at the Battery, look out for a Pictish carving cut into the natural rock, and another on the face of a stone just beside the iron gate leading into the forestry plantation near the north gate of Raasay House. The Christian Cross symbol is accompanied by pre-Christian symbols of mystifying origin and the stones may date back as early as the seventh century.

A burial ground behind Raasay House contains the old parish church built in the thirteenth century and dedicated to St Moluag, one of the most famous Celtic saints and a member of that hardy band who brought Christianity from Ireland to the western seaboard and other parts of the Highlands. He set up a foundation on the island of Lismore, between Morvern and Appin, and may not have actually landed on Raasay (a dedication does not necessarily signify a saint's presence). There is also a mid-nineteenth century memorial chapel here, and a smaller structure probably dating from around the eleventh century. Close to Clachan village is the prominent Dun Borodale broch which dates from the Iron Age and may have been a last-bastion site for people in times of war.

A short stroll on the road takes the walker from Clachan back to Inverarish village.

The entrance to Oban Bay from Ardantrive (photo Màiri MacDonald).

WALK 33: *Strathclyde — The Isle of Kerrera (by Màiri MacDonald)*

Maps: OS Landranger Sheet 49—Oban and East Mull. OS Pathfinder Sheet NM82.92. OS Pathfinder Sheet NM83.93. **Start/Finish:** Ferry Slipway, Sound of Kerrera. **Distance:** 12 miles (19km) complete circuit (allow approx. 6 hours) *or* two separate half-circuits of approx. 6 miles (9.5km) each. **Access:** 2 miles (3km) south of Oban by minor road to Kerrera ferry at Gallanach. Nearest railway station at Oban, Argyll. **Type of Walking:** Easy, over minor, unsurfaced roads, grass or shoreline. **Features of Interest:** Ruined sixteenth-century castle and many other historically interesting sites; beautiful sandy beaches and a superb drove-road; panoramic seaward views. **Accommodation:** Wide selection of hotels, guest houses and B&B's in Oban. Large youth hostel on town esplanade. Further details from Oban and Mull Tourist Information Office, Argyll Square, Oban.

An Adventure Trail in the Wake of West Highland History

No visitor to Oban, the beautiful coastal capital of Scotland's historic West Highlands, can fail to be aware of the long and enticingly rugged Isle of Kerrera guarding the entrance to the town's famous and almost land-locked bay. Yet perhaps because of its very proximity to the town, few realise how much Kerrera has to offer the walker—exquisite scenery, an abundance of history and tradition, and an indefinable, magic typical of all the Hebridean Islands.

A rather strenuous 12 mile (20km) circuit of the entire island can be completed by strong walkers in a day, but family parties or less energetic individuals may prefer to split the distance into two smaller circuits and enjoy the northern and southern sections as separate outings, allowing plenty of time for allied pursuits such as photography, bird-watching, swimming or gazing at the scenery.

The nature of the terrain is not difficult in any way, but it can involve walking over grass which may be wet, beaches which may be stony, or tracks which may sometimes be slightly boggy, and therefore strong protective footwear is advisable.

Transport over to the island is provided by the little passenger ferry which plies regularly, on request, to and fro across the Sound of Kerrera from Gallanach, about 2 miles (3km) south of Oban. A small car park is provided near the slipway for the convenience of passengers, together with a special signalling-board which, when turned to show the appropriate side, will summon the ferryman from his house on the opposite shore.

Having crossed the Sound and arrived at Port Kerrera, the traditional landing-place for visitors for centuries, the route follows the road up from the jetty to a junction near the island's telephone box just below the Ferry House. Here walkers should turn left along the road leading south in the direction of Ardchoirc and Horseshoe Bay, where just below the farmhouse lies the smooth, sloping, waterside meadow known as Dail Righ, or 'The King's Field'. Near here in 1249 lay moored the royal galleon of the ill-fated King Alexander II of Scotland who, on being taken suddenly ill aboard his ship, was carried ashore to die on this historic spot.

Only a few years later, in 1263, the little settlements along the Sound of Kerrera were to see the arrival of yet another splendid royal vessel when the powerful King Hakon of Norway, with a war-fleet of over 160 longships, dropped anchor here on his way to the fateful battle of Largs. The Norsemen were destined to be defeated and from then on their oppressive power and influence over the islands of the Hebrides, including Kerrera, began to wane.

From Ardchoirc the quiet island road continues southwards along the Sound of Kerrera for about a mile, passing pretty Little Horseshoe Bay before swinging slightly inland at Upper Gylen to reach the neighbouring farm of Lower Gylen. Here, immediately left of the fanks beside the house, a gate gives access to a faint green track leading down to the ruins of Gylen Castle, perched dramatically on the cliffs above Port a'Chaisteal. Built in 1582 by Dougal, fifteenth Chief of the MacDougalls of Dunollie, probably as a defensive watch-tower and fire-signalling station, the castle was ideally placed to guard the entrance to the Sound of Kerrera and the Firth of Lorn. It was sacked and burned in 1647 by General Leslie's Covenanters under Campbell of Bragleen who carried off as booty the famous Brooch of Lorn, a priceless heirloom seized centuries earlier in 1306 by the MacDougalls from Robert the Bruce at the battle of Dalry near Tyndrum. The rugged scenery around Port a'Chaisteal is impressive, as are the stunning views out across the Lynn of Lorn to the great hills of Mull and the distant horizon-floating

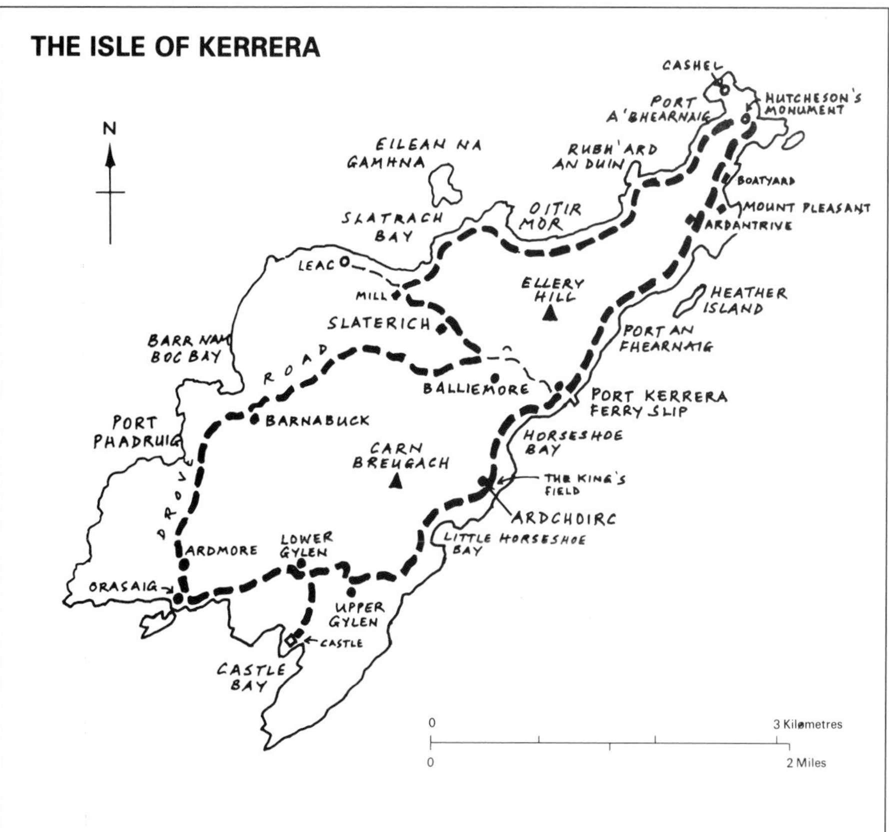

The gaunt ruins of Gylen Castle at the southern tip of Kerrera (photo Màiri MacDonald).

Facing page: ***The view from Kerrera towards Oban (photo Rennie McOwan).***

Facing page bottom: ***The hills of Mull from Rubh'ard an Duin (photo Màiri MacDonald).***

Garvellachs, the sacred 'Isles of the Sea', beloved by St Brendan and St Columba.

On rejoining the route the little island road continues on westwards from Lower Gylen around the spectacular southern coastline of Kerrera, where it gradually deteriorates into a wide green track as it approaches Orasaig. Here, at picturesque Port Dubh, before the building of the large jetty at Barr-nam-Boc Bay on the island's west coast, hugh droves of cattle from Mull and the neighbouring islands of the Southern Hebrides were landed, bound for the great Lowland trysts of Crieff and Falkirk.

The route now follows the old green drove-road from Orasaig up through the narrow pass of Ardmore, continuing on below the steep slopes of Torbhainn Mór past beautiful Port Phadruig to Barnabuck, originally the site of an old change-house. Just before reaching the farm of Barnabuck a short side-track leads off sharp left and runs down to the beautiful sandy bay of Barr-nam-Boc, below the Ridge of the Roebucks from which it takes its name. Here can be seen the remains of the old stone jetty on which the cattle were landed from Mull and, nearer the house, the now-ruinous fanks in which they were corralled prior to continuing on over the ridge to the ferry at Port Kerrera on the east side of the island.

Our walk follows the same route, rejoining the old drove-road at the farm-house and gradually ascending the high, windy pass of Am Maolan, the aptly-named 'Wild Place'. From here there are the most spectacular panoramic views westward to the islands of Mull and Lismore, and northwards along the Lynn of Lorn to the mountains of Morvern and Glencoe, with Ben Nevis itself rising supremely in the distance.

The route now gradually turns inland, conveniently bisecting the island into two separate halves as it continues on over to Balliemore and thence back down to the ferry to conclude the southern half of the walk. It is to this point that visitors aiming to complete only the northern section should make their way from the ferry, joining the route from Balliemore onwards. Those wishing to attempt the full circuit must, however, turn off sharp left at the gated junction just before reaching Balliemore and carry on down to the farm of Slaterich and the lovely sands of Slatrach Bay which, at low water, form one of the island's most beautiful beaches. Here, close to the shore, lie the remains of Kerrera's tiny meal-mill, built in 1732 and kept in use right up until 1843.

It was to the old house of Slaterich that Mary, wife of Iain Ciar the dashing twenty-second Chief of the MacDougalls, fled following the surrender of Dunollie Castle to government troops during the Jacobite Rising of 1715. And it was here, under cover of darkness, that the fugitive Chief would come to meet her from his famous hide-out in the mainland cliffs above the Sound of Kerrera, risking his life to be with her if only for a few precious hours.

Only a short distance around the shores of Slatrach Bay lie the crumbling remains of the little homestead of Leac, marked by the dark outline of a huge sentinel tree. Here in 1865 a poignant domestic tragedy took place; the two young sons of the household were drowned in the narrow channel between nearby Eilean na Gamhna and the shore. Their bodies were never found and the distraught parents forsook the place, leaving the house to crumble away to the haunted, derelict state we see today.

From Slatrach the remainder of the walk around the northern half of the island is virtually trackless, although the going throughout is quite easy and over grass. Simply follow the shoreline around to yet another of Kerrera's beautiful bays, the Oitir Mór, or 'Great Shallows', and then continue on below the high vertical bluff of Rubh'Ard an Duine to the pretty little inlet of Port a'Bhearnaig, the 'Port of the Great Cleft', at the northernmost tip of the island.

On Rubh a'Bhearnaig, above the northern arm of the bay, there is thought to have stood, at one time, an ancient 'cashel', a type of circular stone tower which may have been used by the monks from St Moluag's Early Christian monastery on the neighbouring isle of Lismore, either as a refuge or as a retreat. Only when the bracken is down can this faintly be discerned as a low circular mound with, close by, the remains of a tiny burial-ground dedicated to St Marnock.

Above Port a'Bhearnaig rises the tall obelisk of the Hutcheson Monument which may easily be reached from the shore by means of a gentle ascent eastwards over grass from the southern arm of the bay. The monument was erected in memory of David Hutcheson, partner of David MacBrayne, the founder of the famous West Highland steamship company of that name. It commands a fine all-round panorama which includes Mull, Morvern, Ardgour, Benderloch, Lismore and Oban, the latter bearing a striking resemblance to a Riviera watering-place.

A little track leads down from here to the boatyard at Ardentrive Bay on Kerrera's eastern shore from where a wide, unsurfaced road continues on past the fish-farm near Mount Pleasant to Ardantrive farm. On reaching the farmhouse the road itself turns right and heads back westwards in the direction of the Oitir Mór, so walkers bound for the ferry must take instead a little green track leading around the east side of the farmhouse out to the shore. From here a faint, intermittent track runs south along the Sound, keeping just above the water's edge as it winds its way in and out of numerous tiny bays and inlets. The going is not difficult, and should the track get lost in the bracken in places, simply follow the shoreline until, after about a mile, you reach the ferry and complete the full circuit of this beautiful and historic isle.

The Hutcheson Monument at the northern tip of Kerrera (photo Màiri MacDonald).

WALK 34: *Dumfries and Galloway — Rockcliffe to Sandyhills and Rough Island (by Catherine Mowat)*

Map: OS Landranger Sheet 84—Dumfries, Castle Douglas and surrounding area. **Start/Finish:** Start from Rockcliffe village (5 miles/8km south of Dalbeattie on A710). Finish Sandyhills car park. **Distance:** Up to 6½ miles (10.5km), including Rough Island. Allow at least 5 hours for exploring. **Access:** Drive 5 miles (8km) south of Dalbeattie on the A710. Turn right onto a minor road at Colvend village car park on left before entering Rockcliffe village. No other parking allowed. Car park in Sandyhills village. Return same route or by road. Bus services to Rockcliffe from Dumfries and Dalbeattie on A710. **Type of Walking:** Check tide times locally or buy a copy of the Solway tides timetable, price 30p, available from the Tourist Information Centre in Dalbeattie. Route from Rockcliffe to Sandyhills is clearly signposted but tends to be overgrown and rough in places; strong footwear is essential. The path follows the steep contours of the cliffs for 2½ miles (4km) but from the hamlet of Portling the walk can continue along the shore, tide permitting, to Sandyhills. **Features of Interest:** National Trust of Scotland bird sanctuary on Rough Island; Iron Age fort settlement at Castlehill Point; high cliffs, seabirds and caves. **Accommodation:** Hotel and B&B accommodation in Rockcliffe and Sandyhills. Self catering at both resorts. Nearest youth hostel about 40 miles (64km) at Minnigaff (Newton Stewart). Tel. Newton Stewart 0671 2211.

A Ramble through Folklore, Fantasy and Fact

The immediate impression gained by a visitor to the coastal villages along the Solway Firth is one of quiet unobtrusiveness. Locals welcome visitors, but not commercialism. You won't find many fun fairs, fish'n'chip bars or discos, but you will find peace, beauty and miles of unspoilt coastline to explore at leisure.

Rockcliffe village has an air of gentle dignity. A smattering of well-kept houses and gardens nestles comfortably beneath thickly-wooded slopes facing the estuary of the Rough Firth; a place popular with visiting yachtsmen during the summer months. Until recently this

Facing page **Portling Coves (photo Ross Mowat).**

stretch of coastline was a busy centre for fishing and quarrying. The old mussel beds near Castlehill Point and Hestan Island were worked by local fishermen and soft granite mill stones were worked by the former Glenstocken mill stone quarry from the area around Gutcher's Isle.

At low tide it is possible to cross the mudflats directly across from Rockcliffe to Rough Island, a 20-acre bird sanctuary owned by the National Trust for Scotland. This is definitely welly-boots country—in warm weather it's just as easy to wade across the half-mile stretch in bare feet. Visitors are discouraged from exploring the island during the breeding season (May to June) when oystercatchers and common terns nest along the shore.

Even on a damp, drizzly day the views are worth the muddy trek with the bulk of Hestan Island (Rathan Isle of S R Crockett's historical novel *The Raiders*), looming to the south and the English coastline a smudge on the horizon.

Limpet-and barnacle-covered rocks frame the shoreline which is thick with pink and white tellin and cockle shells. To the south, the shingle beach gives way to larger rock formations and one bears a close resemblance to a sea horse. The sheltered coves are strewn with wild flowers including sea pinks, thrift, and sea bindweed while fern, bracken and wild dog rose cover the middle of the island.

Jellyfish the size of dinner plates are washed up across the causeway and all over the shingle. The causeway, which is uncovered at low tide, leads to Kippford, another attractive seaside village and popular marina. The trip back to Rockcliffe can be made via the Jubilee Path, named after Queen Victoria's Diamond Jubilee, which runs between the two villages, or by a return squelch through the mudflats.

Visitors are not encouraged to park in Rockcliffe. A large car park is provided just above the village and from there it's a short stroll downhill to the start of the walk. A signpost on the left indicates the route to Castlehill Point which winds its way close to the shore giving superb views across the Rough Firth to Rough Island, Hestan Island and Almorness Point. From Castlehill Point, once the site of an Iron Age fort settlement dating back to around 4000BC, the view spans the Solway Firth across to England and the Isle of Man.

The path is clearly marked by arrows and signposts and although rough and damp in places, it is always passable. Keep to the edge of the fields. Steps are conveniently placed across the stone dykes (walls). It is advisable to wear stout walking shoes or similar sensible footwear as the route is often overgrown and the scattered boulders and rocks are popular places for sunbathing adders, harmless as long as they are left undisturbed.

The route follows the undulating cliffs to the hamlets of Port o'Warren and Portling where the cliffs fall sheer into the sea and house many nesting seabirds including razorbills, kittiwakes, common gulls, fulmars and guillemots. In the late evening, parents and young balance precariously on tiny ledges hundreds of feet above the restless sea, perhaps the only witnesses in years gone by to the smuggling that was once rife along this coast. As dusk draws shadows into the many hidden coves, it's not hard to imagine the muffled cries of men unloading contraband to be stored in the caves or taken away on the backs of waiting pack horses.

The rocky outcrop of Gutcher's Isle lies about a mile from Castlehill Point, once the home of a notorious smuggler called Gutcher. Full of strength and daring, he thought little of leaping over sheer cliffs in his efforts to escape the excisemen.

Smuggling was at its height along the Solway during the eighteenth century with large shipments of brandy, rum, wine, tea, salt and tobacco arriving at night on Scotland's southern shores. Everyone took part—farmers and fishermen, lairds and labourers, preachers and politicians. The Church authorities were well aware of the smuggling but their priorities differed from those of the excisemen. An account given in the kirk-session records of 1741 rebukes seven local sinners for smuggling on a Sunday, the breaking of the sabbath-day law constituting the real crime.

Some smuggling stories had more tragic endings. The day before his wedding, a young man from Ramsey on the Isle of Man risked sailing across the Solway with an illegal cargo of fishery salt. He knew he could find a ready market on the mainland and he needed the money to pay for the wedding. The bride's brother went with him. All went well until they reached Hestan Island when suddenly they heard an order to 'stand to'. The cutter, *Prince*

Below left: **'Sea Horse', Rough Island.**

Below: **The Needle's Eye, near Portling Bay (photos Ross Mowat).**

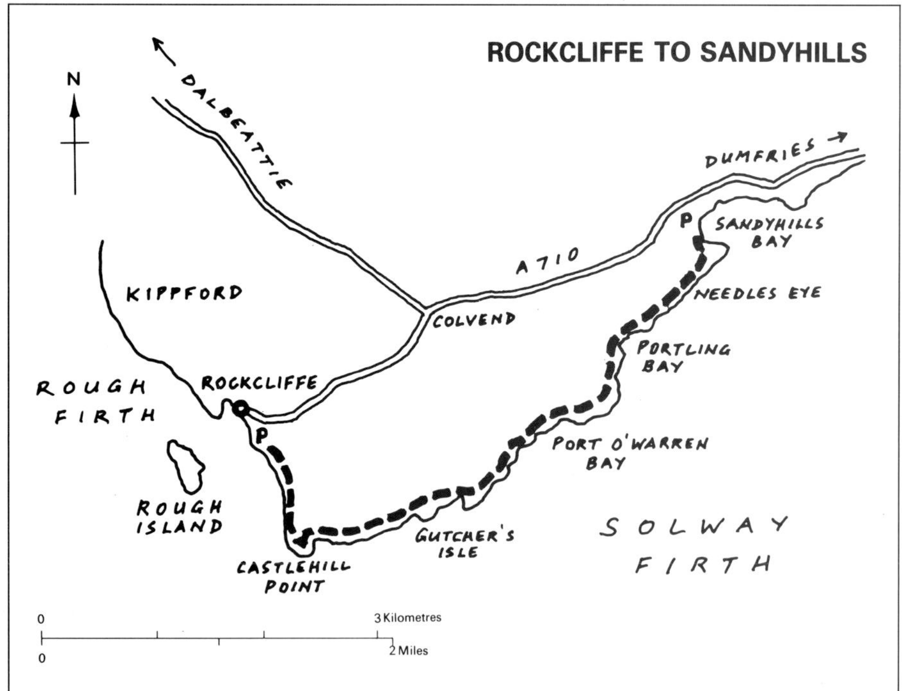

Edward Augustus, had been hidden from sight in Balcary Bay. Pretending to misunderstand, they headed straight for Port o'Warren, a popular landing place for smugglers. They were passing the cutter when a shot was fired, killing the young bridegroom instantly. In a panic his friend ran the boat ashore near Rockcliffe and fled. Their boat, with its unlucky cargo, was towed by the Customs men to Kirkcudbright and the dead man buried on the shore. Later, after a warrant from the Sheriff, his body was taken to the churchyard at Colvend parish.

The bride's brother made his way back to the Isle of Man to break the sad news to his distraught sister and family. It was their wish that the body should be brought home to be buried in the family burial ground. After obtaining the necessary permission, a sad party of friends and relatives, including the bride and her brother, set off for Scotland. On their way home tragedy struck again. The weather became worse and heavy seas and high winds capsized their boat before they got to Hestan Island, at a spot close to where the young man had been shot. The entire funeral party was drowned.

Sir John Reid, who ordered the fatal shot to be fired from the *Prince Edward Augustus*, was charged with murder but later acquitted at the High Court in Edinburgh. For years afterwards local people would point out the first burial place of the young Manxman on the shore near Colvend.

Perhaps it's a trick of the light or the effect of a cross-current, but at a certain point the sea breaks inexplicably into a creamy foam. With no dolphins or shoals of fish in sight, the imagination can conjure up visions of mermaids. This is not as ridiculous as it might sound as local tradition has it that a mermaid of Barnhourie sandbanks fell in love with a handsome young sailor from the town of Dalbeattie and whenever he returned from a fishing trip, she would follow the boat, always careful to keep out of sight, until it moored in one of the narrow creeks near Kippford village.

According to the story, a tremendous summer storm caused the sandbanks of Barnhourie Bank to shift their position. The young sailor was homeward bound, the sea was still rough and the crew were unaware, until it was too late, that the sandbank had moved further west. The keel hit the sandbank and the captain and most of the crew were swept overboard in the wash. The young sailor was flung into the boiling sea and his desperate cries were carried to the mermaid as she sat on the rocks beneath the cliffs of the Needle's Eye, close to Portling Bay. She brought him out of the raging sea to the safety of the Needle's Eye and in the small cave nearby they spent the night. They fell in love and throughout the summer the young man often returned to the cave, but with the approach of autumn he had to go back to sea. Heartbroken, the mermaid swam back beneath the waves and the following spring her baby son was born.

It was 20 months before the sailor returned from the West Indies. Illness had broken out amongst the crew and some of them, including the captain, had died of fever. The mate was unfamiliar with the coastline and before they could reach the safety of the river mouth he ran the ship onto rocks and she foundered within minutes. For a second time, the sailor's cries were heard by the mermaid as she swam with her son near Barnhourie Banks but in spite of her long and frantic search she could find no trace of him. Heartbroken, she was convinced he was dead.

The following morning she saw a huddled shape stranded on the tide line. She managed to pull herself across the wet sand and there, at last, she found him. On the flooding tide she brought him ashore and then, from the hillsides, she gathered special herbs and spring flowers and weeds from the rocks. These she mixed and gave to the young man. Her clear saltless tears, the tears of a mermaid, fell onto his eyes. Slowly he began to breathe and recovered. Realising that he was now more at home in the sea than on land, he joined the mermaid's world. They had more children and over the years the family grew famous with the fishermen of the Solway for their warnings to sailors about the shifting sandbanks of Barnhourie, and any pending storms.

From Portling the walk can continue across the cliffs or, if the tide is out, along the shore. This is a good place to explore the many caves, but take a torch with you as some stretch back into the cliffs for quite a distance.

The Piper's Cave takes its name from a local legend. A piper is said to have explored it, playing the bagpipes as he went. After a while the sound of the pipes abruptly stopped and he was never seen again. The cave has a vertical and horizontal shaft cut into it for copper searching. The Brandy Cave at Portling Bay is traditionally a smuggler's hiding place and has a 12ft long inner chamber.

On a warm, sunny day you can walk barefoot across miles of sand, stopping occasionally to watch the nesting seabirds or laze awhile in the secluded coves. Lines of 'stake nets' are placed by local fishermen all along the shore during the summer months to trap salmon with the ebb and flow of the tide.

Soon the broad sweep of Sandyhills Bay with its caravan park comes into view with the Southwick coastline stretching beyond. There is a car park and shop at Sandyhills where you can buy something cool to slake your thirst before making the return trip either by the same route or by the road back to Rockcliffe.

WALK 35: *Cumbria — St Bees Head*

Map: OS Landranger Sheet 89—West Cumbria. **Start/Finish:** St Bees seafront. **Distance:** 7½ miles (12km)—allow 3 to 4 hours. **Access:** St Bees lies on the B5345 west of the A595 Cumbrian coast road. Nearest railway station—St Bees. **Type of Walking:** Well-walked, undulating cliff path, stony tracks and field paths. **Features of Interest:** Outstanding sandstone cliff scenery; Fleswick Bay; St Bees Bird Reserve; St Bees Lighthouse; wide views of the Lakeland fells. **Accommodation:** Available in St Bees, Sandwith and Whitehaven. Nearest youth hostels inland at Cockermouth and Gillerthwaite.

Sandstone Cliffs and a Lakeland Panorama

Considering the legendary quality of Cumbria's lakeland and fell scenery, much of its coastline is a disappointment. Pockets of industry run from Workington and Whitehaven south past the Sellafield nuclear power and reprocessing complex to Barrow-in-Furness, interrupting miles of low dunes, grassland and an often stony, inaccessible foreshore.

Only at St Bees Head do we find echoes of the Lake District's grandeur. Four miles (6.5km) of towering red sandstone cliffs, carpeted with wild flowers and home to numerous sea birds, form a nipple-like protuberance on the westward swell of Cumbria's coastline. An enclave of considerable natural beauty, the headland is popular with the local population and visitors alike who come, perhaps, to watch sea birds in the RSPB Reserve or walk the cliff path; the as-yet incomplete Cumbria Coastal Way and Alfred Wainwright's well-established Coast to Coast Walk both take in St Bees Head.

Straddling the Pow Beck valley, St Bees stands half a mile back from the sea. St Bee, or St Bega, said to have been an Irish princess

Previous page: ***The coast towards Whitehaven, after rounding St. Bees Head.***

Above: ***The view forward from South Head. St Bees lighthouse is just visible centre top.***

Right: ***Sea pinks by the path.***

Sandstone cliffs at Fleswick Bay.

who took a childhood vow to devote herself to God, established a nunnery here in the seventh century. This was succeeded, 500 years later, by a Benedictine Priory which, though greatly restored and adapted, became the present Priory Church of St Mary and St Bega; its western doorway is an exceptionally handsome example of Norman architecture, built from glowing local sandstone.

The well-preserved body of a local fourteenth-century lord was discovered by archaeologists in 1981 on the site of a ruined chapel on the church's south side. Medieval human remains are rare and this one the more so for its exceptional condition, attributed to the lead sheath and resinous shroud coating which together excluded all air and moisture. Details and exhibits are displayed in Whitehaven Museum.

So much for history! The attractions of an airy seafront may be spoiled for some by a suspicion that the Irish Sea, so close to Sellafield, is not as wholesome as it might be! Infrequent Cumbria Coast trains, nudged by foothills to the very water's edge for much of their course, dodge inland here along the Pow Beck valley to Whitehaven. Roads, however, head seawards, converging to reach the Seacote Hotel near two large car parks.

St Bees' concrete sea wall was installed around 1960 to halt serious erosion and provides a pleasant pedestrian promenade backed by grassy hillocks. If you arrive on a calm day, the presence of Lifeboat House, bright red lifejackets and stout groynes along the grey pebble beach will remind you that sea conditions here can be treacherous.

Cliffs immediately to the north-west, rising above colourful boulders, fallen rocks and a rough bathing pool, are unremarkably grassy, unlike the precipitous bastions of red sandstone beyond and out of sight. Starting the walk along the sea wall 'prom', you pass the end of a caravan park, cross a footbridge over Rottington Beck and climb a worn sandstone path past a Nature Reserve sign. Cliff edge erosion is at work—be warned—but the path soon continues securely enough over brackeny ground. As height is gained, views open up across St Bees' wide sands down the coast to Sellafield and distant Black Combe, a silhouette of high moorland obscuring the Duddon estuary.

Topping a rise by a ruined Coastguard lookout on South Head, the majestic cliff architecture of this unique headland is revealed for the first time. It is an impressive sight, extending to the lighthouse on North Head and accompanied by dizzy glimpses of a bouldery foreshore over 300ft (100m) below. Inland of the path, pasture rises voluptuously to a close horizon; by the pathside itself, sea pinks, cow parsley, gorse and buttercups brighten grassy

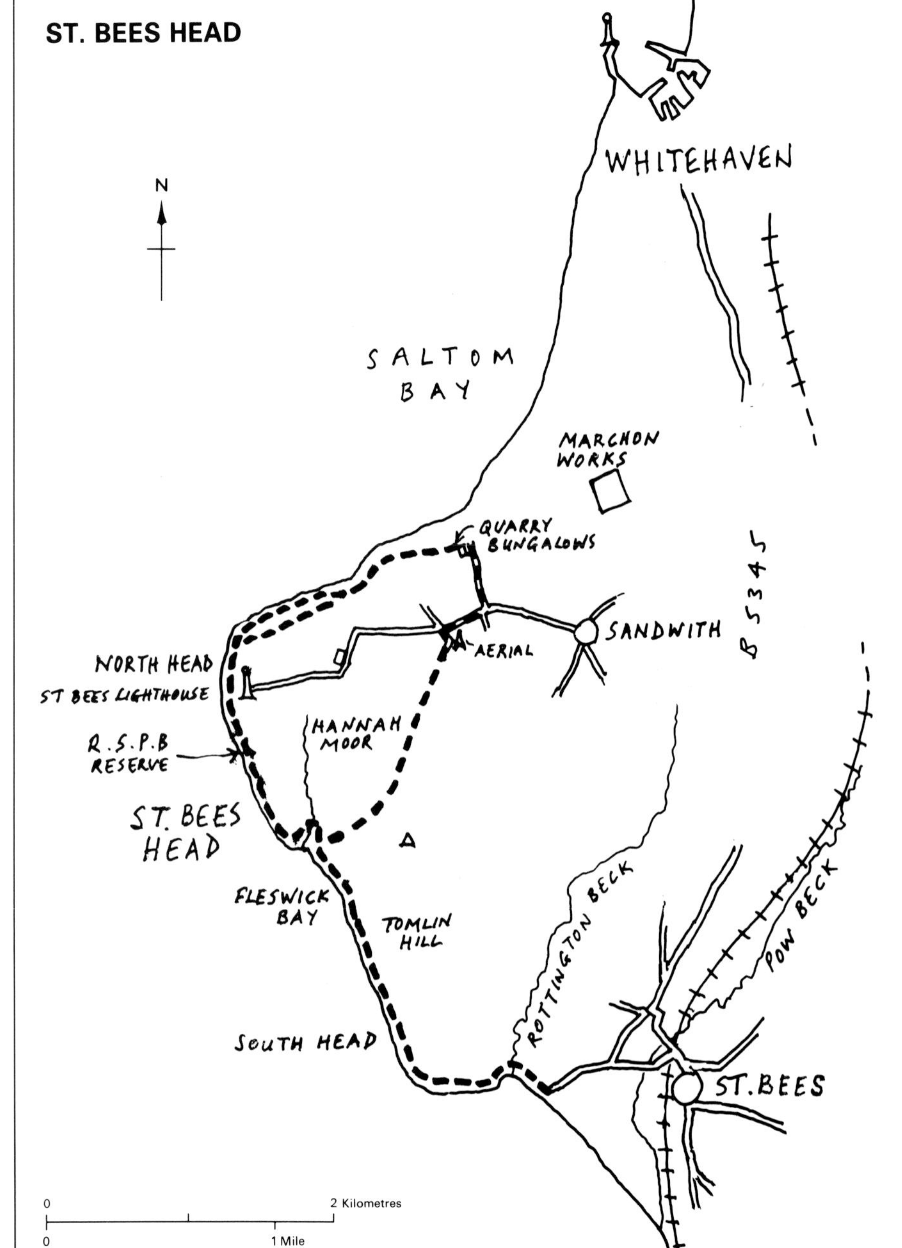

banks.

Undulating along the flanks of Tomlin Hill, you soon approach Fleswick (pronounced 'Flezzick') Bay where the cliff line is riven by a dramatic cleft at a stream outflow. Unless circumstances are pressing, do make a descent to the beach here. On your way down the stream bed, you will pass a veritable hanging garden on the cliffside—sea pinks, scurvy grass and sea campion are common on these rugged cliff faces, with rock sea lavender, rock samphire and golden saxifrage occupying damp ledges and wet 'seeps'. Above a low pebble bank containing the occasional semi-precious stone, such as garnets, soar complex, brown-red cliffs streaked with white gypsum and bedded and eroded into flowing, scalloped and often overhanging forms. A cave at the northern end was frequently used by smugglers to land contraband from small boats.

Accessible slabs of smooth sandstone have been copiously engraved with the names and initials of visitors dating back many decades. Each will last longer than its author's lifetime but none can resist eventual obliteration from the polishing effect of waves and weather.

Your exit from Fleswick Bay is either back to the head of the ravine (where our return loop comes in) or via a short rock climb to a stile on the left. Either course regains the coast path and climbs steps back to clifftop level. The RSPB has provided viewing balconies along their cliff-edge Reserve and they are well patronised by birdwatchers during spring and early summer when breeding activity reaches its height. St Bees Bird Reserve holds one of western England's largest sea bird colonies and is noted for its auks, guillemots, razorbills, puffins and the rare black guillemot; many other species frequent the area.

Rising gently, the path approaches St Bees Lighthouse, set back 487ft (150m) from the cliffs at an altitude of 310ft (94m); visits can be pre-arranged by telephoning the Keeper on Whitehaven 2635. Crossing a concrete pathway to the spick and span Fog Signal building (a place to avoid in poor visibility!), you will have reached the nearest mainland point to the Isle of Man, about 30 miles (48km) distant. To the north-west are vistas of the Galloway hills across the Solway Firth.

Rounding North Head, the path is dangerously close to a precipitous drop for a few metres (great care is needed in a gusty wind, when the nearby fence can be held onto), but quickly reverts to normality. Quite suddenly, into sight swing Saltom Bay, Whitehaven's harbour lighthouse and the coast as far north as Workington. You are left with few illusions. This western seaboard, ravaged by industry past and present, offers little to the walker in search of clean air and unspoiled surroundings, despite its proximity to one of Britain's most popular National Parks. Flanked by pollution to land and sea, the isolated 'specialness' of St Bees Head seems doubly poignant.

At a stone slab stile, two onward routes are available—right to cross easy field tops, or ahead for a more intimate (and strenuous) encounter with cliff geology and flora. The latter way dips and climbs above leaning sandstone beds through profuse clifftop vegetation, eventually rising abruptly on scrambly steps to meet the field path. Veering progressively east, you arrive at Quarry Bungalows above the disused crater of Birkhams Quarry.

Half a mile ahead, the landscape is dominated—many would say blighted—by the Marchon chemical works, owned by Albright and Wilson. Like Sellafield to the south, it is visible from a range of many, many miles, spewing fumes and smoke downwind and depositing foam into the adjacent sea. Its main output is detergent and surfactants—products that foam. In deference to the local economy, the plant does provide some 1900 much needed jobs and although its impact on the environment is inescapably detrimental, Albright and Wilson did co-sponsor (with the National Coal Board) the construction of a coast path past the works back in 1984. The Cumbria Coastal Way continues, in fact, to Whitehaven but with walking quality taking such a nosedive, a return loop to St Bees is infinitely preferable.

To achieve this, you turn right past Quarry Bungalows on a sunken, stony lane. In 500m you reach the private lighthouse road (a pedestrian right of way from Sandwith village) and turn right, uphill, to a crossroads by a conspicuous aerial near a covered reservoir. Taking the farm track on the left which heads off between fields, you cross a ladder stile and continue along by a hedge. Between gaps, especially towards the far end, there is a quite superb panorama of the Lakeland fells above a dipping foreground of cultivated fields. By keeping to the coast, you are denied such spectacular views by the intervention of Tomlin Hill and Hanna Moor, so this short inland loop gives you the best of both worlds!

Emerging into a hilltop field, the path peters out but at the next walled bank you swing right, downhill towards the sea. A stile halfway down and another in the field's bottom corner take you to steeper ground where the coast path is met above Fleswick Bay. It is now a simple matter of reversing your outward walk along the cliffs to St Bees.

A panorama of Lakeland fells from the field path over Hannah Moor.

WALK 36: *Isle of Man — Raad ny Foillan (by Aileen Evans)*

Maps: The Isle of Man Public Rights of Way and Leisure Map—Scale 1:25,000. OS Landranger Isle of Man Sheet 95. NB Route marking includes 3 errors on both maps. Waymarks on ground correct. **Start/Finish:** Douglas or Castletown circuit. Return to Douglas from towns en route by bus or train. **Distance:** 96 miles (154km). Allow approx. 40 hours total. **Access:** By sea—Douglas. By air—Ronaldsway, Castletown. **Public Transport:** Bus routes connecting main towns with Douglas. Steam train Port Erin—Castletown—Douglas, May-Sept. Electric train Douglas—Laxey—Ramsey, May-Sept. Timetable from IOM Dept. of Tourism or Information Offices. **Type of Walking:** Well waymarked throughout. Easy to moderate walking. Clifftop footpath can be narrow and overgrown in places but is generally well maintained. Mountain section more arduous. Beach sections tide check advised. Conglomerate cliffs unstable. Main Road walking 2½ miles (4km). **Features of Interest:** Castle Rushen, Castletown; Peel Castle; Viking excavations; traditional Manx crofters village, Cregneish; Maughold churchyard—Unique Celtic crosses; Mull Hill, Ballafoyle Cairn—ancient burial Sites; many sites of Neolithic and Celtic Habitation; Nature reserves—Scarlett Point, Calf of Man, The Ayres; vast areas of unspoilt Heritage coastline. **Accommodation:** Hotels—book through IOM Dept. of Tourism, 13 Victoria Street, Douglas, Isle of Man. Farmhouse acc. and B&B—list from IOM Dept. of Tourism. Camp sites—list from IOM Dept. of Tourism or local Information office. Many farms allow camping on request. Numerous backpacking pitches throughout the walk.

Raad ny Foillan–Way of the Gull

The Raad ny Foillan is a 96 mile (154km) footpath around the coastline of the Isle of Man. It was completed and waymarked in 1986 to mark the island's Heritage year.

The coast of this beautiful island is mainly virgin territory; real heritage coastline with a rugged unspoilt air that is truly captivating. Although the island is relatively small, the variety of shoreline introduced to the walker, together with its flora and birdlife, provides a video of surprises and delights. The secret of this diversity lies in the island's foundations. In the south, very old hard rocks of the Cambrian period stand proud, defying the waves of time. In the north, new sands and gravels ride the breakers eager to enlist. On the east and west

Facing page: **At the Chasms, the Sugarloaf centre bottom (photo. Aileen Evans).**

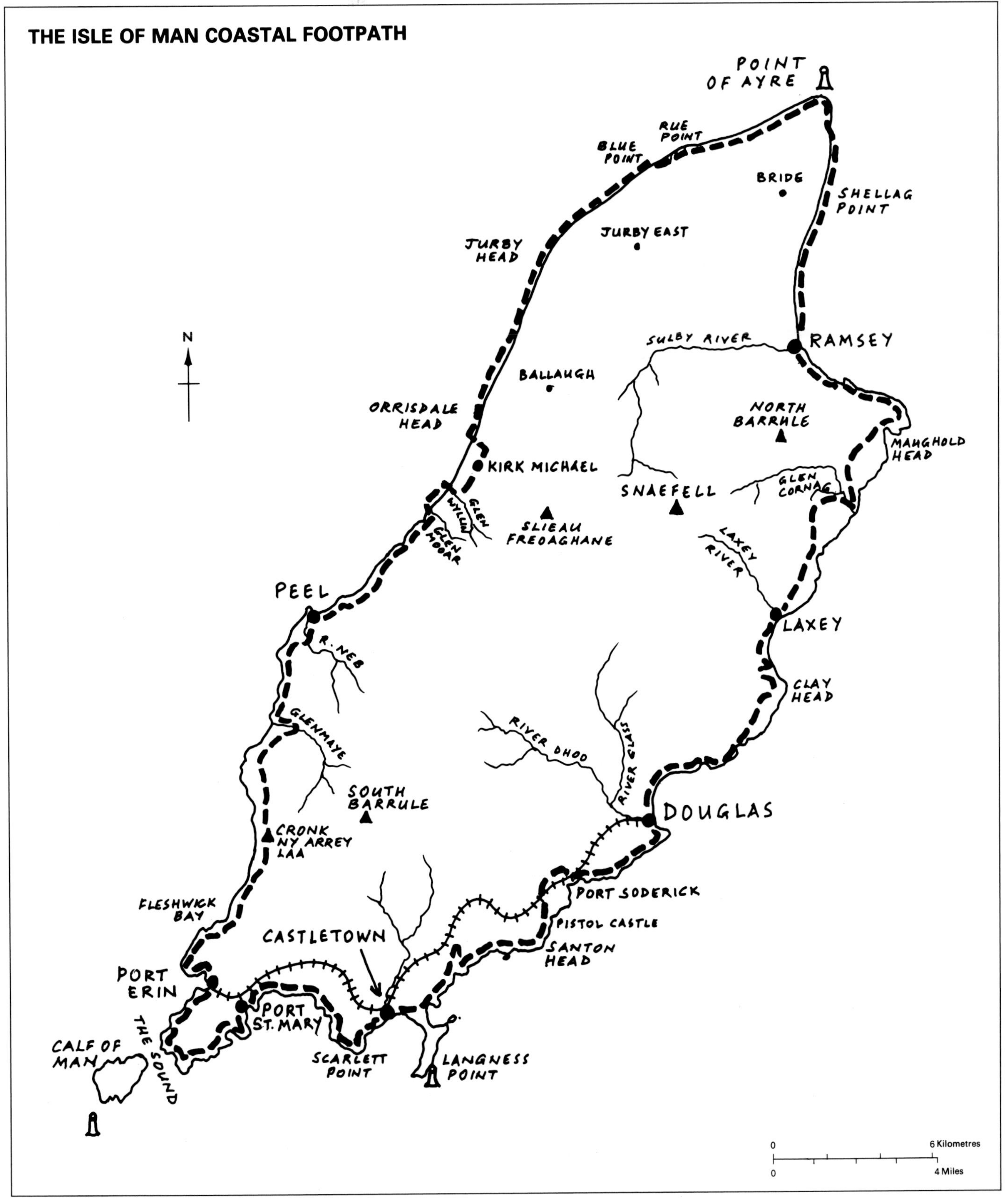

Left: **Dawn over the Tower of Refuge, Douglas Bay.**

Bottom left: **Across Port Erin Bay to Bradda Head (photos Aileen Evans).**

coasts appears a geological cavalcade which provides the walker with an ever changing sea-borne tableau. The footpath passes over spectacular sea cliffs, moors and hills, winds through gentle glens, visits sheltered havens, descends to isolated beaches and pauses by picturesque fishing villages. The footpath is never far from the sound of the sea or the cry of the gull.

In a few places the passing years have left their mark but the fashionable Victorian visitors who changed Douglas and Ramsey into busy holiday resorts have gone; peace and quiet have returned. No caravan sites draw your eyes from the view. No tourist hotspots cause a hurried bypass and no cheek by jowl traffic gives rise to concern.

The walking is easy to moderate with one more arduous mountain section and distances can be regulated to suit the party. A fast walker travelling light can complete the circuit in 5 days, whilst a family party of backpackers visiting the many sites of interest on the way could take a fortnight. The starting point depends on your choice of transport, but as the footpath passes the sea terminal at Douglas and skirts the airport at Ronaldsway you will alight literally on the footpath.

Douglas to Castletown ($15\frac{1}{2}$ miles/25km) Grade Easy

Starting from Douglas, a clockwise circuit of the island will put the prevailing wind at your back when on the west coast mountain section. The blue and white waymarks showing a soaring gull, are carefully and frequently sited. They lead south-east over the river and up onto the level of the Marine Drive. The views of the distant Lake District hills, unfamiliar to me from this angle, adorn the horizon while underfoot the airy, unused road gives you a neighbourly acquaintance with the magnificent Manx Slate cliff scenery. This is followed by the little beach of Port Soderick and its pretty glen. The isolated sea cliffs at Pistol Castle host rock climbs and, as the height of the cliff decreases, the first of many sites of ancient habitation are passed. Derby Haven, a wide shallow bay, attracts hundreds of hungry birds as the tide recedes. They seem to ignore Ronaldsway airport over the fence and remain oblivious to walkers. The footpath, shunning the Langness peninsula, cuts across the ancient towboat isthmus and turns to Castletown.

Once the ancient capital of the island, Castletown's Castle Rushen is a rewarding visit. The camp site, however, is the only one I have come across which does not allow camping!

Castletown to Port Erin (14 miles/23km) Grade Moderate

Excursion to Cregneish & Mull Hill ($1\frac{1}{2}$ miles/2.5km)

Fast progress can be made to Port St Mary if you are not captivated by the plants and pools of the Scarlett Point Nature Reserve.

As the Raad ny Foillan rises onto the southwest headland of the island, the prime part of the footpath, the west coast, is revealed. Here begins the National Trust Area of Public Ramblage where you can stay on the footpath or wander its acres at will.

The footpath climbs from Perwick Bay until it stops abruptly where the cliffs fall sheer 250ft (76m) into the sea at The Chasms. These are real chasms, great slits down through the earth to sea level, loved as sheltered nesting sites by many varieties of sea birds, deadly for the unwary walker. The view from the protected balcony shows the surf sweeping around the Sugar Loaf, a giant sea stack; wheeling seabirds will pin you hypnotically to the spot but the sighting of Spanish Head and the Calf of Man persuade the feet to turn northwards.

The walker with an easy schedule and an interest in Manx history can visit the beautifully restored, yet informal village of Cregneish and the Neolithic stone circle of Mull Hill.

The narrow channel between the island and the Calf of Man is aptly called The Sound. When the tide race is in full flow its roar will flood your senses as you climb over the shoulder of Aldrick Moor, then lull as you descend into the sunset haven of Port Erin. Here is a chance to meet the local fishermen who take passengers on a tour around the Calf of Man collecting their lobster pots at the same time—an opportunity to see the Raad ny Foillan from a different angle.

Above right: ***Between surf and cliffs at Jurby Head (photo Aileen Evans).***

Port Erin to Peel ($14\frac{1}{2}$ miles/23km)—Maximum Height 1434ft (437m); Actual Height Gain 2850ft (869m) Grade Strenuous

The traverse of the Carnanes begins with the well-trodden Coronation Footpath up Bradda Head to the spot from which a world's winning photograph was taken. At the Milner Tower say goodbye to civilisation for a while. The three summits—Bradda Hill, Lhiattee ny Beinnee and Cronk ny Arrey Laa—follow, each higher, wilder and more remote than its predecessor. From the summit of Bradda Hill (766ft/233m) a steep descent is made to the beach at Fleshwick Bay, followed by a climb across the heather and gorse clad slopes of Lhiattee ny Beinnee. The heather is short and the gorse is a dwarf variety which flowers in late summer when the footpath threads its way through a carpet of purple and gold.

The summit of Lhiattee ny Beinnee (988ft) provides an excellent viewpoint and one's gaze is drawn north-east to Snaefell, cushioned in its surrounding hills and glens. Looking westward the Mountains of Mourne join the sea to the sky.

The Sloc is the next gap, where a busy farm flourished in Neolithic times, and the site of the village can be clearly seen as you ascend Cronk ny Arrey Laa ('The Hill of the Morning Watch'). From the Bronze Age Burial Mound on the summit the way north is spread before you. The single white building in the distance emphasises the remoteness, whilst the height of the cliffs baffles the sound of the surf. As you descend and curve west nearer the sea a shy footpath crosses the way. Following a line of springs across the steep hillside it leads to a secret grassy balcony. Here in a sod and thatch hut lived a hermit priest tending his tiny keeill ('church'). Built in AD 430-700 it was last used for a funeral only a hundred years ago. Little has changed, only the pattern of the footprints by the spring.

The footpath now crosses the merry stream of Gloin Mooar and winds through the Creggan Moor Broughs to Dalby and the beautiful Glen Maye. What a place in spring! Waterfalls reflect countless shades of green and bluebells thigh deep.

Back on the clifftop path, home of the friendly stonechat, easy progress is made. A visit to the prominent tower on Corrin's Hill is a very poor exchange for the velvet path where the seabirds preen themselves on its western side. My feet began to drag over Peel Hill but it was the sudden view of Peel castle shielding the harbour which brought me to a standstill. A worthy finale to an excellent day.

Peel to Kirk Michael (7½ miles/12km) Grade Easy

The Raad ny Foillan's character is now changed by the island's geology. Red sandstone cliffs adorn the tideline and a mile out from Peel the footpath takes to the track-bed of the abandoned Peel to Ramsey railway. Wide views stretch out from the embankments and cuttings have been taken over by wild flowers and attendant butterflies.

Glen Mooar leads the way to the beach where the younger cliffs of glacial drift now trap the footpath between their towering walls and the surf. Now is the time to check the tide. This mile of beach walking is just a curtain-raiser before the cliffs break at Glen Wyllin and allow the path to regain the track bed into Kirk Michael.

Kirk Michael to Point of Ayre (15 miles/24km). Grade Easy

After Kirk Michael and a quick goodbye to the railway track the footpath slips down Glen Trunk and lands on the beach. Check the tide then set the automatic pilot for the Point of Ayre.

The sand is firm and although the cliffs of Orrisdale Head look forbidding, company in the form of seals and birds are a constant delight. Just as the legs are starting to sing the desert song the cliffs become lower and the gentle heath of the Ayres Nature Reserve brings you refreshed to the lighthouse at the Point of Ayre.

Point of Ayre to Ramsey (7miles/11km). Grade Easy

The Point of Ayre is the watershed of the Raad ny Foillan. The beach walk to Ramsey freewheels below the red conglomerate cliffs of Shellag Point and the familiar Manx slates in the distance take on new shapes in the form of Maughold Head and North Barrule. The picturesque busy port of Ramsey snuggles close to the foot of the hills. Its swimming pool and café may delay you but this is just one of many pleasant surprises the Way of the Gull drops on you before the circuit is complete.

Ramsey to Laxey (13 miles/21km). Grade Moderate

The cliff profile on the east is lower than that on the west coast but equally attractive. The slopes above Maughold Head are the domain of the four-horned Loughtan sheep, whilst Maughold village churchyard displays a magnificent collection of sixth to twelfth century carved stone slabs and crosses telling the story of Sigurd. The churchyard is just over the wall from the footpath. In a series of climbs and swoops to the shore the path visits the Ballafoyle Cairn (a neolithic burial site), the beech glades of Glen Cornaa, and continually runs the gauntlet of the amazing electric railway to arrive at Laxey Harbour.

A worthwhile diversion can be made to visit the famous Laxey wheel and the recently instituted mines trail.

Laxey to Douglas (9½ miles/15km). Grade Easy

After wandering through the patterned fields of Clay Head the end is in sight. The approach to Douglas summed up for me the friendly spirit I had received all round the island; the way was barred by private, well-tended lawns, yet there was the waymark. The owners have donated the gift of passage allowing the Raad ny Foillan to pass through their gardens. This generous act enhances the accumulated pleasure as the stroll along Douglas promenade brings the circuit of the Isle of Man to its conclusion.

USEFUL ADDRESSES

British Trust for Conservation Volunteers
36 St Mary's Street
Wallingford
Oxon
OX10 0EU

Camping and Caravanning Club of Great Britain
11 Grosvenor Place
London
SW1W 0EX

Coastal Anti-Pollution League
94 Greenway Lane
Bath
Avon
BA2 4LN

Countryside Commission
John Dower House
Crescent Place
Cheltenham
Glos.
GL50 3RA

For Scotland:
Battleby
Redgorton
Perth
PH1 3EW

English Tourist Board
Thames Tower
Blacks Road
London
W6 9EL

Friends of the Earth
26-28 Underwood Street
London
N1 7JQ

Greenpeace
30-31 Islington Green
London
N1 8XE

Long Distance Walkers Association
11 Thorn Bank
Onslow Village
Guildford
Surrey
GU2 5PL

Marine Conservation Society
4 Gloucester Road
Ross-on-Wye
Herefordshire
HR9 5BU

National Trust
36 Queen Anne's Gate
London
SW1H 9AS
For Scotland:
5 Charlotte Street
Edinburgh
EH2 4DU

Nature Conservancy Council
Northminster House
Northminster Road
Peterborough
Cambs.
PE1 1UA

Open Spaces Society
25a Bell Street
Henley-on-Thames
Oxon
RG9 2BA

Ramblers Association
1-5 Wandsworth Road
London
SW8 2LJ

Royal Society for the Protection of Birds
The Lodge
Sandy
Beds.
SG19 2DL

Scottish Tourist Board
23 Ravelston Terrace
Edinburgh
EH4 3EU

South West Way Association
Membership Secretary
1 Orchard Drive
Kingskerswell
Newton Abbot
Devon
TQ12 5DG

Wales Tourist Board
3-6 Bridge Street
Cardiff
CF1 2EE

World Wildlife Fund
Panda House
11-13 Ockford Road
Godalming
Surrey
GU7 1QU

Youth Hostels Association
Trevelyan House
St Albans
Herts
AL1 2DY

For Scotland:
7 Glebe Crescent
Stirling
FK8 2JA